THE POLITICAL ECONOMY OF SOVIET MILITARY POWER

The Political Economy of Soviet Military Power

Leo Cooper
Research Associate
Department of Politics
Monash University, Australia

Foreword by Murray Wolfson

M
MACMILLAN

First published 1989

Published by
THE MACMILLAN PRESS LTD
Houndmills, Basingstoke, Hampshire RG21 2XS
and London
Companies and representatives
throughout the world

Printed and bound in Great Britain at
The Camelot Press Ltd, Southampton

British Library Cataloguing in Publication Data
Cooper, Leo
The political economy of Soviet military power.
1. Soviet Union. Military power
I. Title
355'.0332'47
ISBN 0-333-47279-9

Contents

List of Tables

Foreword

This book is about the central question of our times – peace or war. The author understands the confrontation between the superpowers in all its aspects – not only military. He sees that war and preparations for war involve the allocation of economic resources. Hence the arms race entails more than threatening gestures and proxy wars. The arms race itself involves a competition in the collectively wasteful use of resources as the US and USSR are driven to match one another in threat potential.

It is clear then, that the arms race itself may not be a prelude to war, but is an essential aspect of an ongoing conflict. The weapons are the forced diversion of resources of the enemy from consumption and investment to military expenditures. Thus, this diversion serves to undermine the capacity of the opponent to wage war in the future. That, Clausewitz told us, is what war is all about.

The author's great contribution is to analyse, record and explain the influence and conduct of economic war in the Soviet system. He has elucidated the interface between the economic and the political and military institutions. His grasp of Soviet literature and the understanding of the complex nature of the interrelationship between the economic system of the USSR and its performance on the one hand, and the effectiveness of the Soviet military on the other, is quite impressive. The author has not hesitated to make judgements but at the same time has avoided simplistic conclusions which characterise so much of Soviet studies. Not all of them will be met with universal assent. Never mind. This book is a treasure of information and analysis, for in its attempt to draw together the diverse strands that go to make up the subject of the book, it integrates the relevant disciplines of economics, politics, history and international relations. I commend it to the informed public as well as the specialist.

California State University MURRAY WOLFSON

Acknowledgements

Writing a book is said to be a lonely job, but one is never alone searching for material which can be of use in course of writing. This was of special importance during the research stage since I have set out to find sources of information originating from the Soviet Union. A number of persons and institutions were extremely helpful in this task. My thanks go to the Office of the United States Information Service in Melbourne, especially to Mr George Forner, for providing up to date writings on the American point of view. Some original Soviet material was supplied by the Embassy of the USSR in Canberra, but a substantial volume of Soviet political literature was provided by the State Library of the Czech Socialist Republic in Prague, as well as by the National Szechenyi Library in Budapest during my visit there. My appreciation goes also to the British Library of Political and Economic Science (London School of Economics and Political Science), especially to Mr B. R. Hunter, for allowing access to the Shapiro Collection in the library. Mr Geoffrey Jukes of the Australian National University was very helpful in providing Soviet publications not normally available in the National Library.

Much of the credit must also go to Monash University itself. The Travel Grant provided by the University was of immense value as it allowed me to visit some of the institutions abroad where important material was located. In this regard, I must mention the assistance in arranging and speeding up the procedure at the last minute by Professor Hugh Emy.

As for the book itself, there are many people to whom I owe my thanks. Dr Ian Ward of the Economics Department of Monash University read some of the chapters on economic matters and his suggestions were of great value. I am very grateful to Professor Murray Wolfson of California State University for his comments and help in the publication of the book. But my greatest appreciation and gratitude must go to Harry Redner whose incessant constructive criticism and attention to details made the completion of this book much more manageable. Last, but not least, my sincere appreciation and thanks go to my wife Fanny whose moral and practical support made this book possible. Her patience in typing the manuscript and attending to the editing and corrections were of immense help. My son Mark also deserves my appreciation for his share in this work.

LEO COOPER

List of Abbreviations

CIA	Central Intelligence Agency
DIA	Defence Intelligence Agency
JEC	Joint Economic Committee Congress of the United States
Narkhoz	Narodnoe khoziaistvo (statistical yearbook)
USIS	United States Information Service

1 The Political Economy of the Arms Race: An Introduction

Nikita Khrushchev once commented, 'The case of international tension is like a cabbage, if you tear off the leaves one by one, you come to the heart. And the heart of the matter is relations between the Soviet Union and the United States' (*New York Times*, 11 May 1959, quoted in Caldwell, 1985, p.6). This is still as true today as it was nearly three decades ago. The international situation at present is still dominated, as it has been since the end of the Second World War, by intermittent tension in the relations between the superpowers. This is reflected in the ongoing arms race which, despite attempts at arms control, shows no signs of slackening. What aggravates the state of tension is that each side perceives the other's military capabilities in terms of aggressive intent while proclaiming its own peaceful objectives. This approach to the assessment of the opponent's military power – one that shapes the military policy of both superpowers – appears to be based on the often repeated principle that the best clue to the adversary's intentions is his military potential. The implicit answer to the question whether defence policies and planning should be responsive to the enemy's capabilities or to his intentions (Brodie, 1966, p.85) is reflected in the continuing arms race itself.

Not surprisingly, the conflict between the superpowers and the arms race are subjects of voluminous analysis and debate among political scientists in the West. But, generally, most of the material published on that subject deals primarily with the strategic aspect of the arms race; more specifically with the military balance between the Soviet Union and the United States. Much less has been written on the Soviet military effort within the context of the Soviet political and economic system.

A common feature of most Western writings on the subject of the East–West conflict is an approach which takes a Western perception of the problem as an analytical tool. Many analysts take the simplistic view that Soviet policies are determined by Marxist ideology. They advocate policies that do not take into account the

Soviet perception of economic issues linked to the arms race and of its domestic problems. Diplomacy, political skills and economic sanctions may be effective means of influencing the policies of even the most ideologically committed of powers, but if we have no understanding of the adversary, we have no means of knowing whether they can be successful. As Bernard Brodie (1966, p. 147) once said: 'what we need...is a thorough knowledge of the special idiosyncrasies of the adversary...the interpretation that an opponent widely removed from us in culture and in political doctrine puts upon our actions'.

This book examines what these relevant issues look like from the Soviet point of view, and in doing so attempts to develop a better understanding of the nature and essence of the Soviet Union as a political and economic order different from the Western system and to study the implications of these differences for East–West relations generally, and the arms race in particular.

While examining the arms race, we devote a great deal of attention to the political economy of the Soviet Union; especially to the interaction between the military and the civilian sectors of the economy, and to the issues that arise within the Soviet system and its society as a result of this interaction. It takes a view of the Soviet Union as an entity whose prevailing feature is the centrality of the economy as the backbone of its military power. The major emphasis will be on the effects of the Soviet military effort on the civilian economy and the population at large.

CONTRASTING POSITIONS

A common view prevailing at the present time is that the state of international tension is due mainly to the different ideologies of the superpowers. According to this view the Soviet Union is a revolutionary force, and whether or not Soviet leaders believe in their revolutionary ideology, they are prisoners of that ideology and are inevitably bound to conduct an ideological struggle against Western liberal democratic institutions. Furthermore, the Soviet Union sees itself as an aspirant to world preponderance and in that sense the conflict is about areas of influence (Beyond Containment, 1985, p.17). Others see the root of the conflict in the fundamentally different historical perspectives. For centuries the Russians have looked at the outside world with distrust, fright, insecurity and uncertainty. The traditional expansionism of the Russian Empire has been incorporated by the Soviet Union into its own expansionary course. Consequently, on this view, the danger of the Soviet Union to the West is of the same kind that other societies faced from Alexander the Great, Napoleon, the Kaiser, and Hitler (ibid., p.18).

The Soviet Union, on the other hand, sees all conflicts, particularly those that took place since the end of the Second World War, as the 'result of aggressive colonial policies of imperialist states of the West' (Oleandrov, 1966, p.12). The ideological principle from which the Soviet leaders perceive and evaluate the outside world creates an image of a world conspiring against socialism (Brzezinski, 1963, p.18). By applying Marxist theory of class antagonism and class struggle, the Soviets seem to adopt a rather extreme and uncompromising attitude regarding the present global situation and consider it as part of the continuing battle between socialism and capitalism. According to this view the struggle takes on many different – although not always violent – forms. The military dimension of the conflict which is reflected in the arms race is, therefore, not the only one. The assault by imperialism is being waged, in the Soviet view, not only by military means but also through economic pressure and as a matter of ideological warfare.

The Marxist–Leninist element, which is usually present in Soviet writings on that subject, has confirmed the conclusion by many Western analysts that Soviet military policy represents the application of communist dogma. It also strengthened the belief that ideology is central to any analysis of Soviet policies (Kubalkova and Cruickshank, 1980, p.82). The debate on that subject is usually about the means of containing Soviet expansionism; thus for the adherents of this view it is the military dimension of the conflict that is the most important one. This perception by the United States' politicians of the growing Soviet military power, coupled with the apparent Soviet quest for spreading communism and even for world domination, led a number of Western analysts to conclude that 'it is unlikely for any nation, especially the Soviet Union, to continue making great sacrifices for the sake of accumulating military power without having any intent to excercise it' (Hardt, 1961, p.36). In other words, any increase in military power, whether relative or absolute, would be a clear pointer to political and strategic objectives. Consequently, American national security concern always included an assessment of the capabilities and intentions of a potential adversary, in this case the Soviet Union (Schultze *et al.*, 1972, p.26). According to this approach, the Soviet Union has built up its forces to such an extent that it makes evident Moscow's intention to press its challenge to Western interests in nearly every corner of the world, and that the Soviet long-term ideological objective of world domination remains relatively consistent (*Soviet Military Power*, 1983, p.83).

The latter assumption is reinforced by the fact that the USSR has greatly increased its offensive military capability and has significantly enhanced its ability to conduct military operations worldwide. A document published annually by the US Department of Defence since 1983 indicated that the Soviet Union has created the world's largest military industrial base and has committed vast resources to military related areas of science and technology. Soviet military expenditure in recent years has absorbed 15 per cent of the Gross National Product, compared to less than 7 per cent of the United States', and was estimated to reach 20 per cent by the late 1980s (ibid, p.74). In a later document, the US Department of Defence assessed the dollar cost of Soviet procurement of arms and other military assets during the period of 1973 to 1982 as exceeding that of the United States by some 240 billion dollars (ibid., 1984, p.99). Such defence expenditure when translated into military power clearly pointed to a continuing upgrading of the USSR's armed forces. The document reported many examples of continuing Soviet build up, but concluded that the United States and its Allies have made progress towards restoring the military balance (ibid., pp. 4–5). A subsequent edition of *Soviet Military Power* (1986) was essentially a repetition of the previous edition, the main emphasis being on the projected development of Soviet military capabilities: 'recognition of these facts is the basis of [US] strategic and nonstrategic modernisation programmes and arms control policies. It is also the basis for the SDI' (p.149). A more recent issue (1987) estimated Soviet defence expenditure as absorbing 15 to 17 per cent of their GNP for supporting the military build up.

The Soviet official view on the strategic balance is in direct contrast to the American assessment of the relative state of military power of the USSR and the United States. In response to the US Defence Department claims, in documents published in 1983 and 1984, the Soviets challenged the Reagan Administration's contention that the USSR has achieved military superiority over the United States. The documents made a detailed comparison of strategic and conventional forces of the superpowers and concluded that 'an approximate military balance has arisen and is being steadily maintained between the USSR and the USA, and between the Warsaw Treaty and NATO, both in the world at large and in Europe' (*Otkuda iskhodit ugroza miru*, 1983, p.63). It accused the United States of a bid for military superiority and in its turn pointed to the increased military expenditure which represented, in 1980, 5.2 per cent of US GNP and was estimated to rise to nearly 10 percent by 1990 (ibid., p.49). In response to the American publication of *Soviet Military Power* in 1984, the Soviets have again published their assessment of the state of military strength in which they attempted to disprove American assertions. In particular, they claimed that the United States has adopted as its main objective 'to achieve a scientific–technological superiority in the exploitation of outer space for military purposes'. The latter was a reference to SDI, which the Soviets perceived as an attempt by the United States to create an 'effective shield' and a potential for a first nuclear strike capability (ibid., 1984, p.40). A more recent publication analyses in greater detail the implications of the SDI (*Star Wars*, 1985).

In turn, in the 1987 edition of their document, the Soviets have put their estimate of American defence expenditure as having doubled from 140.7 billion dollars in the fiscal year 1980 to 284.9 billion dollars in 1987. Furthermore, according to Soviet estimates, the share of allocation for military purposes in the expenditure part of the US Federal Budget has risen from 22.7 per cent in 1980 to 29 per cent in 1987. It concludes that 'the threat to peace comes from the US war machine, the militarist policy pursued by the US Administration and its efforts to conduct international affairs from the position of strength' (*Otkuda iskhodit ugroza miru*, 1987, p.3).

A QUESTION OF BALANCE OF POWER

The conflicting claims by the superpowers about the intentions and military capabilities of their respective opponent have focused the attention of political and military analysts on the strategic weapons balance and its significance for the relations between them. More often than not, the question of strategic balance has been answered on the basis of comparison between quantities and technical characteristics of various types of nuclear as well as conventional weapons, by the so called 'bean counting'. But depending on who did the counting, widely different assessments were offered.

The attempts to assess the respective military potentials of the superpowers and their military capabilities had as one of their objectives to determine the extent to which military power can be used as an instrument of foreign policy. It followed the traditional approach to the question of balance of power on which were based classical theories of international relations. If it is still widely used today, it is partly because of a tendency to fit new situations into well established modes of thought (Hoffman, 1968, p.199). However, the traditional notion of balance of power – on which analysts used to base their whole assessment of the state of international relations – is less applicable today. In the pre-nuclear era the security of a nation was thought to be based on achieving military power that would match or exceed that of any potential aggressor. The general view was that disparities in military power, as perceived by an opponent, encouraged aggression (Nash, 1975, p.13). In such a situation military alliances were of the utmost importance and the balance of power tended to be more effective as the number of participants increased. It meant that the increase in power of any one state could be offset by shifting alliances (ibid., p.26). War itself had been considered in Clausewitzian terms as an instrument of national policy and justified as being in the national interest. According to the Clausewitzian philosophy war was a political instrument; a mere continuation of policy by other means. Clashes of interests between states were typically resolved by 'an act of violence intended to compel [the] opponent to fulfil [the] will...Violence, that is to say physical force [was], therefore the means' (Clausewitz, 1978, p.101).

Clearly, to look at the global situation from the point of view of balance of power in the classical sense and to consider the achievement of political objectives through a nuclear war becomes rather meaningless, for the balance of power can no longer be much disturbed by shifting alliances but by a perceived real or imaginary superiority of one superpower over the other. Whether a balance of military power between the superpowers really exists or whether a so called 'superiority' is held by one or the other of the adversaries is the subject of incessant debate among military experts who specialise in the area of strategic weapons. But if we assume that the nuclear deterrent is still operative, then we must also accept the assumption that a relative military balance does exist at the present – a balance that may or may not be disturbed in the future. This may be the reason for the recent apparent willingness by the Soviet Union to enter into negotiations with the United States, regarding the reduction in the number of nuclear weapons to a level which will still allow each to retain a mutual deterrent.

On the other hand, the arms race does not appear to abate but, on the contrary, it mobilises more human resources for the development of military technology, as well as material resources to cover the cost of research and production of more sophisticated weapons. For the arms race is not so much concerned with the present state of military capabilities as with what it may be at any future time. One Soviet commentator quoting Lenin as saying that 'it is illogical, even criminal, for any army not to prepare itself to absorb all kinds of weapons, all means and ways of battle which are or could be in the possession of the enemy', drew attention to the words 'could be'. He concluded that the assessment of the military, economic and scientific potential of the would-be adversary must be based on the accurate study of the present situation as well as on projections of what the enemy might have in the future (Lagovskyi, 1969). A similar approach appears to be adopted by the Pentagon, hence its analysis of the Soviet military potential takes into account not only the existing state of Soviet military power, but also its future development given the economic resources of the USSR and the performance of its economy.

THE ECONOMIC FACTOR

If the ever accelerating arms race may be considered as an insurance against a possible future imbalance of military power, it has quite different and, to some extent, immediate implications which have so far received less attention than they deserve. As the arms race continues, the USSR, as well as the United States, is forced to divert extensive resources to military areas. The arms race, therefore, takes on a different, although not entirely new, dimension of not only a race for strategic superiority but a contest of economic strength. There exists a general consensus in the West, as well as in the East, about the direct relationship between military expenditure and the economic resources that a country is able to divert for building up its armed forces. Consequently, one of the limiting factors on defence spending would be the capacity of an economy to sustain it. A larger GNP reflects a greater capability to satisfy defence and civilian needs; which means that a complex relationship also exists between military policy and the performance of a national economy (Campbell, 1973, p.127).

The estimates of the Soviet GNP as being between 50 and 60 per cent of that of the United States, and the Soviet military expenditure as constituting roughly 12 to 15 per cent of that GNP or about equal or exceeding that of the United States in absolute terms, leads one to conclude that in order to match the projected increase in American defence spending, the Soviet Union will have to use a greater proportion of its economic resources for military purposes. This assessment of Soviet military power presents, therefore, two facets of the same problem. One is purely strategic, involving the evaluation of Soviet military forces and their likely development in the future – an aspect outside the scope of this book – the other, mainly economic, related to the interdependence between the level of military expenditure and the performance of the Soviet economy. The connection between the economy and the military effort of the Soviet Union, the link between defence spending and the operation of the Soviet economy, is thus of prime importance for the analysis of the Soviet military power. Furthermore, the interdependence between the Soviet military effort and the economy is closely linked to the question of the relationship between the military and the civilian sectors of the Soviet economy; consequently, it raises the question of the 'defence burden' and its implications for Soviet domestic and foreign policies. It is on the above aspects of Soviet military power that we shall concentrate our attention.

There is a tendency among many Western political analysts to present a picture of the Soviet economy as a cumbersome machine that a bureaucratic hierarchy tries to manage in a most inefficient way. The result seems an enormous waste of resources which affects economic growth and leads to poor economic conditions in a country endowed with an abundance of natural resources. On the other hand, in relation to the military power, the size of the Soviet military machine – which, according to Moscow, has reached parity with that of the United States – would seem to suggest either that Soviet military expenditure is far greater than is generally estimated, namely that 'the Soviet leadership can devote a large percentage of the national income to defence programmes' (*Soviet Military Power*, 1986, p.3), or that the Soviet military establishment operates in a most efficient manner – an assumption adopted by a number of Western analysts. However, the latter assumption would be certainly contradicted by the evidence of gross inefficiencies in the operation of the economy as a whole and which, even according to Soviet sources, are also applicable to the military sector. We shall attempt to throw some light on this apparent contradiction.

METHODOLOGY

However, the understanding of the Soviet Union cannot be limited to the examination of the link between the military and economic aspects of the Soviet approach to the arms race. For in trying to understand the Soviets the West is facing an opponent with a different social and political structure, a society that appears basically apolitical or, at least, lacking political culture in a Western sense; a government that claims an adherence to a Marxist philosophy, and a country whose very different history and traditions still influence present attitudes. One must, therefore, look behind the purely ideological facade of the Soviet political and economic structure and explore other factors that enter into the shaping of Soviet policies.

We shall argue that the present attitudes and the way the Kremlin perceives the position of the Soviet Union in the world arena has its source in Russian historical experiences and Russia's militaristic traditions. Chapter 2 examines the historical and traditional roots of Soviet thought and their significance for the understanding of the Soviet military doctrine. In this respect, the role of historical experiences in the forming of the Soviet society as it exists today is clearly of some importance. As one philosopher once said: 'to understand a man you have to know his memories'; the same could also apply to a nation. This is probably even more appropriate for the Soviet Union than it is for any Western country. The Russians have come to feel the imprint of history through their own experiences and this appears to be far more important to them than it is for the American people. Therefore, whether the Soviet Union represents the continuation of the history of Imperial Russia or constitutes a historical break expressed in the application of the communist ideology is a question that will be explored before proceeding to the more specific analysis of Soviet military thought.

Chapter 3 deals with the Soviet approach to military policy and analyses the factors that are instrumental in the shaping of the Soviet military doctrine. It examines Soviet views on national security and Soviet interpretation of the military aspect of the arms race. As with all matters related to Soviet policies, the ideological and pragmatic aspects of Soviet military thought are examined in detail so as to present the contrast between the Soviet and American approach to military policies. Even a random selection of Soviet and Western writings on political and military aspects of the arms race would indicate the gulf that exists between the Soviet and Western modes of thought. It would reveal the absence of a common language and of a terminology that has the same meaning for both sides in the conflict. There is a generally accepted assumption among Western political and military analysts that the Soviet perception of the arms race is based on the same concepts adopted in the West. Terms such as 'balance of terror', 'counterforce', 'damage limiting targets', 'limited nuclear war', etc., are new concepts that have appeared as a result of changes in modern warfare and the advent of nuclear weapons. Let us note that these terms have been coined in the West and represent Western strategic concepts. Although the equivalent of the relatively new military jargon can be found in Soviet military literature, it is only used within a critical appraisal of Western ideas. A quote from Marshal D. Sokolovsky (1963, p.2) indicates the Soviet attitude to Western concepts: 'the modern theories of "limited war", "massive retaliation" and "global war" etc. advanced in such profusion by bourgeois military theoreticians...reflects imperialist policy'.

Generally, the difference in military thought lies in the whole approach to the arms race. While the United States looks at the arms race from a purely military point of view and concentrates its thinking on the assessment of the strategic balance, the Soviets look at the problem from a much broader and far more complex perspective that embraces many aspects of war and peace such as military power, ideology and the economy.

The economic aspect of the arms race and its perception by the Soviet leadership is the subject of Chapter 4. It examines the link between Soviet military thinking and the Soviet economy, taking into account the much more extensive application of state power in the USSR as a factor of its economic and political system. The interdependence between the economy and national security is a central theme in all Soviet comments on its military policy and in the statements and addresses of Soviet leaders. It indicates Moscow's perception of the American military policy as part of an ongoing economic attack upon the USSR (Faramazan, 1981, p.14).[1]

The link between the Soviet economy and defence expenditure has been recognised for quite some time as vital for the assessment of the Soviet military effort. The chief objective of such assessment was to find out the level of Soviet defence spending and to translate such expenditure into military capabilities. Many Western analysts also asserted that defence spending is an indication of the direction in Soviet military strategy and was, therefore, useful for those American policy-makers who have a say in budgetary decisions. Chapter 5 of the book looks at the various approaches to the assessment of Soviet military expenditure.

The search of the Soviet budget allocations for defence is also important for those in the American Administration who advocate the use of economic power as an alternative for influencing Soviet international conduct. It was thought that given the Soviet political and economic system, there ought to be a direct correlation between defence expenditure and the economy. The impact of the arms race on the Soviet economy as a whole, the effects of defence spending on the civilian economy in particular, was thought to be vital if economic pressure is to be successful.

The analysis of the economic potential of the USSR – as it relates to its military power and the economic burden that this implies – has been generally concentrated on the question of the extent to which Soviet defence expenditure is limited by the capacity of the economy and, to a lesser degree, about the impact of the arms race on the civilian development and on general welfare. The latter aspect has not attracted sufficient attention, despite the fact that the situation of the Soviet population in terms of real welfare has important socio-political and economic implications and – as can be deduced from Soviet sources – is the subject of constant attention by the leadership. This question takes on additional significance if one adopts the view that increasing military expenditure may have destabilising effects upon the Soviet economy and consequently upon the mood and morale of the population. The above implications will be examined in Chapters 8 and 9. But first, we shall look in Chapter 6 at the domestic aspect of the Soviet military effort and its impact on the general welfare of the Soviet population. This chapter is devoted to an analysis of the functioning of the Soviet economy and of the problems it faces in trying to satisfy consumer demand and expectations. In this connection the means by which the Soviet leadership hopes to achieve these objectives will be examined.

The role of foreign trade and economic relations with the West, especially the question of Soviet acquisition of Western technology, will be the subject of Chapter 7. The latter aspect of Soviet economic policy has a bearing not only on the domestic economy as a source of supply of consumer goods, but also on American policy which is geared to denying the Soviets access to Western technology and know-how on account of its military and strategic importance. It is a well known fact that the United States has been exerting considerable pressure upon its European allies to limit as much as possible the export of goods of military significance or 'dual use' to the USSR. The question of technological transfer and the problems faced by the Soviets in their pursuit of Western know-how is also discussed.

Based on the evidence presented in the preceding chapters, an attempt will be made to assess the extent of the defence burden of the Soviet Union and its implications for Soviet foreign and domestic policies. How does the Soviet leadership perceive the impact of defence expenditure upon the economy? Is the military effort becoming an obstacle to Soviet economic growth? Specifically, an answer will be sought to the question why the problem of the defence burden does not appear to be a vital issue in Soviet political and economic analysis of the present situation.

If the Soviet leadership does not seem to be excessively perturbed by the defence burden that its military effort may entail, it certainly indicates an increasing concern about the general mood of the population and its attitude to the economic effort on which the Soviets rely as a solution to a number of domestic difficulties. The question of general morale acquired additional importance in Soviet thinking in view of the ideological offensive launched by President Reagan. This is viewed by the Soviets with a certain degree of concern, and judging by the volume of writings on this subject, it is taken quite seriously by the leadership. Chapter 9 looks closely at Soviet perception of the American propaganda effort as a form of ideological war waged in order to destabilise the Soviet system.

The emergence of the new leader, Mikhail Gorbachev, and the seemingly radical reforms that he has introduced since coming to power, presents an opportunity to test empirically some of the conclusions arrived at in the preceding chapters. This we shall do in Chapter 10 of the book. It will deal exclusively with the internal situation in the USSR following the introduction of *perestroika* and *glasnost*. It will examine the nature and scope of the new policies and their implications for East–West relations

Finally, the concluding chapter will bring together all the issues discussed so far in the book and interpret them in the context of American foreign policy. It will also address the question whether American strategy aimed at changing Soviet behaviour by means of a continuing arms race, economic pressure and an ideological offensive can be successful given the Soviet perception of the arms race and its approach to issues connected with military power.

SOVIET SOURCES AND STATISTICS: A QUESTION OF INTERPRETATION

The present study relies, to a large extent, on original Soviet sources so as to reflect as closely as possible the underlying thought and motivations which constitute the basis of Soviet policies and attitudes. Soviet primary material consists of writings by Party theoreticians and political commentators as well as Soviet statistical data.

The question of reliability of Soviet data and of the extent to which official sources represent the views of the Soviet leadership has arisen from time to time; questions were raised especially about the connection of Soviet information with state propaganda. Ideas and new trends in Soviet policies always originate from above and are formulated at the highest level of the Party hierarchy – the Politburo. They are usually made public during the Congress or Plenary Meeting of the Central Committee of the CPSU. The strict adherence to the official views and the principle by which the decisions of the Central Committee are enforced is formalised in the Soviet Constitution as 'the principle of democratic centralism...the...mandatory fulfilment of the decisions of higher organs by lower organs' (Art. 3). Essentially, published statements and comments express basic ideological principles upon which the Soviet system claims its legitimacy. Consequently, political comments by Soviet writers must conform to the official line. Nevertheless, from time to time divergences of views do surface and a change in the official attitude is very often the evidence of debate that takes place at the top. The problem which arises when a new policy is adopted is usually solved by readjusting the Party line and setting all the resources of the state propaganda machine to publicise and explain the new doctrine as being now in force (Barrington, 1965, p.421). This is necessarily reflected in Soviet political writings, and commentaries in the press never show the slightest deviation from the official line. Deviation from the official policy by Soviet spokesmen – as is sometimes the case in the West – is practically non-existent. Even the policy of *glasnost*, which on the surface appears to be an invitation to voice different opinions, is in reality a directive coming from above to which the Soviet media must conform; the limits to which opinions can be expressed are well understood by the writers. Thus, what the Soviets say in their openly published literature represents genuine Soviet thinking – even if not all that they think.

However, the complexity of modern domestic economies and contemporary international relations, the technological advance, and the increasing sophistication of military command, creates problems of communication for the leadership. It becomes imperative for the Soviets, especially the military, to be able to communicate their views, as well as any changes in strategic policies, to the armed forces and to the mass of reservists. It also becomes necessary to have recourse to the advice of experts outside the top hierarchy (Pipes, 1976, p.59), and it is difficult to see how important decisions can be made if they run counter to the opinion of experts.

> In this regard, serious attention must be given to military-scientific conferences and to the improvement of the content of military-theoretical journals whose objective must be to enable wide exchange of views; for it is known that anything new, as a rule, finds its way with difficulties. (Kulikov, 1976, p.46)

The necessity to seek expert advice and to communicate new trends is also reflected in Soviet statistical data. The realisation that a modern and complex economy cannot function efficiently without adequate information about its performance has already resulted in a marked quantitative increase as well as qualitative improvement in the output of data. Although the secrecy surrounding information in the military field is still a feature of Soviet statistics, the interconnection between economic planning in general and the defence sector in particular, makes it difficult for the Soviets to isolate the civilian from the military branch of the economy (an issue that will be discussed at length in Chapter 6). It is now, at least, possible to detect trends in military spending while examining the performance of the Soviet economy.

The view held for a long time by some Western analysts was that 'Soviet economic data are fragmentary, misleading and, on occasion, simply untrustworthy' (Bergson, 1972, p.185). Although it is fair to say that the above conclusions are to a certain degree still valid, Soviet statistics must be seen in the context of the role that they fulfil within the requirements of Soviet economic and political objectives. The political, or rather ideological, objective of gathering statistical data and generally the work of Soviet statistical bodies is 'to prepare the publication of materials that would reveal the development of the socialist economy under Soviet power, of its science and culture, of the improvement in national welfare, and the fundamental superiority of socialism over capitalism' (*Materialy*, 1979, p.33). It is only natural that in meeting the ideological objectives, the element of propaganda and the emphasis on achievements is usually present in all commentaries on economic matters. This is also reflected in the way Soviet data is presented. The arbitrary choice of periods of years for the purpose of favourable comparison of results, the use of values instead of unit numbers and of quantities where appropriate for the indication of a positive trend, recourse to percentage increase rather than quantities, and sometimes selected omissions – all these are some of the methods used for propaganda purposes.

But it would be wrong to assume that what the Soviets publish is only propaganda and that it is being 'doctored' at the highest level of the Soviet statistical service. The distortion of data – spurred by the constant emphasis on fulfilment of economic plans – begins at the lowest level of economic activities, as was openly admitted at the All-Union Conference of Statisticians in 1977. The conference debated the role of statistical information and, although the ideological content of statistics was often mentioned, the message to the conference from the Central Committee of the Party and from the Council of Ministers of the USSR spoke of statistics as a 'powerful weapon of social knowledge' and of their primary role for 'helping the Party and the Government in the scientifically based management of the economy, to secure the planned and proportional development of the national economy and control over the fulfilment of the plan' (ibid., 1979, p.6). It called for improvements in the system of accounting, reporting and statistical information.

The conference debated extensively the problems of reliability and authenticity of statistical information, particularly the widespread practice of 'upward distortions of results' (ibid., p.29). The chairman of Gosplan commented that as a result of wrong information about the fulfilment of plans, which often come from ministries, it became necessary to revise annually the plan of capital works after it has already been approved. During the discussions it was revealed that the 'upward distortions' begin at the level of primary accounting of the enterprise, *kolkhoz, sovkhoz*, etc. and the suggestion was made to combat this practice by legal means (ibid., p.32).

Despite the marked improvement in the quality and increased volume of reporting that makes the task of objective economic analysis more manageable, there is still some scarcity of information in the area of policy-making. It is still difficult to determine the process of policy debate and conflict resolution at the level of the Politburo. But at the lower level of the hierarchy, especially the bureaucracy, there is the possibility of understanding Soviet politics (Warner, 1977, p.11). Articles by relatively junior military and economic specialists and theoreticians are likely to reflect the opinions of much higher authorities or, at least, have their approval. Therefore, everything that is expressed in Soviet publications has some true meaning (Scott and Scott, 1979, p.xiv). It is rather surprising to find how much valuable information is available and the variety of questions that are discussed by Soviet political and economic analysts. In the opinion of one former Soviet social scientist; 'there is enough Soviet material available to expose some "secrets" – for Soviet secrets are first of all secrets from the Soviet people' (Birman, 1981, p.xiii).

However, while the inherent Soviet secrecy is diminishing to some extent, due to the requirements of modern military organisation and a modern economy, there remains the problem of interpretation of the available information. What is significant in this respect is the fact that Soviet political and economic commentators do not speak any longer with one voice. The unanimity of views expressed in Soviet writings which was the practice for decades, especially during Stalin's rule, gave way to more diversified opinions on economic, social and, sometimes, on military matters. Discussions about the economy reflect a search for solutions to economic difficulties, while the differences of views in the military area indicate the existence of two trends in Soviet thinking: a conservative one that attempts to cling to Marxist dogma and a more pragmatic trend searching for practical answers to questions of national security. Thus, it is sometimes difficult to separate the ideological element contained in Soviet material from the pragmatic because almost every discussion is expressed in terms of Marxism–Leninism and usually includes a reference to an opinion voiced by the Party leaders.

If the lack of access to some Soviet sources of information and the problems of interpretation complicates the understanding of Soviet military policy, it is the overabundance of Western data and the plethora of various opinions expressed in the West that probably confuses Soviet understanding of the United States and the West in general (Ermath, 1981, p.54). Because they face a surplus of information – many of them conflicting – Soviet assessors face similar problems (Collins, 1980, p.13). The fact that the West does not speak with one voice – the debate in the US between the Executive Branch and the Congress and powerful pressure groups presenting opposing views – may send conflicting signals to the Soviets. Ironically, similar difficulties face a Western analyst who attempts an assessment of American foreign policy. While Soviet information indicates a general consistency in foreign policy matters, voices emanating from the United States do not present a uniform picture in matters affecting US–USSR relations. More often than not one encounters contradictory statements from various government sources.

Although, as mentioned earlier, this book relies mainly on original Soviet sources, it must obviously seek to clarify and interpret US policies as they are being presented by government spokesmen. This method necessarily raises the question of validity. Are they representative views? Because this problem imposes certain limitations on the interpretation of US foreign policy objectives, it was necessary to emphasise those areas of US policy where there appears to be least contradictions. We have, therefore, concentrated our attention on three distinct areas – military policy, economic policy, and propaganda – as instruments of

American foreign policy. These appear to be rather consistent as can be judged by President Reagan's State of the Union message to the Congress on 27 January, 1987. In his address Reagan emphasised the necessity to retain a 'sound military balance', the use of economic power when dealing with the Eastern bloc, and the communication of 'information and ideas on a worldwide basis' through an 'expansion of America's international broadcasting capacity'. The Soviet perception of the US–USSR relations is, therefore, analysed in the context of the above stated objectives of American foreign policy.

An added complication in interpreting Soviet material is the tendency by Soviet leaders and writers to idealise any situation or any development in a manner that makes it appear as if it were already a reality. Such tendency is especially evident in the analytical treatment of the state of the Soviet society where the normative becomes fused with the positive statement – what ought to be becomes in such a statement what already is. For example, since a socialist society is by the Marxist definition the more creative and potentially more productive, it follows that the defence forces of a socialist state must be superior to the army of a capitalist state. Such an attitude sometimes acquires a sinister connotation in the eyes of a Western observer who can no longer decide where the ideological element ends and pragmatism takes over. These problems may be attributed to the attempts by Soviet analysts and commentators to reconcile an ideological principle with the reality of a given situation. This book takes into account the inconsistencies that are often present in the Soviet interpretations of political and economic questions and by doing so tries to evaluate critically Soviet material rather than accept it at its face value.

We shall, therefore, begin with an examination of the most commonly discussed question concerning the role of Marxist ideology on which the CPSU and the Soviet government claim their legitimacy. The subject of the ideological determinant of Soviet policies is very important in the context of Soviet military thought and practice. For if we are to grasp the principles which guide Soviet behaviour then we must investigate the nature and essence of this ideology and its sources.

2 Soviet Russian Ideology: The Source of Soviet Military Thought

INTRODUCTION

The relevance of ideology to politics lies in the fact that ideology is often a guide to political action and – as the French and Bolshevik Revolutions revealed – ideology can be used deliberately for most political ends, above all the achievement of power (Plamenatz, 1971, p.137). While the pursuit of power is always one of the attributes of politics, ideology can sometimes be a justification for those involved in its pursuit as well as their followers. But sometimes it is 'a false front behind which the element of power is concealed', that is, the actor on the political scene, whether an individual or a group, may be using ideology as a disguise for the real motive of his action (Morgenthau, 1973, p.89). To look behind the ideological facade and to find the real motivation for political action is a most important and difficult task for a political analyst (ibid., p.98). Such a task becomes even more complicated when it is applied to the search for the real sources of Soviet international conduct and domestic policies. It is this area of political research that has become the subject of much debate since the Bolsheviks came to power and even more so after the end of the Second World War.

The discussions have been focused mainly on the role of communist ideology in Soviet foreign and domestic policies. To those who perceived the Soviet Union as a threat to the non-communist world, the foreign and military policies of the USSR appeared as geared for world domination, an ultimate objective which it hoped to achieve either through world revolution or the use of military power whenever favourable conditions presented themselves. Others, who were inclined to disregard the importance of ideology as a determinant of Soviet policies, saw international relations in purely Clausewitzian terms; the USSR simply being a great power attempting to expand its sphere of influence by various means not necessarily motivated by ideological considerations.

The difficulty faced by political analysts in relation to the Soviet Union is the fact that Soviet policies over the years do not seem to be very consistent. At times they seem to support the view that Marxism–Leninism, or any other variant of this ideology, cannot be left out from an analysis of Soviet conduct (Kubalkova and Cruickshank, 1980, p.82), while at other times Soviet political activities seem to point to state interests. Thus, the assumption that Soviet policies are determined by state interests ought not to exclude the role of ideology in Soviet politics. Consequently, the analytical problem that one faces in order to understand Soviet behaviour is to define the kind of ideology that affects Soviet policy. The systematic modifications of Marxist tradition seem to have removed from the theory, to some degree, its economic determinism (although this is still the officially promoted theoretical principle) and what is left of Marxism is what is useful (Rostow, 1967, pp.85–6). Nevertheless, ideology is still needed for the Soviet leadership in order to give them a sense of legitimacy and as a rationale for their policies. But 'the persisting and important role of ideological assumptions in the thinking and actions of Soviet leaders (which is essential for an understanding of their conduct) can be appreciated only if it is seen in a perspective that takes into consideration all various elements that enter into the shaping of this ideology' (Brzezinski,1967,p.132). It will be defined in this study as Soviet Russian ideology.

In this respect it is essential to devote a great deal of attention to the question of the influence that Russian history, tradition and her geographical location exerted on the shaping of Soviet society as we know it today, and especially to the role that these factors together with Russian nationalism play in Soviet military thought. As this study will indicate, the Soviets have succeeded in fusing communist ideology with Russian national traditions – a fusion which meets the need of Russian society to retain its links with the past. History plays an important role not only as a factor used by the leadership in the formation of military theories, but also as a source of pride for the Russian people as a whole. Of all beliefs and ideas that permeate Soviet society patriotism still appears to be most pervasive and very powerful (as the course of the Second World War indicated).

It is Russia's cultural and political heritage, not only its communist ideology, that makes the Soviet Union and its society so different from the West. Russia's history, culture and traditions have always contributed, and to some extent still do, to the retention of national peculiarities which even today assume some significance in Soviet military, foreign and economic policies. In the words of the nineteenth-century Russian historian, Miliukov, the process by which Russia established herself as an Empire was 'a national experience and a national existence radically different from the West; it created a social and political system, a national character, a mentality, a way of life, utterly dissimilar to the patterns evolved in Western Europe' (Szamuely, 1974, p.12). Indeed, one can find a great deal of similarity between contemporary Russia and what she had been in the past. Consequently, if we are to understand the Soviets we must look beyond the obvious, the ideology and the system which claims to be based on Marxist principles. As we shall see, the ideology as it evolved from the Russian experience and the system itself point to a continuation of a historical process rather than a break caused by a revolution.

RUSSIAN MILITARY TRADITION IN HISTORICAL PERSPECTIVE

An important determinant of Russia's relation with the West was her geographical location and climatic conditions. Both the geography and climate left an imprint upon Russian national character for it kept Russia isolated from the West for centuries as there was little commercial, let alone cultural, contact. Poor soil and unreliable rainfall coupled with primitive agricultural methods resulted in very low yields and productivity lagged very much behind Western Europe. As late as the nineteenth century, one acre under cultivation yielded only about one-seventh of the English crop and less than half of French, Prussian and Austrian output (Pipes, 1982, p.8). For most of its history the country has been unable to produce a surplus and whatever was produced went for domestic consumption and for the maintenance of the state apparatus. Economic progress was thus very slow and commercial activities with the West practically non-existent. This was primarily due to the remoteness of Russia from European commercial centres.

Until the eighteenth century Russian trade remained oriented towards the Middle East, especially Iran. The conquest of Kazan and Astrakhan in the 1550s, both important bases for oriental and Middle Eastern goods, increased Russian involvement with Eastern markets. This long tradition of trade with the Levant left a lasting impression on the Russian merchant class that did not disappear even after Russia's participation in trade with the West. Russian merchants almost never ventured on business to Western Europe, it was the merchants from the West who came to Russia to explore trading possibilities. There they found a type of Russian merchant whose business mentality retained a strong Levantine imprint. There was very little of the capitalist ethic with its stress on industry and thrift. The dishonesty of the Russian merchant was proverbial at the time (ibid., p.205).

The geographical location, which made Russia the object of invasions, initially from the East, coupled with the economic necessity for constant expansion and colonisation essential for her survival, was a powerful factor in the establishment of a military organisation capable of both defending the country against invasions and expanding the frontiers of the Empire. Russia's military tradition is, therefore, as ancient as her history.

A fact rarely mentioned is that the status of a superpower and the position as an equal among the great powers in Europe has not been achieved by Russia only since the Second World War, but at the beginning of the eighteenth century following a long struggle against foreign invaders. In the historical context it can be seen that the role of the state, of its military strength and the impact of wars in general, was incomparably more powerful in Russia than in the West. All through Russia's history, her military power and wars were important factors in shaping her society and the politics of the state. From the early days, following the invasions from the East, Russia has adopted from the Mongols the concept of society and the state, a system of government and administration that was suitable for a large and expanding state, especially in the two most essential areas: military affairs and finance (Szamuely, 1974, p.20). The Russian system and social structure have evolved mainly through the organisation of the nation's defence that became the justification and legitimation of the all-powerful state. The establishment and maintenance of a large standing army for permanent duty was, therefore, the main concern of the government. It was dictated by incessant wars that Russia waged in the sixteenth and seventeenth centuries. During these two centuries there was scarcely a year without war on the southern and south-eastern borders of the Empire. In the West, on the border with Poland, Lithuania, Sweden and Germany there was an average of a war every second year (Pipes, 1982, p.20). Sometimes the Russians succeeded in advancing westwards in the quest for access to ports, at other times it was the Western countries who pushed the Russians eastwards. It was also in the course of the sixteenth and seventeenth centuries that Russia developed its distinctive social and political structure whose main feature was a largely military organisation of the state. From her early ages of existence as an Empire, Russia was organised for warfare much more than the Western monarchies. This may not be surprising in view of the fact that no European country had so long and exposed a frontier as Russia, no such mobile population expanding outwards in search for land, and no such vast territory to garrison.

But the problem was then, as it is today, how to support a vast military machine in a country as primitive as Russia was at the time. This vital task of creating an efficient system for the mobilisation of Russia's scattered human and material resources has been taken over by the central government and its bureaucracy. The state began to channel the major resources of the Empire into military purposes. A large proportion of the country's labour went directly to supporting or 'feeding' the military. In addition, the bulk of the funds secured from taxes collected from the 'tiaglo' people – those that had to bear the load of taxes and labour, mainly peasants and artisans, 67 per cent of whom lived on land owned by secular proprietors – was also channelled into the military area (ibid., p.115).

However, despite the huge military expenditure, the results hardly justified the financial burden imposed upon the country. While, under Ivan IV, the Russians had successes in their wars against the Tartars, they suffered defeat in wars against the Poles and the Swedes. This was due mainly to the traditional manner of waging war which was effective as long as the adversary waged war in a similar manner – relying on cavalry supported by commoners serving on foot. But no matter how tough and undemanding the Russian soldier was on the battlefield, he could not stand up to the technological changes in warfare introduced by Western European states in the late sixteenth and early seventeenth centuries. The latter had developed the art of war into a system of professionals and mercenaries who fought with new weapons – the flintlock and bayonets against pikes and slow-firing muskets (ibid., p.116).

The task of modernising the Russian army was subsequently undertaken by Peter the Great, the creator of Russia's military might. His firm belief in military power as essential for every country's welfare, and his constant emphasis on the dominant role that it played in history, led him to establish a large standing army. In 1699, Peter conscripted 32 000 commoners into the army and thereafter the bulk of Russia's armed forces consisted of men drafted from the tax-paying classes. Russia, in fact, became the first country with compulsory (although not universal) military service, nearly one century earlier than Western Europe.

Another first for Russia was the use of conscripted labour. Saint Petersburg that was to be Russia's 'window to the West' was built largely by labour that Peter had to bring in from other regions. Requisition orders, calling for 40 000 peasants to perform several months of labour in Saint Petersburg, were issued every year; it was, in fact, forced labour.

The period of Peter the Great's rule was mainly characterised by the impact that wars exerted upon the politics of the Russian state. The wars with Sweden (1700–21) led to most of the financial and administrative reforms and to a further militarisation of the Russian Empire. The initial defeat at Narva resulted in the creation of a powerful navy which was subsequently instrumental in Russian victories against the Swedes in 1709 and 1714 at Poltava and Hangohud. At the end of the war the Russian army and navy were second to none in Europe (Mirsky, 1942, p.184). It was also under Peter that militarism of the Empire made the army and navy officers socially and politically a dominant group (ibid., p.186). An extreme expression of the militarist spirit of the time was the establishment of 'military settlements' under which several hundred thousands of crown peasants became hereditary soldiers.

The Swedish War, as did others, provided the driving force for military reforms introduced by Peter – the establishment of a permanent standing army organised, trained and equipped along the most modern European lines. This was also reflected in the military budget which had already then consumed two-thirds of the greatly increased level of state expenditure. The armed forces needed up-to-date armament and equipment. Therefore, industry had to be established, the fiscal system reformed, and a new administrative structure had to be devised.

Peter's approach to the task of modernisation of Russia was one of pragmatism. In order to establish the Russian Empire as a great military power there was a need for European technology and efficiency, but for the rest Europe remained an object of hostility and distrust. Despite Peter's interest in the West and Western thought, he was more interested in military power than in Westernisation. According to Peter: 'we shall need Europe for a few decades and then we can turn our backside to her'. Peter's promotion and support for Russia's industry was motivated by a desire to free his military establishment from dependence on foreign suppliers. This had the long-term effect of greatly expanding the foundation of Russia's industry (an objective reminiscent of Lenin's and Stalin's approach to post-revolutionary industrialisation of the Soviet Union). The standing army which Peter created required weapons, which he was reluctant to import not only on account of lack of funds, but mainly not to become dependent on the West for supplies of commodities that affected national security. He therefore embarked upon the building of an independent defence industry. Under Peter, nearly all new industries worked for the military and the manufacturers and mines worked exclusively for the state. However, the industrial development that he launched, though new in spirit, was basically traditional in practice. The state owned the means of production, set prices and absorbed all the output. It was not industrial capitalism in the true sense, it rather resembled a system that is defined today by some economists as state capitalism. Despite Peter's efforts, socially and economically Russia remained for centuries a primitive and backward country.

It needed the disaster of the Crimean War finally to expose the inadequacy of Russia's obsolete social system; to set in train a chain of events leading to the radical reforms of 1861. The economic growth of Western Europe and the spread of industrialisation in the nineteenth century revealed to the Russians their weaknesses. The backwardness of the Russian state became even more obvious during the Crimean War and made it clear to the rulers that without an effort at modernisation the international position of Russia would decline (Kemp, 1971, p.119). Russia's deficiencies in internal communications, the lack of modern transport and inferior equipment of the army resulted in the military defeat by the Anglo-French invaders in the Crimea. It would appear that, just like today, the economic development of Russia was tightly linked to the international political role which the rulers wished her to play. The interconnection between political considerations and modernisation of the armed forces was thus always present (ibid., p.123).

THE POLITICAL HERITAGE

It was not only the military imperatives that were instrumental in the creation of a state based essentially on absolute authority. As Russia's structure developed into what is usually defined as a state with supreme powers vested in a political hierarchy dominated by the tsar, there arose the necessity for preserving that power. The centralised autocratic state came to hold every aspect of the nation's life within its grip. There was no room left for autonomous activity for either the individual or social class (Szamuely, 1974, p.36), and any deviation from that principle, any independent thought, came to be known as a political crime. This in turn led to the establishment of the political police. Under the tsar Ivan the Terrible (1533–84), the first political police in Russian history – the Oprichniki – came into being. The methods used by the Oprichniki were not dissimilar from those employed centuries later by another ruler; after a few years of unrestrained activities by the Oprichniki, some of the most powerful among them were executed in their turn. This period in Russian history (1564–72) has been known as the 'Oprichnina Terror'.

But it was only in 1649 that the notion of political crime was defined for the first time as a crime against the tsar and his realms and codified under the category of 'Words and Deeds' offences. At the time, the tsarist government relied mainly on denunciation by private citizens, but the perception of the existence of a vast number of enemies of the tsar scattered among all strata of society led to the creation of a separate police bureau – the Preobrazhenski Prikaz. This appears to have been the first organisation in history to deal exclusively with political crimes. It may be considered as a prototype model of a basic organ of all modern police states (Pipes, 1982, p.130).

Subsequent rulers in Russia practised political repression in a rather haphazard manner, but as contacts with the West grew rapidly and Western ideas began to infiltrate into the intelligentsia, it became necessary to undertake measures for 'internal' defence. This became particularly evident in connection with the Decembrist uprising. The first move in this direction was to give the Empire a regular political police force. It was established by Nicholas I in 1826 when he formed the Third Section of the Imperial Chancellery. The duties of the political police force included, in addition to uncovering and forestalling subversive activities, surveillance of foreigners, dissenters and a certain amount of censorship. Censorship in fact began much earlier in 1790 under Catherine. Later, many foreign books were prevented from entering Russia and hundreds were banned under Paul. Nicholas I went one step further; not only had the printed material to be free from harmful ideas, but it had also to make some positive contribution to public morals – an early form of 'positive censorship' forshadowing 'socialist realism' practised under the Bolsheviks in the Soviet Union.

The Russian Criminal Code of 1845 bears a striking resemblance to the Soviet (RSFSR) Code of 1927 and 1960. The tsarist Criminal Code provided for 'persons guilty of writing and spreading written or printed material or representation intended to arouse disrespect of Sovereign Authority or...Government...may be exiled with hard labour from ten to twelve years'. The Soviet 1960 Code (art.70) speaks of 'propaganda carried out for the purpose of slanderous fabrications which defame the Soviet state and social system, or circulating or preparing or keeping for the same purpose literature or such content; shall be punished by the deprivation of freedom for a term of six months to seven years, with or without additional exile for a term of two to five years'. Whether due to political necessity or political tradition prevailing in Russia for centuries, from the instant that the Bolsheviks came to power, they began to organise a police apparatus, a political police – the CHEKA – and continued this practice with some variations throughout Soviet rule. For example, the internal passport system that existed in Imperial Russia for the purpose of keeping control over the movement of individual Russians, a practice severely criticised by Lenin and abolished after the Revolution, was fully restored by the Soviet government in 1932 for the same purpose. These methods and many other aspects of the former Russian political behaviour were continued by the Soviet regime (Barghoorn, 1956, p.163).

THE POLITICAL CULTURE HERITAGE

The consolidation of the powers of the tsars, the creation of a state based on military power for the purpose of either defending or expanding the Empire, and the establishment of a political police to eliminate any traces of foreign influence and dissent, have all contributed to the political and cultural isolation of Imperial Russia from the rest of the civilised world. Russia's isolation became in fact an integral part of tsarist policy, whereby the militarised Russian state developed methods of governing and diplomacy which were to be a trait of the Russian political culture heritage. Suspicion of foreigners and of foreign influence was inherent in tsarist despotism (ibid.).

In contrast to this official xenophobia, the history of Russia offers abundant evidence of susceptibility to foreign influence. As far back as the sixteenth and seventeenth centuries, individual Russians who came in contact with foreigners and succumbed to the influence of foreign ideas attempted to flee their native land. Political emigration and the importance for Russians to travel abroad in the pre-Soviet period is a well known fact. As late as 1913 the Duma debated the government policy of permitting only politically reliable students to study abroad. On the other hand, severe limitations were always imposed on foreigners wishing to enter Russia. In 1914, an American or European traveller could cross the borders of any country without a visa, except Russia and Turkey. The Frenchmen, the Marquis De Custine, in a book on travel to Russia in the 1830s, commented that 'the Byzantine government and indeed all Russia have always looked upon the diplomatic corps and Westerners in general as envious and malevolent spies' (ibid., p.160).

But despite all the efforts by tsarist governments to eliminate or limit foreign influence, Russian isolationism was being gradually broken down by the growing forces of foreign trade and contacts – a process interrupted by the Revolution. The influence of Western ideas and the initial resistance to those ideas by conservative forces in Russia both came to a head in the controversy that arose within the intelligentsia in the late 1830s concerning Russia's historic mission. The origin of the controversy can be traced to some German thinkers who, influenced by Hegelian philosophy about the contribution by every country to the advancement of civilisation, tended to denigrate Slavic participation in the progress and classify the Slavs as an 'unhistorical' race. Reacting to this image of Russian culture, the intelligentsia created the so called 'Slavophile' theory. They presented Russia as the country of the future. On the other extreme were the 'Westerners' who rejected the missionary role of Russia. They admitted that Russia was different from the West but claimed that this was due to her backwardness rather than uniqueness. Peter Chadaev argued that Russia's contribution to civilisation was negligible due to the Byzantine form of Christianity adopted by Russia which led to her isolation from the European mainstream, and created a social structure that impeded cultural progress. According to Chadaev, 'Russia is a whole separate world, submissive to the will, caprice and fantasy of a single man, whether his name be Peter or Ivan...Russia moves only in the direction by her own enslavement and the enslavement of all the neighbouring peoples' (Pipes, 1982, p.268). The Slavophiles, however, created the first ideology of Russian nationalism. Russia was to become the country to solve the problems plaguing mankind.

In many ways, the internal situation and the social and cultural trends within Imperial Russia resemble those prevailing even at the present time. Although the controversy between the Slavophiles and Westerners has been diffused in the course of history, some of its aspects still remain. In the area of foreign influence, the Slavophiles have succeeded in instilling, so to speak, the fear that Western ideas may subvert the socialist consciousness of the Soviet people (a problem that will be investigated in detail in Chapter 9); while 'Westerners' advocate increased contacts with the West in order to benefit from the technological progress. The uniqueness of Russian society in the guise of progressive ideas of socialism which is to be the future of mankind, indicates a striking parallel to the Slavophiles view about Russia's messianic role.

SOVIET RUSSIAN NATIONALISM

The role played by the history of Russia in Soviet thought, especially military thought, can best be judged by the way historical events and ideas are interpreted by Soviet historians and by the method used to integrate them within general ideological tenets. References to Russia's past invariably include praise of Russian military theories especially those which, they say, preceded or paralleled those of the founders of Marxism. On military science, generally, they assert the superiority of Russian military science and trace it back to medieval Russian princes such as Igor, Vladimir Monomakh and others. Peter the Great is considered in this respect to be the founder of the Russian military school whose principles were further developed in the second half of the eighteenth century by Suvorov and Rumiantzev (*Istoria*, 1967, vol.III, p.251). They also make a point that despite Russia's economic and political backwardness and despite the retarding influence of Tsarism on the development of military ideas, Russian military theory 'far surpassed' that of other countries. By the eighteenth century, according to one Soviet assessment, the Russian army was already similar in terms of recruitment, composition and numbers to armies formed in the West much later in the first half of the nineteenth century. Suvorov's use of massed troops instead of linear tactics, before its introduction in the West by Napoleon, was another example of Russia's superiority in military matters quoted by a Soviet military figure (Sokolovsky, 1963, p.111).

In this context, the rule of a particular tsar is very often evaluated in a positive light when the changes in the military area introduced by him led to the expansion of the Russian Empire. The reorganisation of the state apparatus by Peter and the military reforms which he introduced are seen by Soviet historians as contributing to the attainment by Russia of the status of a great power, and the building of a powerful navy as a necessity to secure an outlet to the Baltic sea.

> The Russian navy honourably withstood the trials of war. Victories at Hangohud, Grenham and in other sea operations, gave the Russian navy the right to be considered as one of the most powerful in Europe . . .without an army and navy Russia could not have achieved her foreign policy objectives....In the centre of all these efforts stood Peter: 'really a great man', according to Engels, while Tshernishevski saw Peter as the 'ideal patriot', even if he represented the ideology of absolutism. (*Istoria*, 1967, vol.III, p.249)

It was also under the rule of Peter, according to Soviet historians, that military service began to be considered as a 'service for the homeland' and military art as 'most important for the defence of the fatherland' (ibid., p.247).

Noble as these attributes of service in the Imperial army may have been considered by Soviet historians, they seem to contradict a fundamental Marxist principle which states that the armed forces of the state exist only to defend the interests of the ruling classes. To resolve this apparent contradiction Soviet historians applied a dialectical method that often characterises the Soviet approach to ideological questions when they run counter to classical Marxism. In this case, they took great care to differentiate between the Russian people and Russian society as developing according to the Marxist theory of economic determinism and the regime of the tsar. Every victory of the Imperial Army was a victory by the Russian nation; while military defeats were those of Russian Tsarism (ibid., vol.IV, p.568). The reconciliation between the history of Imperial Russia as a process of a growing military power and territorial expansion, and the social development of Russian society took place within the context of nationalism and patriotism: 'the struggle against foreign invaders became fused in the conscience of the nation with the struggle against class enemies and the idea of defending the homeland with that of social liberation' (ibid., vol.IV, p.562).[1]

There can be little doubt that Russian patriotism is still a powerful factor in Soviet society and, as the Great Patriotic War had shown, can still be relied upon by the leadership in times of national emergency. After the German attack against the USSR, the official communist ideology has been largely replaced by the idealism of Russian patriotism. The all out effort to defeat the German invaders was not to be in defence of socialism and the Revolution – a slogan used during the intervention – but of Mother Russia: 'to defend freedom, honour and the motherland in our patriotic war against Germany' (Stalin, 1967, vol.XV, p.9). Stalin correctly assumed that nationalism is still an effective force and that 'the moral strength of the army consists in the fact that it defends the motherland' (ibid., p.7).[2]

His confidence in Russian patriotic feelings did not deceive him, and he was ready to recognise it when at a reception in the Kremlin on 24 May, 1945 he toasted the Russian people as 'the leading force in the Soviet Union...because it has a clear mind, strong character, patience...and...faith in the Soviet government'. On another occasion, he referred to political events which took place well before the Revolution. After the signing of the unconditional surrender by Japan, he reminded the Russians of the 'special account...with Japan'. The defeat of 1904 – said Stalin – 'left in the conscience of our people bitter memories. We – men of the old generation – have waited forty years for this day' (ibid., p.204).

MARX AND ENGELS IN SOVIET MILITARY THOUGHT

So far the emphasis of this study has been on those features of Soviet ideology that are reflected in the continuation of historically rooted traditions: militarism, isolationism coupled with fears of foreign influences, and other political and cultural remnants of Russia's history. But Soviet nationalism, although it has many important links with Russia's past, is not a purely 'Russian' product; it also represents the ideology of the new regime that came into power after the Revolution. The leaders of the Communist Party needed Russian nationalism to fill the void left by the destruction of beliefs and customs capable of satisfying the Russians (Barghoorn, 1956, p.260); they had to amalgamate Russian patriotism with socialist virtues and use it in the political process whenever necessary. The role of military power and its link with Russian history, patriotism and national security, on the one hand, and communism, on the other, found its expression in ideological terms of Marxism–Leninism – Russian nationalism became equated with Soviet patriotism, and the supremacy of everything that was Russian with the superiority of the Soviet system.

Subsequent treatment of the Great Patriotic War by Soviet historians incorporated a Marxist scientific approach. While the predominant role of the Russian people was generally emphasised when dealing with the Second World War, its outcome was seen as proof, indeed confirmation, of Marx's theory. The victory over Nazi Germany has been viewed not only as the result of a great national effort, but as the effect of the immutable laws of historical materialism which 'once more proved to be correct', and the final outcome as evidence of the superiority of the socialist system.

> The victory was not a matter of luck, but was preordained by the course of history...the war was a close race between the science, technologies, and economies of the opposing social systems. The Soviet defence economy proved to be more powerful...and the socialist system...demonstrated its vitality and efficiency. (Grechko, 1977, p.149)

Frequent references to the virtues and advantages of the socialist system are a common feature of Soviet analytical method and is often applied to questions of policy and military power. Any Soviet advance is predetermined by the laws discovered and formulated by Marx and Engels. According to these laws, Soviet military power and its structure as a system of economic, scientific, social, moral and political factors, which constitute its potential, must by definition achieve its supremacy, 'for it consists of the non-antagonistic nature of socialist society' (Volkogonov *et al.*, 1977, p.173).

The point of departure of the Soviet analysis of the role of military power and the nature of war itself are the ideas of Marx and Engels on the essence of war and its relation to politics (ideas which were later further developed by Lenin and adapted to Soviet reality by the Party leadership). The application of the Marxist interpretation of history to Soviet military theory is the basis of what the Soviets call military science, or rather of the part which deals with military doctrine: 'Marxist teaching on war and the army is an integral part of historical materialism, which became an important starting point and the guideline for Soviet military science' (Korablev, 1977, p.170).

Such a scientific approach seeks as its objective to adapt the military doctrine, military policy and strategy, as well as the composition of the armed forces, to the 'immutable laws of historical materialism', to justify scientifically the correctness of Soviet military policy and, at the same time, to confirm the truth of Marxist principles. Everything that is written in the Soviet Union on military matters must contain references to Marxist theory.

However, while dialectical materialism and economic determinism are referred to as important factors which determine the economic and social development of Soviet society as a whole, it is Engels to whom Soviet military theoreticians attribute the application of Marxist ideas to the theory of military power. Lenin himself referred to Engels as 'the greatest expert' on military matters and stressed the importance of military science (Lenin, 1964–65, vol.36, p.116). The importance of Engels in Soviet military literature can be attributed to his theoretical treatment of questions connected with the state of military power and economic development, with the link between the methods of waging war and, as he described, 'the nature of social relations prevailing at a given time in history'. With the help of specific examples, Engels attempted to show how the conditions of the army and the outcome of military operations are influenced by the level of socio-economic development and the political system of a country: 'the influence of the class structure of society on the organization, equipment and composition of armies, on the methods of conducting war operations and the development of art of war' (Marx and Engels, 1980, vol.18, p.xv).

Soviet theoreticians found Engels' approach to the analysis of the history of warfare original and attractive because it conformed to Marx's views 'that the armed forces of every society were the product of a certain social system, that every social formation tended to create a corresponding type of army and an equally corresponding way of waging war' (Engels, 1980, vol.18, p.xvi). Specific arms, according to Engels, were the weapons of the bourgeoisie against feudal nobility. The infantry and artillery were used by the bourgeoisie while the armour-clad cavalry disappeared with the defeat of the nobility. But, according to Engels, the decisive weapon in the struggle of the bourgeoisie against feudalism was nothing else but its economic power. 'Economic power supplied the means by which force could be applied – the instrument of force is armaments, the more perfect of which gets the upper hand over the less perfect' (Engels, 1962, pp.229–30).

The principle on which Engels based his so called 'Force Theory' emphasised the role of economic power in the transformation of society and in the class struggle. Force – said Engels – is no mere abstract notion but is based on concrete factors and comes into being as a result of the existence of instruments of force, namely, weapons. But as these weapons have to be produced, it follows that the producers of superior armament will have a great advantage over producers of inferior equipment. 'The triumph of forces is dependent on production in general – therefore, on "economic power"...on the material means which force has at its disposal' (ibid., p.22).

Force then, in the form of armed forces, requires huge funds for its maintenance which must be provided through production. So, according to Engels, it again depends on the economy which supplies means for the equipment of the army. Nothing depends more on economic conditions than the composition, organisation, armament, strategy and tactics of an army. While weapons are the basic requirements of the armed forces, their production depends directly on the level of the productive capacity of the state (Volkogonov *et al.,* 1977, p.22). In the final analysis, the level of the army and the weapons at its disposal reflect the level of economic development of a given society. The outcome of a military confrontation, a potential victory in a war – Marx is quoted as saying – is dependent on the production of weapons and this in turn on material factors (Lagovskyi, 1969). A more developed society, a more advanced economy, must be able to produce better and technologically superior weapons. Thus, 'superiority in the military field belongs to the country on a higher level of civilisation', and since, according to Marx, socialism is a higher stage of the development of society, it follows that the Soviet Union has all the attributes necessary to achieve economic and military superiority.

Despite the application of Marx's ideas to the Soviet situation and the references to Engels in military matters, Soviet analysts had to come to terms with the somewhat embarrassing fact that Marx and Engels were, on the whole, bitterly anti-Russian. The Soviets were particularly sensitive to the opinion about the Russian military expressed by Marx and Engels. They accepted criticism by Marx of Russian expansionism as originating from Russia's history and her link with the Mongol tradition, but rejected Engels' criticism of Russian military power. They objected to his assessment of Imperial Russia's position in Europe in the middle of the last century, and of the state and nature of her military power, because it ran counter to Russian nationalistic sentiments.[3]

Engels, in his days as a war correspondent reporting on the Crimean War, published a number of articles and essays dealing with military matters in which he made an analysis of military questions in the context of contemporary politics. He saw the political and military situation in Europe at the time as being basically a conflict between the more developed and more civilised West and the backward, despotic East. Militarily he assessed the advantage of Russia as 'being constantly in a state of impending war, while the West [he said] must still mobilise'. But this advantage was more than offset by the 'higher degree of industrial perfection existing in the Western countries' (Engels, 1980, p.128). The victory of 14 000 Allies over 30 000 Russians at the battle of Inkerman was due to a large extent, according to Engels, to the higher level of civilisation and superiority of armament and firepower of the British (ibid., p.534).

Analysing Russia's geographical and strategic position and her need to maintain a permanent large army equipped with arms equal to that of the West, Engels remarked that 'it is impossible to maintain permanently such an army on a war footing in a country with only partially developed resources' (a question subject to much debate even today). Engels concluded that the only reason for Russia to have a large army on her European borders was to maintain in subjection the Western non-Russian part of the Empire and to 'hang like a threatening cloud over the West of Europe' (ibid., p.126) – a conclusion which some contemporary Western analysts would fully endorse as being applicable to the present day situation.

It is also interesting to note that as far back as 1854 there already existed a controversy about the real military strength and capabilities of Russia – overrated by some, underrated by others. Engels was interested in the assessment of Russia's military power but, as today, he was hampered by the extreme secrecy of the tsarist regime and by the lack of expression of opposing views to its official policy. 'The West', said Engels, 'would soon scatter to the winds assertions which in Russia pass for Gospel truth, because there the opponent has no right to reply', but, he concluded, 'even that Russian military writings always glorify the tsar and Holy Russia, and in spite of the attempts at distortions, there remains enough positive information' (ibid., p.124).

Engels had also often expressed his disdain for the East as being barbarian and his belief in the superiority of Western civilisation. Criticising the 'Panslavism' movement theory as anti-historical, he accused it of intending to subjugate the civilised West under the barbarian East: 'behind this ludicrous theory stands the terrible reality of the Russian Empire...which for the last 150 years has never lost, but always gained territory by every war it commenced' (ibid., p.47).

Engels' uncomplimentary comments about the Imperial army were particularly offensive to Stalin, for whom Russian nationalism was an important political factor. He objected to the forthcoming publication in a Soviet journal of an article written by Engels on 'Foreign Policy of Russian Tsarism' on account of the opinion expressed in the article that the Imperial army owed her successes to foreign elements who, although 'dishonest but talented, have done more than all Russian armies to advance her borders' (Stalin, 1967, vol.xiv, p.4).

One Soviet commentator attributed Engels' attitude towards Russia to the influence of anti-Russian bias of the Western European press and the biased works of Western historians at the time. 'This, and also the political slant of articles against Russian Tsarism, explains the exaggerations and one-sided opinions held by

Engels' (Marx and Engels, 1980, vol.14, p.xxiv). An attempt has been made to 'correct' Engels on many points and to 'Russify', so to speak, Marx himself. Every scrap of evidence of favourable interest in Russia on the part of Marx and Engels has been exploited to the full in Soviet writings. Some of it was found in the praise that Engels had for the Russian soldiers, for 'the brilliant operation of the defenders of Sebastopol, the skills of the military engineers, combined with their usual tenacity'.

CONCLUSION

The survey of the main elements that appear to play an important role in Soviet thought on matters of national security and military force indicates the existence of some traditional features of the former Russian state and society; features that even today can be detected in Soviet attitudes. The survey has also revealed the extent to which these features have been incorporated into the ideology of the state. This ideology, which on the surface appears to represent most of the classical Marxist tenets, contains a large element of the Russian past and her historical experiences. As will be shown in the subsequent chapters, the recourse to an ideological interpretation of contemporary political, military and economic questions by the Soviets, although containing a fair dose of Marxism, is rarely devoid of the Russian historical and nationalistic elements which now carry the official definition of Soviet patriotism.

Within the context of the above conclusion we shall now turn to an important aspect of this study, the military policy of the Soviet Union, especially in its theoretically based military doctrine. The understanding and interpretation of the Soviet military doctrine is essential for the understanding of Soviet military policy as it pertains to the ongoing arms race. The ideological features that appear in the doctrine will be examined, as well as the pragmatic elements. An attempt will be made to indicate the link between Marxist principles and the historical experiences which shaped Soviet military thought and influenced the formation of its military doctrine.

3 Soviet Military Thought – Theory and Practice

INTRODUCTION

A comparison between the Western mode of analysis of war and military force and that of the Soviets underlines the different conceptual approach to military theory and practice by the East and the West. While in the West, due to the different political and social order and the totally different ideological basis of thought, such analyses do not form part of an aggregate scientific discipline, the Soviet approach presents a conceptually well structured (even if not always consistent) Marxist–Leninist theory on war and the army (Lider, 1983, p.180). In contrast to the Western structure of government which clearly separates the functions of the military and the civilian administration, these functions are integrated into the overall Soviet state system. Very often Soviet political leaders comment on military matters and it is not rare for the military to voice their opinion on political, economic and social questions. Military doctrine in the Soviet concept has a much wider scope than in the West; it embraces all aspects of military power in war as well as in peace time, and reflects the essence of the Soviet political and economic system that subordinates all facets of activities of the Soviet society to national security objectives. Consequently, an analysis of Soviet military doctrine and strategy must take into account the peculiarities of the ideological and theoretical approaches by the Soviets to questions of national security, for there is always the danger of a mirror-image analytical approach, which 'may distort the adversary's ideological premises and conclusions by attributing to him one's own values, criteria and way of reasoning' (ibid., p.314).

A doctrine, according to the Soviet definition, is understood to mean a philosophical and scientific theory – a system of guiding principles. It represents the officially adopted views on the character of war, on the method of warfare and on the preparation of the country and the army for war. In that sense, one can say that the Soviet military doctrine is war oriented; it attempts to foresee the circumstances which may lead to a war and the appropriate military policy to be adopted prior to the actual outbreak of hostilities. Military doctrine is considered as part of military science and the study of war and the army (peculiar to Marxism–Leninism) (Volkogonov *et al.,* 1977, p.390).

THE MILITARY DOCTRINE

The reliance of Marxism–Leninism on dialectical materialism means that the Soviet military doctrine must be scientifically justified in terms of 'objective laws' discovered by Marx and Engels.

> The theory of art of war, the means and methods of warfare, and military operations worked out by Soviet military science, is the outcome of the principles laid down by Marxism and developed by Lenin, about the dependence of art of war on the social and economic order, the level of development of production, science and technology, and the morale of the army. (Ogarkov, 1981, p.85)

According to Soviet theoreticians, Marxist–Leninist ideas determine the general theoretical and methodological principles of the science of war and military power. But as will be shown, Soviet military doctrine is not only the product of ideological motivations, but pragmatic ones as well, reflecting the interests of the Soviet state similar to Russia's imperial ambitions, as outlined in the previous chapter. Thus, one must not go to the extreme of viewing Soviet strategic policies as being determined exclusively by Marxist philosophy. Such perception of the Soviet position would necessarily disregard the ambiguities and inconsistencies that can be often detected in Soviet military literature and would not consider the conflict that arises between Marxist theoretical principles and questions of practical military strategy. It is for this reason that there is a constant attempt by Soviet military experts to reconcile ideological principles with a realistic approach to military policy through the differentiation between the concepts of military doctrine and military strategy; the former based on Marxist–Leninist theory of war and the army, the latter on pragmatic considerations.

The basis of a military doctrine, in the Soviet view, is the interpretation of the essence of war (ibid.), and it is guided by

Lenin's definition of war (borrowed from Clausewitz) as being a continuation of policy by other, namely, violent means. Lenin often quoted Clausewitz whom he considered as 'one of the most profound writers on the problems of war', and it was Lenin who introduced the notion of 'violent' means to describe 'other'. To understand war, according to Lenin, it is necessary to 'examine the policy pursued prior to the war, the policy that led to and brought about the war' (Grechko, 1977, p.274). It follows, that Soviet analysis of the nature of war implies, above all, its political content, political objectives and operating social forces. Accordingly, Marxist–Leninist definition of the nature of war would be equally applicable to a world nuclear war (Sheliag, 1974).

The source and origin of wars are viewed as the result of the appearance of antagonistic class societies and the exploiting system based on private property of means of production. But, since socialism became victorious in one country, Marxism–Leninism needed to move the revolution from the political stage of class struggle within a nation to that of a war between socialist and capitalist states (Semmel, 1981, p.17). Soviet theoreticians saw the class struggle as taking place not only within Western nations but also on an international plane between the two opposing camps – for the contradictions between the two world systems were class contradictions. The maintenance of the aggressiveness of imperialism is, therefore, the continuation of the historical conflict between the two socio-economic systems and of the general crisis of capitalism which is perceived by the Soviets as deepening constantly and revealing its internal contradictions (Volkogonov *et al.*, 1977, p.40). Thus, a future war would take on the ferocity of a revolutionary civil war. It would be 'a decisive armed collision between two opposing social systems'. The application of the Marxist principle of class struggle to the international arena clearly contradicts the Soviet stress on the operation of objective social forces within bourgeois countries as a factor which will bring about the victory of socialism. This contradiction has been subsequently modified in arguing that although the outcome of the class struggle is inevitably the triumph of socialism, it does not mean that it must inevitably lead to a global war.

While the official position of the Soviet Union concerning the possibility of an armed clash between the United States and the USSR has been modified to allow for the view that war is not inevitable, this was not reflected in the writings by some Soviet political analysts and theoreticians. The apparent contradiction between the historically determined inevitable armed confrontation and the possibility of peaceful coexistence was explained by one Soviet source in these terms: 'peaceful coexistence is a continuation of the conflict between two social systems but employs peaceful means without war. This conflict is an economic, political and ideological struggle, not a military one' (Sokolovsky, 1963, p.171).

An extension of the Marxist based analysis of the sources and origin of war as being the expression of the ongoing class struggle is the Leninist notion that the policy of which war is a continuation – that is, the class that is waging the war and the aims for which it is waging war – determines the character of a war (Lenin, 1964–5, vol.25, p.363). Consequently, he divided wars into 'just' and 'unjust' and classified them according to their socio-political content into wars between capitalist states, civil wars between the proletariat and the bourgeoisie, wars of national liberation and finally wars between capitalist and socialist states. While a Marxist solution to the problem of war assumed a situation in which world capitalism is overthrown, 'the victory of socialism in one country would not exclude at once all wars', according to Lenin. On the contrary, 'it presupposes war, since socialism cannot be victorious simultaneously in all countries, it will provoke an attempt to crush the socialist state's victorious proletariat by bourgeois of other countries'. Thus, 'wars of victorious socialism in one country against other bourgeois...states are a possibility'. The Marxist–Leninist analysis of the nature of different wars constituted for Soviet theoreticians an important principle that allowed them to determine the kind of enemy in a probable war. This could only have been a capitalist state or a group of states, for 'a bourgeoisie armed against the proletariat is one of the fundamental facts of modern capitalist society'. The classification of wars according to their socio-political content, which is one of the theoretical principles of Soviet military doctrine, is important for our analysis for it reveals one of the contradictions between the ideologically motivated approach to military questions and that attuned to political reality. Marxist theory of the origins of war and the Leninist classification into types of possible wars did not allow for the eventuality of a war between socialist states – Marxism–Leninism considers such wars as unconceivable and unthinkable.

FORMS OF WAR

The application of Marxist theory to the military doctrine is not limited to questions of a purely military nature but embraces a much wider area, and Soviet views on war as a continuation of policy by other means is much more complex than it appears. By adopting Marxism as the theoretical base together with the Clausewitzian principle, Soviet theoreticians have extended their understanding of the essence of war to include other forms that a war may take and which, from Moscow's point of view, are just as threatening to the security of the USSR as is a military confrontation. Although war in its strict definition is an armed struggle, it does not preclude other forms which by their nature are also a continuation of politics by other means. Economic warfare, ideological and psychological wars are, in the Soviet view, 'other' means of achieving political objectives and can be used without resorting to actual war: 'it is incorrect to view a war as only an armed struggle, although the latter represents a specific indication of war. Therefore, preparations for war and victory must include economic, political, psychological and ideological factors' (Usachev, 1976, p.42).

The total approach to the question of war in all its forms and manifestations, as seen by the Soviets, is in contrast to the West, where non-military aspects of war are not given sufficient attention in theoretical writings (Lider, 1983, p.12). But for the Soviets it is not a new concept and had always been reflected in the notion of 'capitalist encirclement' and the call for greater economic effort and ideological vigilance. Increasingly, they began to perceive the arms race as being imposed by the West as an instrument of economic pressure to put a break on the growth of socialist economies. 'The United States and other bourgeois countries seek through the arms race to weaken economically the socialist states. They want to slow down the economic development of the USSR and its allies and to exhaust their economies' (Faramazian, 1981, p.14).

The Soviets may have been reinforced in that conviction by the openly proclaimed objectives of the Reagan Administration, to which reference was made in the introductory chapter of this book. Thus, it should not come as a surprise that the Soviets were making strenuous efforts to become economically independent – a traditional Russian attitude examined in Chapter 2. The close connection between the Soviet economy and its military power constitutes an important feature of the Soviet military doctrine and influences, to a large degree, Soviet economic policies. A detailed examination of the theoretical basis of Soviet policies in this area will be the subject of Chapter 4, in which the Soviet perception of an economic war and its implications for Soviet relations with the West will be analysed.

Another variant of war which excludes an actual armed struggle is the ideological and propaganda war waged by the United States, according to the Soviets. The place that ideological warfare assumed recently within the Soviet military doctrine is evident from the increased volume of literature devoted to that subject. Such war appears to the Soviets as an attempt to subvert their society and to undermine the very ideological foundation on which the regime claims its legitimacy. The notion of ideological warfare constitutes an integral part of Soviet military doctrine and the means of response to the perceived danger of ideological subversion are part of the military strategy. As with other aspects of the Soviet military doctrine, the perception of ideological contamination is, to some extent, linked to Russian traditional trends towards the isolation of Soviet society from Western influence, to which we referred earlier, but we shall examine the question of ideological war in greater detail in Chapter 9.

In recent years, the Soviets have also shown a marked concern with psychological effects that the international situation may have on the population. The term psychological warfare has appeared in the Soviet classification of non-military forms of war. According to one Soviet source, 'psychological war is a means of exerting political and emotional pressure on the Soviet Union and the socialist community'. The purpose of the 'psychological war', comments the same source, is to influence the mood of the Soviet population by making it aware of the gravity of the world situation and the dangers the Soviet Union is facing. This is being done through disinformation aimed at creating a war-psychosis (Tolkunov, 1982, pp.93–4). The psychological war thus becomes part of the more general classification of the ideological war.

THE MILITARY POTENTIAL IN THE SOVIET DOCTRINE

A significant feature of the military doctrine of the Soviet Union is the assessment of the factors that will be instrumental in achieving victory in a potential war with the capitalist enemy. This is of the utmost importance for, in the context of the determination of the features of military and non-military forms of warfare, it allows the Soviets to adopt corresponding measures in their military strategy (Tiushkevich, 1978, p.478).

Military power in its structure is looked upon by the Soviets not only in its quantitative and qualitative aspects of strategic and conventional weapons, but as a system of economic, scientific and technological, moral and spiritual factors embracing the human element (Milovidov, 1973). They all contribute to the military potential of the USSR and will determine the course and outcome of a military confrontation. Factors or potentials that affect the final outcome of a war are a basic analytical tool in Soviet military literature and have replaced Stalin's thesis (1942) on the five permanent acting factors of war (Berman and Baker, 1982, p.111).

The most important factor, one that in itself embraces the potential for superior military strength and fighting capability, is the economic potential of the Soviet Union which 'through its productive forces forms the military power of the state' (*Siezd*, 1978, p.235). The theoretical basis for this view are the ideas of Engels about the relation between the outcome of a war and the level of technological development of a society, to which we referred in Chapter 2. The economic potential of a state is determined by the capacity of its economy to satisfy material necessities of an individual and society as a whole, while at the same time producing everything necessary for its defence needs. (An analysis of the two conflicting objectives within the Soviet economic and military policies will be the subject of Chapter 6.)

Taking the Marxist position, the Soviets assert that the economic potential depends upon the level of development of productive forces. Consequently, within the socialist type of organisation of the state, which determines the economic structure and the 'material productive relations', the process of planning and development of the economic potentials of the USSR, and by implication its military capabilities, is considered by the Soviets to be far superior to a capitalist one. The correctness of this view is usually confirmed by quoting Lenin who predicted that 'the defence capability of a country that threw off the yoke of capitalism...would be many times greater than the defence capabilities of capitalist countries' (Lagovskyi, 1969).

The assessment of the economic potential as a factor of military power is also extended to include the economies of the Warsaw Pact countries, as well as other socialist states which form part of a 'world socialist system'. The military–economic integration of Eastern Europe is perceived as an important factor of the military–strategic position of the USSR, and although the process of integration of the West is recognised by the Soviets as giving the 'imperialists some particular advantages by enhancing the distribution of military and industrial resources and the advantages of economies of scale in the production of weapons', it is seen as an unstable situation which will eventually create and sharpen the contradictions inherent in capitalism – each member of the Western coalition attempting to resolve its problems for its own benefit (Volkogonov *et al.*, 1977, pp.186–8). By contrast, within the framework of an alliance of socialist states, there is a total absence of antagonistic contradictions.[1]

The importance of the economic factor within the concept of the military potential of the USSR is an essential part of the Soviet military doctrine.

> The economic readiness for war represents the embodiment of part of the economic potential and an active part in peacetime in order to secure supplies for military operations during war time. The military-economic potential being part of the total economic potential of the country constitutes the link between economic preparedness of the state in peacetime and the course and outcome of a war (ibid., p.192)

In respect of the industrial potential of the USSR, the importance of the geographical location of sources of raw material and other 'productive forces' is part of the overall military strategy and its defensive aspect is often stressed (Shuvalov, 1965, p.12). Special attention is to be given to the need for dispersing industrial power sources (Sokolovsky, 1963, p.326). Generally, the USSR should take advantage of its geographical position which gives it the possibilities of dispersing its industries, while the military and economic foundation of the Western bloc would be highly vulnerable to a nuclear attack due to its concentration in limited regions and its dependence on imports. In a future war, it will be the West that will suffer because of its population and industrial concentration (Khrushchev, *Pravda*, 15 January, 1960).

The emphasis is also upon mobility of industry, the relocation of production facilities and on the ability of adaptation of industries for war production (Volchkov, 1971). It echoes the experience of the Second World War when a large part of Soviet production capacity had been moved and relocated deep within the Soviet Union (this will be taken up in some detail in Chapter 4). At the same time, the Soviets seem to realise that under the conditions of modern warfare that task may not be so simple. This, according to one Soviet analyst, will be an important problem because of the decrease of the role of the territorial factor in a missile war, and a most complex task as there may not be sufficient time for moving industrial capacity (ibid.).

Another factor which will play an important role during war operations, one that always assumed a far greater place in the Soviet military doctrine than it did in the West, is the human element. The stress on the role of the human factor is based on a Marxist view of technological progress and the relation between man and technology in a modern war, on the one hand, and the role of an individual and the morale of the troops – a Clausewitzian notion – on the other. Both approaches take as their point of departure the apparent belief that nuclear weapons may not decide the outcome of a war.

The Soviets assert that 'man was and remains the decisive factor in war. A nuclear war cannot be considered through computer models only without taking into account the human element' (Arbatov A., 1981, p.106). Accordingly, no matter how powerful nuclear weapons are, they must not be considered as the decisive factor to achieve the objective of the battle (Reznichenko, 1984, p.42), and since it is the man on the battleground who may determine the outcome of the combat, he must be psychologically prepared (ibid., p.63). The emphasis on the human element reflects Lenin's interest in Clausewitz who did put morale as an essential factor in a war. It is also a reflection of the traditional role of ground troops in pre-revolutionary wars of Imperial Russia. The view on the place of ground troops is also reflected in Soviet military tactics, the operation of ground forces under actual nuclear war conditions, which will be examined in the final part of this chapter.

In view of the stress on the human element, it is not surprising that the Soviets show an increasing interest in psychological problems that may arise in the course of a nuclear attack. Such questions were not revealed, let alone discussed, in earlier writings, and the area of applied psychology was previously neglected and practically ignored in Soviet military literature. One Soviet source stresses the fact that the outbreak of a nuclear war will introduce a new element into the psychology not only of the army but the population at large because of the extraordinary dynamics of operations and the huge scale of losses and destruction. The application of a previously unknown weapon will 'catch the mind by surprise, above all in the emotional sense' and the possibility of mass fear is freely conceded by the commentator: 'as is well known, people blinded by fear cease to evaluate reality. Their world becomes confined to personal imagination distorted by fear' (Volkogonov *et al.*, 1977, p.246).

Psychological problems resulting from a nuclear attack are even more highlighted by the Soviet military in relation to army personnel. The role of psychology in this respect consists in the preparation of the population and the troops for conditions that will follow the outbreak of a nuclear war. The capacity of the individual, whether on the front or in the rear, to overcome the potential problems which a nuclear war may create is, what the Soviets call, the spiritual factor of the military power. The means for overcoming these problems are contained in ideological indoctrination which stresses the need for optimism based on faith in the political and moral principles of Soviet policy, 'all of which add to the spiritual potential of the people and the army' (Yegorov *et al.*, 1970, p.88). The role of the spiritual or moral factor is considered to be of first-rate importance and, according to the late Marshal Grechko (1977, p.165), 'under certain circumstances may reduce the enemy's superiority to nil for it will mobilise...and restore the fighting capacity of the surviving armed forces'.

MILITARY STRATEGY

The general theoretical concept of Soviet military doctrine, examined so far, ought not to be confused with the notion of military strategy which, although rooted in the doctrine, considers the more practical questions of composition of the armed forces, method of warfare, and planning, development and production of armament.

One Soviet source defines the link between the two concepts in the following terms:

> Military strategy occupies a subordinate position to military doctrine in the sense that the latter determines general positions, while the former, starting from general considerations, investigates and develops concrete problems affecting the nature of a future war, military preparedness of the country, organisation of the armed forces and method of warfare (Sokolovsky, 1963, p.421)

Another important feature which makes Soviet military strategy distinct from its doctrine is that strategy is being adapted to changes in the means of warfare and 'is being amended and developed according to the alignment of forces in the world and the state of the Soviet economy' (Grechko, 1977, p.273), while the military doctrine remains basically unchanged.[2]

This can be illustrated by looking at Soviet military policies from a post Second World War historical perspective with a special emphasis on Soviet responses to changes taking place in the outside world and in the military technology in particular.

As we have indicated earlier, the fundamental principle upon which rests the Soviet military doctrine, one that had been adopted by Lenin from Clausewitz, is the view of war as a continuation of politics and as an instrument of policy. The advent of nuclear weapons and the prospect of a nuclear confrontation between the USSR and the USA did not initially change the view of Soviet theoreticians regarding that principle – 'even a nuclear war would be a continuation of policies by other means'.

At first, the Soviet leadership attempted to play down the strategic importance of the atom bomb and in fact the American raid on Japan had not been given much publicity. Strategically, Soviet thinking was still dominated by the recent experience of the Second World War and Soviet strategists claimed that the decisiveness of nuclear weapons was overrated. They may have followed Stalin's personal opinion who, in an answer to a question by a *Sunday Times* correspondent, declared that he does not consider the atom bomb such a serious power as some politicians are inclined to think: 'atom bombs are intended to frighten those with weak nerves, but they cannot decide the outcome of a war' (*Bolshevik*, November 1946).

Even after the elimination of the nuclear monopoly, the strategic objective of keeping large ground forces reflected Soviet thinking dominated by historical experience, while the rapid devlopment of strategic nuclear capability was aimed at creating an effective deterrent against a possible American nuclear strike. The two objectives also reflected various opinions among the military and the political leadership about the composition of the Soviet armed forces. Until the matter of ground troops versus nuclear missiles came to a head during Khrushchev's rule, the conservative view that 'strategic bombing will not decide the outcome of war, but soldiers on the battlefield' seemed to have prevailed, but after the announced first flight of the Russian ICBM in August 1957, there was an increased emphasis on creating nuclear rocket forces and, at the same time, the relevance of respective branches of Soviet military forces became an important issue and subject of debate within the Soviet leadership.

It was Khrushchev who was putting a 'one sided' emphasis on the ballistic missiles and suggested a substantial reduction in the number of troops. He claimed that the reduction was made possible because the USSR has 'new types of weapons – nuclear missiles – that can strike at any part of the world', therefore, the defence capability of the Soviet Union will not be determined any more by the number of troops. In a speech on 15 January 1960, Khrushchev also stated that the decision to reduce the numerical strength of the armed forces had not been taken by the government unilaterally, but as he said: 'we have examined the problem in details and in every aspect. We have asked for advice the military and the chiefs of staff.' Khrushchev was supported at the time by Marshal Malinovsky who considered rocket troops as the main branch of the armed forces, as well as by Major General N.Talensky. The new strategy, which relied on nuclear missiles rather than ground forces, has not remained unchallenged and is said to be one of the reasons of Khrushchev's downfall (Semmel, 1981, p.32). Under the pressure of the military Khrushchev was forced to announce, in July 1961, a temporary halt to the planned reduction of Soviet troops.

The reorientation towards a balanced development of all types of armed forces became especially marked after the October 1964 Plenary Meeting of the Central Committee of CPSU when the 'mistaken' views within the military circles of overestimating the capabilities of nuclear weapons and their role as a deterrent gave way to the new strategic policy. Marshal Grechko (1977), stressed the new principle of Soviet military policy of not placing a 'particular branch of the armed forces above all others' in these words: 'For all their formidable power and vital role, nuclear strategic ICBM's cannot attain every objective of war. This is why efforts are continuing to develop new and improved existing types of conventional weapons' (ibid., p.159).

At the same time, Soviet military literature began to show an implicit acceptance of American strategic concepts. One well-known commentator, in a book published by the Ministry of Defence in 1978 (Tiushkevich), analysed the probable ways in which a nuclear war might begin and the ways in which it would be conducted. The analysis revealed a large degree of resemblance to Western mode of military thinking.[3]

It presented variants of a nuclear war: a sudden nuclear strike as a beginning of a war, a sudden nuclear strike in the course of a conventional war, or a sudden mass use of nuclear weapons following a limited use of tactical weapons – in other words through escalation. According to the author, nuclear conflicts can be divided into three kinds: strategic (general) war with unlimited application of the whole arsenal of nuclear offensive; a 'limited' strategic war in which nuclear strikes would be directed only on military targets; theatre war, mainly in Europe where tactical weapons would be used; finally a non-nuclear war was also considered as a possibility. He concluded that the correct determination of the characteristics of a modern war was of immense importance for the adoption of 'corresponding measures for the organization and equipment of the armed forces' (Tiushkevich, 1978, pp.477–8).

The controversy among the Soviet military leadership regarding the role of strategic nuclear missiles versus ground forces and conventional weapons has not been entirely resolved. It would appear, nevertheless, that a compromise has been reached between the two opposing views, but while Soviet military effort was directed towards a general and all embracing development of its military power, strategic nuclear forces were still considered as the basic element of Soviet strategy and as an effective deterrent.

> The most important component of Soviet military might in contemporary conditions, is its strategic nuclear force which serves as a basic factor to deter aggression...The launching of modern ICBMs is automated and their technical characteristics

allows them to strike at the opponent's targets with sufficient accuracy in practically every corner of the globe. (Ogarkov, 1981, p.87)

The shifting emphasis from the quantitative to the qualitative aspect of the Soviet military effort, indicated an attempt by Soviet strategists to respond to the American military doctrine with its heavy emphasis on sophisticated technology. But at the same time, the Soviets expressed the fear that deterrence which was based on 'mutual vulnerability and on unacceptability of damage caused by a returned nuclear strike' (Usachev, 1976, p.171), may give way to a situation when it 'will be practically impossible to determine through national means, the overall quantity, the nature of the charge, the mode of deployment and the likely targets of the new weapons' (Sergeiev, 1981, p.35). Furthermore, modern war technology has blurred the distinction between attack and defence. According to Sokolov, the former Soviet Minister for Defence, the latest trend in military technology, the SDI, which on the face of it is a defensive system, contains as an ultimate objective a first-strike capability (*Pravda*, 2 March 1986).

Although the Soviets constantly stressed that they do not believe in a limited nuclear war (Lavrionov, 1982) they began, nevertheless, to diversify their military efforts to allow for many forms of a potential war: short nuclear exchange, full scale nuclear war, as well as a conventional and protracted one requiring large ground forces. Present Soviet military strategy takes into account the eventuality that the first massive nuclear-rocket attack may not immediately influence the course of war.

The role assigned by the Soviets to ground forces in a future war stems partly from historical experience of Russian wars, mainly the Second World War, and partly from the perception of the political objectives of a war. This assumes the final defeat of the enemy on the ground and the capture of his territory. According to Marshal Sokolovsky, 'political objectives of the establishing of proper order and peaceful settlement of all problems after the war, can only be attained as a result of operations of the ground forces'. One of the reasons for maintaining a large standing army and the constant buildup of conventional weapons, appears to be the view that even after a surprise attack, conventional forces will play a decisive role. While 'missiles and nuclear weapons are powerful military means, they cannot conquer the territory of another state' (Sokolovsky,

1963, p.xv). Finally, although Soviet military strategy considers that nuclear rockets will determine the speed and the course of a war, the possibility that it may be protracted is not excluded (Tiushkevich, 1978, p.429).

MILITARY OPERATIONAL TACTICS

We have analysed, so far, the Soviet doctrine which is based on ideological principles that define the essence and nature of war, its various forms and, generally, the theoretical grounds for war preparations. We have also surveyed the Soviet concept of military strategy 'the highest area of military art which includes the theory and practice of preparing the country and the armed forces for war and the planning for conducting strategic operations' (Reznichenko, 1984, p.7). We shall now proceed to perhaps the most revealing aspect of Soviet military thought, to the so called 'taktika', or mode of operation of army units under actual war conditions that may involve the use of nuclear weapons. The tactical aspect of Soviet military thought is of utmost significance for it represents the purely practical application of the theory of the Soviet doctrine and strategy, while at the same time, it reveals the kind of military training practised in the Soviet armed forces.[4]

A manual published by the Ministry of Defence, in 1984, designated for the commanding staff of the armed forces and trainees in military academies, considered very carefully and in precise terms the conduct of war operations by Soviet troops using conventional as well as nuclear weapons. The theory and practice of the application of tactics during war operations is still based on the assumption that the decisive factor in any war, including a nuclear one, is the man on the battlefield.

The importance attributed to the role of the man on the ground is not an outcome of a philosophical principle alone, but a realistic view that technology no matter how developed must still depend on the human element that controls it. In contrast to the physical characteristics of modern weapons, whose performance can be tested and determined beforehand though not necessarily under actual combat conditions, the results of theoretical research in the area of military science are not able to substantiate the established principles, nor is research accompanied with concrete evidence which will determine with sufficient precision the course of military operations under actual battle conditions. It is for the man on the battleground, 'in our times as in the future', to assume the decisive role in this respect (Reznichenko, 1984, p.6).

It is not surprising that the rules to be followed according to Soviet military tactics indicate an approach to military operations under conditions of nuclear warfare reminiscent of the Second World War. In fact there seems to be little distinction made between nuclear strikes and the use of conventional weapons. Attack, counterattack, and defensive actions during military operations are dealt with in classical terms of troop movements.

> What could happen is that as a result of a massive nuclear and conventional strikes, the advancing enemy may succeed in breaking the defence line. In such a situation the defending units must take all the necessary measures to retain their positions before going over to a counterattack which can only be successful if it contains the element of surprise, as was the case during the Great Patriotic War (ibid., p.210–11)

Defence is also considered in terms of classical methods as if conventional weapons were used. But clearly, defence operations will have to be conducted in areas devastated by mutual strikes with nuclear weapons which will make the conduct of combat operations extremely difficult. According to the manual, large zones of radioactive contamination might 'temporarily' stop the movement of troops, but in the meantime and prior to a situation when the threat of a nuclear strike by the enemy becomes apparent, the army personnel is to take cover in dug-outs, shelters, bottom of trenches, in armoured vehicles whose hatches, doors, slits, blinds, etc. will be closed (ibid., p.239).

While it is admitted that there will be a large number of casualties, the affected army units are to 'await the reduction of the level of radiation and restore their fighting capacity' (ibid., p.224). This will presumably involve the restoration of the command links, the removal of the effects of the nuclear attack, clearing of roads, and search for ways of bypassing contaminated areas. Affected personnel are to be evacuated to the nearest hospital and damaged armament and other military equipment that cannot be repaired on the spot is to be handed over to an officer in charge of evacuation and repairs. The same procedure is to be followed after an aerial attack in which nuclear-tipped rockets of large and 'superlarge' calibre will be dropped (ibid., p.250). Units that have retained their fighting capability after a nuclear strike are to continue their forward movement. Nuclear weapons, nevertheless, are considered of great importance for Soviet offensive operations, 'for they will allow the annihilation of the enemy in a very short time' (ibid., p.74). But it will be for the ground forces to follow up a nuclear strike by an advance despite the enemy's counterattack.

Of additional interest is Soviet strategy in case of an attack by neutron weapons. Since, as it appears, the Soviets do not possess, so far, operational neutron weapons, they quote the technical characteristics and their effects from Western sources. For example, an explosion of a neutron bomb of about 1000 tons – the equivalent to 30 000 tons of TNT – will affect the army personnel within a radius of 1300–1400 meters, and those in tank units within 1000 meters. The Soviet manual emphasises that the effectiveness of a neutron bomb explosion is drastically diminished with the distance from its epicentre. At a distance of 1600 meters its effect is weakened a thousand times and a protective layer of 35 cm of moist soil or 25 cm of concrete will further reduce the effects of the explosion by ten times. A doubling of the thickness of the protective layers will reduce the effects by up to 100 times. Also forming a marching column in a V-shape with increased intervals between the subunits should bring down the casualty losses to only 30 per cent (ibid., p.17). However, the main defence against a nuclear attack is to 'be able to uncover and destroy the nuclear means of the advancing enemy before he can use them' (ibid., p.178). This can be taken as an indication that a pre-emptive strike is not excluded.

Our survey of the changes in Soviet military thought since the end of the Second World War would not be complete without an examination of the changes that took place in the Soviet military doctrine. Contrary to the Soviet view that it is only military strategy that alters according to the prevailing technology and balance of military power, the military doctrine of the Soviet Union also underwent a fundamental change. An analysis by the well-known G. Arbatov is most revealing in this regard (*Kommunist*, no.2, 1987). There are two main aspects of the changed doctrine. First, the old Clausewitzan principle of war as a continuation of policies by other means is no longer part of the doctrine. According to Arbatov, 'the advent of the nuclear era constituted the end of an historical period when it was possible to exploit the war and military power as an instrument of policy – its continuation with other means'. The same opinion was expressed by the former Minister for Defence, Sokolov (*Pravda*, 9 May 1987).

Secondly, the Marxist interpretation of war as being the result of the existence of capitalism has also been modified, as was the assumption that only the victory of socialism in the whole world will bring about the end of wars 'because war ceased to serve the interests of the bourgeousie. A modern war would be just as disastrous for the bourgeoisie as for other classes, just as suicidal for capitalism as for socialism' (Arbatov G., 1987).

As a corollary to the above, the question of deterrence acquired an increased significance in Soviet military thinking. While earlier the Soviets always denied the concept of deterrence as being instrumental in preventing a nuclear war, their latest view on that subject is almost identical with opinions expressed in the West. In the words of Arbatov (ibid., p.108):

> the destructive power of nuclear weapons almost automatically excludes the possibility of their use. More than that, nuclear weapons by making the big powers more careful, help to restrain dangerous local conflicts in which conventional weapons are used. Thanks to this mankind has been able to live for forty years without a world war.

In fact the idea of a nuclear deterrence is being publicised within the Soviet Union in a manner unthinkable only a few years ago. Following the new trend of *glasnost*, Soviet social scientists embarked upon a programme of opinion polls in order to study attitudes and opinions of the Soviet population on a range of political and economic issues. In one particular poll, a question was asked whether the elimination of nuclear weapons will increase the possibility of a conventional confrontation between East and West (Ivanov, V., *Kommunist*, no.5, 1987, p.118). The results of the poll indicated that opinions were almost equally divided between those that answered affirmatively, negatively and undecidedly. But the significance of this poll is not so much in its findings as in the fact that it was published. It seems as if the Soviet leadership would like the population to see the strategic parity between the superpowers, which the Soviets claim exists, as preventing a nuclear war.

In the context of this assumption, the negotiations that have been taking place between the superpowers for a number of years and the apparent willingness by the Soviets to offer substantial concessions, can be explained as an attempt by them to retain the nuclear balance as an effective deterrence. One can also interpret fierce Soviet objections to the American SDI programme as an indication of a perceived threat to that balance. The Soviets still seem to be convinced that the ultimate objective of the United States is to 'force the USSR to change its foreign policy and domestic order' (Arbatov, G., 1987, p.105).

CONCLUSION

By analysing Soviet military thought we have attempted to dissect it into the various factors which determine Soviet military policies, and to indicate the complexity of approach to questions of military importance by the Soviet leadership. The analysis revealed that Soviet military thought and policies are not based exclusively on purely military–strategic concepts but look at the question of national security and war in their totality. The separation of the theoretical concept of military doctrine from the more practical notion of strategy and tactics, allows the Soviets to incorporate into their thinking some of the classical Marxist tenets and combine them with historical traditions.

The military doctrine, which is based essentially on theoretical principles, indicates an attempt to make it conform to the general objective of socialist ideals which, if achieved, would provide the Soviet armed forces with the advantages over capitalism and military superiority. Within the context of the military doctrine, the economic potential which constitutes the base of Soviet military power will be superior as well. A socialist economy will be by definition more productive than would be a capitalist one, while the morale of the armed forces thanks to a developed socialist consciousness will be the decisive factor over an enemy deprived of real motivation. The Soviet military doctrine is thus relying on an ideal to be attained in the future. This is the normative feature of Soviet ideology referred to in the preceding chapter.

By contrast, the Soviet military strategy takes a more pragmatic position in relation to military questions; one that takes into account the existing state of Soviet technology as compared to that of the United States and puts into practice policies that would counteract any American initiative. The Soviets also appear to rely on a more conventional approach to military strategy that very often is reminiscent of methods used in the Second World War and even earlier wars. It is, in a way, an implicit recognition of technological inferiority. They still appear to put great emphasis on the belief in territorial advantage, on dispersion of production potentials of the country, as well as on the morale factor – the ability to mobilise the population in a national emergency.

As we have also seen, in the area of military policy the economic factor is considered as decisive for the maintenance of a strong military posture. As the Soviet themselves would admit, a military doctrine and military strategy, no matter how theoretically correct, while they determine policies, are not of much use unless they are backed by material factors such as production of weapons, modern technology and abundance of manpower. In other words – by the economic potential of the country.

The economic factor within the overall Soviet military policy is of prime importance and, as we shall see in the following chapters, is a powerful determinant of Soviet domestic as well as foreign policies. Domestically it is important for the solution of economic difficulties connected with economic efficiency – a problem more relevant to the Soviets than military expenditure, as we shall suggest in Chapter 8.

4 The Economic War: Economic Power and National Security

INTRODUCTION

The classical dictum about the ultimate objective of war as being 'to submit the enemy to our will' is as valid today as it was when first formulated by Clausewitz. At the time, war had been viewed in its ultimate form 'as an act of violence', a confrontation using military means to achieve the above objective. In the contemporary situation, however, the physical force – the military option as a solution to the conflict between the superpowers – is generally considered as not feasible for it would spell a global disaster. But the concept of forcing a change in the behaviour of the adversary, the 'submission to [the] will' by other than military means, if the latter is not possible for the time being, is still applicable at the present time.

The American objective of negotiating with the Soviet Union from a position of strength, to which reference was made earlier, could be considered as the modern application of the Clausewitzian principle. The rearmament programme launched by the Reagan Administration was to be the main option of the American foreign policy aimed at a change in Soviet conduct. It had also been suggested that simultaneously with the intensification of the defence effort by the United States, use was to be made of a second option – that of economic pressure. An assessment of the Soviet economy as being in crisis, due to inadequate productivity and incapability of changing internally, led some Western thinkers to the conclusion that 'the West would be well advised to do all in its power to assist the indigenous forces making for change in the USSR, on the one hand, and to deny the Soviet bloc various forms of economic aid in order to intensify the formidable pressures which are being exerted on their creaky economies'. Such policies, coming increasingly under the term of the 'Reagan Doctrine', simply mean 'pushing Soviet influence back inside the borders of the Soviet Union with the combined pressure of a military buildup along with...economic measures' (Bode, 1986, p.21).

The consideration of economic means of exerting pressure upon the Soviet Union, in order ultimately to change its behaviour by other than military means, is being evaluated by the Soviet leadership as an American effort which, they say, is directed on the one hand towards achieving military superiority so as to be able to dictate to the Soviet Union conditions it will not accept, and at the same time, to affect the USSR economically as well. Such a course is considered by the Soviets as an 'economic war'. From the Soviet point of view, the arms race is being used by the United States as an instrument of military, political and economic pressure in order to put a brake on the growth of socialist economies, since it 'forces the USSR and its allies to use considerable resources for the strengthening of its defences' (Ponomarev, 1977).

The Soviets do agree that the arms race has a negative effect on the economic growth of the socialist countries, but are quick to point out that the hope to 'exhaust' the USSR economically by drawing it into costly military programmes will be in vain as the course of the post-war economic development of the Soviet Union has proved.

> The expenditure that the USSR and other socialist countries are forced to make to safeguard their security, naturally reduces the resources available for their economic development programmes. However, the advance of the Soviet economy shows that the main targets of the national economic plans are being successfully fulfilled...(Zhlobin, 1975, p.200).

Assertions of this kind are not rare in Soviet political literature. They usually contain a large dose of propaganda and are clearly made for home consumption. But for a Western analyst the problem to be investigated is the relationship between the Soviet economic performance and its defence effort.

The relationship between military expenditure and the economic resources that a country is able to divert for building up its armed forces is an important aspect of the analysis of the arms race. One of the limiting factors on military expenditure is the capacity of an economy to sustain it, and would be equally applicable to the Soviet Union, the United States or any other country. A larger GNP reflects a greater capability to meet defence requirements and, at the same time, to satisfy civilian needs. But as the arms race continues, the USSR as well as the USA are forced to divert additional resources to military areas. The American Administration openly calls for more funds and increased military budget, and while the Soviet Union claims not to have raised its military expenditure it may be reasonable to assume that in order to match the projected increased military spending by the American Administration, the USSR will have to use a greater proportion of its resources for the same purpose. The arms race, therefore, takes on a different, although not entirely new, dimension of not only a race for strategic advantage, but also of a contest of economic strength.

DEFENCE AND THE SOVIET ECONOMY IN HISTORICAL PERSPECTIVE

As indicated earlier in Chapter 2, the theoretical-ideological grounds for the belief in the capacity of the Soviet economy to meet the defence requirements are rooted in the ideas of Marx and Engels. But the emphasis on the role of economic development and industrialisation in particular is not based exclusively on ideology. It can be traced back to the last century when Russia's military defeats have been the catalysts for state intervention directed towards the development of a strong industrial base. The same problem arose during the Second World War when the poorly equipped Russian army had to fight against the well-structured and technologically superior German army. Even Lenin himself saw Russia's military failures as a result of her backwardness. The call for a full transformation of Russia's economy to a socialist one, which Lenin launched in September 1917 just prior to the Revolution, may have been motivated not only by ideological considerations but by his perception that a highly centralised economic system 'will not only solve [Russia's] domestic problems but her military [ones] as well' (Lenin, 1964–5, vol.25, p.360). From a practical point of view Lenin saw that the only way to make Russia capable of defending herself was 'to destroy with Jacobin ruthlessness everything old and to renew and rebuild Russia economically'. Rebuilding a sound economic base was then the primary task of the new regime. Lenin expressed his belief that with the establishment of socialist means of production, 'no capitalist enemy will be a threat to us' (Zhlobin, 1975, p.117). He already claimed at the time that the 'link between military organization of the country and its economic and social order was never as close as it is today' (Lenin, 1964–5, vol.9, p.156), and he was convinced about the superiority of the socialist mode of production.

On the other hand, Lenin's pragmatic approach to problems which the new Soviet state had to face can be found in his views on the question of a separate peace with Germany. Defending the decision to negotiate it, Lenin pointed out that the state of the army 'coupled with the incredible chaos in the area of food supply' necessitated such a step. He saw an urgent need for a few months of relative peace for the consolidation of power, reorganisation of the political and economic order and 'the creation of a solid economic base for a 'mighty worker's and peasant's Red Army' (ibid., vol.26, p.449). Following the signing of the Brest–Litovsk Armistice Agreement, Lenin called for an all out effort to take advantage of the respite to 'bring about an economic revival without which a real increase in [the]...country's defence potential is inconceivable' (ibid., vol.27, p.238). Except for the short period of NEP when problems of internal stability of the regime were of prime concern, the preoccupation of the Soviet leadership with building a sound economic base through industrialisation and collectivisation of agriculture had as its source national security considerations.

> [T]he successful completion of the first Five-Year Plan...the consistent implementation of the Leninist course toward the country's industrialization and collectivisation of agriculture...meant a further strengthening of economic and defence capacity of the Soviet state (Sarkisiant, 1980, p.27)

The coordination of economic planning with defence policies is a feature inherent in the Soviet political system to this very day, but the view about the necessity of a strong economy for the security of the Soviet Union stems from the perception of the capitalist world as being basically hostile, and had always been expressed in the notion of capitalist encirclement. This is usually attributed to Lenin who, according to Soviet historians, foresaw the possibility of socialist victory in one country and 'thus the fact that a socialist state must exist surrounded by capitalist states will make a solid defence system an unavoidable necessity' (Korablev, 1977, p.28). Western intervention during the Civil War is often pointed out as a confirmation of Lenin's prediction that the Soviet state will have to stand by itself against the entire capitalist world. The words of Lenin that 'no revolution is worth anything unless it can defend itself' became a constant reminder of the inherent capitalist menace and influenced subsequent economic planning. It implied rapid industrialisation of the country in order to create the foundation of a strong defence industry

> Building the army was an inseparable part of the great task of socialist construction. The combination of economic and military goals was a necessity born of hostile capitalist encirclement. Without a strong army, peaceful economic development would have been impossible. On the other hand the strength of the army depended on the country's economic achievements (ibid., p.189)

Frequent references are also made to the Leninist approach to the relationship between war and the national economy which, within the traditional concept of war against imperialism as being unavoidable, imposes a duty 'upon the Party to follow the directions given by Lenin to prepare for war'. The necessity to prepare the country for a potential war along with the development of the economy and the maintenance of economic independence are a common feature of Soviet military literature and can be detected in practical directives by the military economic planners.

It was only in the middle of the 1930s that the Soviets began to devote increased attention to the technological and qualitative aspects of the army equipment. They were observing with particular interest the course of the Civil War in Spain where the Germans began to test their weaponry and new methods of warfare. A retrospective analysis by Marshal Grechko stressed the fact that the Red Army did not follow up the new trend of warfare: 'on the basis of a one-sided approach to studying the limited experience of the war in Spain, that an unsubstantiated conclusion was drawn about the inadvisability of having large tank formations' (Grechko, 1977, p.261). 'What was needed at the time', said Grechko, 'were practical recommendations on the improvement of technical equipment'.

According to Soviet historians, discussions did take place during the 17th Party Congress in 1934 regarding the re-equipment of the armed forces with new and up-to-date hardware. But the question of rearmament was closely linked to problems of the economy and defence (Korablev, 1977, p.189). The Congress decided on a policy of expanding the mobilisation capacity of the Soviet economy as a whole and of the industry in particular. Industrial facilities were to be built and used in such a way as to be placed quickly on a war footing should the necessity arise. The decision by the CPSU to give first priority to the branches of the economy closely connected with the strategic objectives of strengthening the material base of Soviet armed forces, was reflected in the output of the war industry which in three and a half years of the last pre-war Five-Year Plan grew by an average of 39 per cent annually compared to 13 per cent annual growth of the industry as a whole, according to one Soviet source (Grechko, 1977, p.54). There was also a correspondingly rapid increase in total military expenditure from 23 billion (old) rubles in 1938 to 57 billion (old) rubles in 1940. The share of defence spending in the state budget of 1940 was over 32 per cent and its share of GNP (Soviet national income produced) has grown to 17.8 per cent (Narkhoz, 1981, pp.522–3).[1]

The redirection of some enterprises in the heavy industry sector towards war production began well before the German attack on the USSR, and the construction of plants and factories for civilian needs had already been planned to be able to divert their activities for the production of war material. Tractor, automotive, locomotive, machine building as well as some naval construction yards have switched to the production of weapons and ammunition. The Cheliabinsk tractor plant began producing tanks in June 1940 (Tiushkevich, 1978, pp.226–7) According to the same historian, Soviet industries continued to develop much faster than the rest of the economy. While the overall growth of Soviet industry has been in the order of 16 per cent in 1939, defence industry plants grew by 46.5 per cent in the same year. From 1938 to June 1941 capital investment in defence related areas reached 25 per cent of the total capital investment in industry as a whole (ibid., p.228).

Notwithstanding the efforts to build up the industrial capacity of the USSR to meet the aggression by Nazi Germany, the results were far from satisfactory. In retrospect, it is clear that Soviet economic development was at an insufficient level to meet the requirements of the war. For despite the tremendous efforts for industrialisation, as an essential factor of Soviet national security, the country had not been put on a war footing prior to June 1941. One Soviet historian puts the situation at the time as unfavourable for the USSR not only in the military sense but in the economic as well. By 1941 Nazi Germany's military and economic potential had absorbed the resources of the countries it occupied in Western Europe. Germany was producing five times more coal than did the USSR, three times more steel and two to three times more electric power. According to the Soviet assessment the German army had a numerical superiority in weapons as well – it had 50 per cent more tanks, three times more airplanes, and 25 per cent more guns (Korablev, 1977, pp.193–4).[2]

In this respect, it is worthwhile to point out the debate within the Soviet Union over the 1941 disaster and its causes. If, as the Soviets claim, their military doctrine, based on Marxist scientific principles, was the most advanced military theory, why then did not the doctrine produce the required results? The answer, offered by Soviet military analysts themselves, is that it was not the imperfection of the doctrine that led to the initial defeat but insufficient material backup, in short, inadequate and poor equipment of the armed forces (Tiushkevich, 1978, p.230). Khrushchev himself later commented in the 'secret' speech at the 20th Congress: 'from the first days of the war it became clear that our army was poorly equipped, that we did not have enough artillery, tanks and aircraft to repel the enemy. We did not even have enough rifles to arm the mobilised man-power' (Khrushchev, 1959, p.33).[3]

It would appear from a Soviet historical account that immediately prior to the outbreak of the war, in February 1941, a last minute attempt had been made to reorganise the armoured corps and create twenty mechanical divisions, but the necessary 30 000 tanks, including 16 000 new T-34 and 7 000 armoured vehicles had not yet been produced. Most of the tanks at the time were of 1931–35 production, and furthermore, at the beginning of the war, the mechanised units already existing had no more than 40 per cent of their needs in artillery (Tiushkevich, 1978, p.240). The Soviet army suffered also from insufficient cover against attacking German aircraft because 'the testing of a new type of anti-aircraft gun against low-flying targets has not been done in time and they were in short supply at the beginning of the war'. The supply of war material by the Allies is considered to have been of marginal importance. According to one Soviet source, what has been received by the armed forces relative to Soviet production constituted no more than 12 per cent of aircraft, 10 per cent of tanks and 2 per cent of artillery. It did not add substantially to the Soviet Army's fighting capabilities (Kosygin, 1980, p.10).[4]

The emphasis is on the fact that it was possible under extreme difficulties to move to the East and South-East of the USSR a great number of industrial complexes and rapidly restructure the whole economy towards military production (Sarkisiant, 1980, p.27). The substantial increase of production and productive capacity for war has been achieved primarily by a total mobilisation of all material resources and manpower, as well as by a drastic increase in the working day, compulsory overtime, and the cancellation of all leave. These measures increased the rate of utilisation of plant and equipment by about one-third without an increase in the workforce (Kosygin, 1980, p.6).

Since defence-related expenditure always received first priority and even more so during the war, it was natural that consumer goods production had been severely curtailed. Some indication of the impact on the civilian sector of the economy caused by the expansion of war production can be seen from Soviet statistical data showing a 20 per cent decline of GNP between 1940 and 1945, a decline of 40 per cent in the output of consumer goods (group B) and an equal 40 per cent drop in gross agricultural output (*SSSR v tsifrakh*, 1980, p.37). If one accepts Soviet information and takes into account that during the war years the USSR had produced 142 000 aircraft, 110 000 tanks and other self-propelled guns, and 523 500 pieces of artillery (Kosygin, 1980, p.10), one can comprehend the enormity of the war effort in economic terms and its impact on the living standard of the population.

With the end of hostilities began the task of rebuilding an economy that was almost totally mobilised to fight the war. Although the resumption of production of consumer-related goods and the development of the agricultural sector have been given priority by the Soviet leadership, the problem of reconciling further growth of general welfare, with the objectives of national security as perceived by Stalin, arose again. The problem became even more acute because of the political situation in Europe related to the occupation of Eastern Europe by Soviet troops and the beginning of the conflict between the West and the USSR, on the one hand, and the expectations by the population for a better deal after the great victory, on the other.

The installation of communist governments in Eastern Europe may have been justified by Stalin in terms of national security, but from the Western point of view it meant that Stalin intended to spread the area of Soviet rule. The conflicting perceptions of each other's intentions regarding Eastern Europe sowed the seeds of future conflicts and the Cold War. The perception of hostile intentions was formally confirmed, on 9 February 1946, in an election speach by Stalin in which he announced a new Five-Year Plan designed to rebuild the devastated regions of the Soviet Union, and the restoration of industry and agriculture to their pre-war level. He suggested a tentative target of producing annually 50 million tons of cast iron, 60 million tons of steel, up to 500 million tons of coal and 60 million tons of oil. Only under these conditions – said Stalin – would it be possible to 'guarantee the country's security against any eventuality' (Stalin, 1967, p.20). He promised, at the same time, to abolish food rationing in the near future, to direct special attention towards an increase in the production of consumer goods, and generally to lift the living standard through lower prices (ibid., p.19).

The perception by US politicians that the Soviet Union's military power rested upon a rapidly growing economy and a sustained allocation of a large proportion of its economic resources for military purposes, led them to interpret the plan for massive industrial expansion as a threatening step. The then US Secretary of Defence, James Forrestal, reported a comment on Stalin's election speech by Justice Douglas as 'the declaration of World War' because it contained 'a five-year programme of industrial and armament expansion on a huge scale' (Millis, 1951, p.134).

But even a close reading of Stalin's speech did not reveal any direct reference to an extensive rearmament programme. The American interpretation of the plan as being implicitly military oriented was probably based on the usual lack of details of the plan, on the usually excessive projection of industrial targets and on the rising perception among American politicians of the link between industrialisation and the growing military potential of the Soviet Union. The above conclusion appears as one of the earliest signs of American concern with Soviet economic development as a factor of its military power. Subsequent American Administrations began to consider the implications of Soviet economic capacity for US military and budgetary decisions.

The perception by the United States government that Soviet military power rests on its economic capacity and technological possibilities may have been a result of the constant claims by Soviet theoreticians about the link between the economy and military power. But as long as the level of the Soviet economic development and the state of its military power had been considered inferior to that of the USA, such a perception has not been reflected in American policies. It was only immediately after the end of the Second World War that the economic aspect of US military policy in relation to the Soviet Union acquired increased importance. By contrast, the Soviets always looked upon the state of the economy as an essential factor of development of the armed forces. But, as is usual in all areas of Soviet politics, the economic factor was also closely connected with the perception of the outside world as attempting to gain influence over the policies of the Soviet Union – a decisive element that determined to a large extent Soviet trade relations with the West.

DEFENCE AND FOREIGN TRADE

Surveying past Soviet military–economic activities, one cannot fail to notice the almost total reliance on indigenous sources of economic resources and the reluctance to exploit the possibilities of international trade for the advancement of Soviet economic development. This may have been caused partly by purely economic circumstances due to the inability of the USSR to pay in hard currency for any purchases, and the reluctance by the West to grant credit facilities. But the political element was never absent in the consideration of economic independence. Because of the historically perceived threat of military aggression, a view still held today, the Soviet Union always strived for economic independence and avoided as far as possible close economic ties with the West. This was in accordance with the Leninist view on the relationship between war and the national economy – 'the economic independence and defence capabilities being organically linked' (Lagovskyi, 1969).

Historically the Soviet attitude to economic relations with the West has been reflected to a large degree in the pre-Second World War economic policies of the USSR, characterised by the quest for self-sufficiency and economic independence sometimes bordering on autarky. Under Stalin's rule the major economic objective of industrialisation was to be achieved as far as possible without dependence on Western economies, and any economic interdependence with the West was regarded as an attempt by the capitalist world to achieve economic domination. The Marshall

Plan, which at first had a favourable reaction from Poland and Czechoslovakia, was perceived by the Soviet Union as an attempt to detach some of the Eastern European states from the Soviet sphere of influence. It was denounced as trying 'to restore the power of imperialism in the countries of the new democracy and force them to abandon their close economic and military collaboration with the Soviet Union...to form a bloc of states linked to the United States' (Claudin, 1975, p.469).

It was only after Stalin's death that the Soviet Union emerged from its economic isolationism and began to trade increasingly with the West. The Soviet leadership apparently came to the conclusion that exchange of goods with only ideologically compatible partners was not always a sound economic proposition (Pisar, 1970, p.20). It was also realised that without access to Western technology, the technological gap could only widen and this in turn might affect economic growth. It is probably for this reason that the expansion of trade with capitalist countries, which by 1969 reached 35 per cent of Soviet global turnover (ibid., p.15), was mainly concentrated on the acquisition of Western know-how. But Soviet historical analysis of economic achievements prior to the Second World War are usually attributed to the fact that the 'socialist economy overcame its dependence on imports of industrial equipment and raw materials'. According to one commentator: 'under conditions of capitalist encirclement the strengthening of Soviet economic independence has been a very important factor for the development of all branches of the national economy, particularly for the growth and strengthening of defence capabilities' (Kosygin, 1980, p.4).

The priority assigned to the development of the industrial sector of the economy at the expense of the consumer goods sector, which had always been a feature of Soviet economic planning, can therefore be explained by a desire to build up the productive capacity of the Soviet economy with a view to 'ensuring economic independence and, at the same time, to increase the defence potential of the Country' (Khachaturov, 1977, p.218).

Even in more recent times, when the necessity for trade with the capitalist world imposed itself on account of the need for Western technology, the concern about economic independence as a factor of national security is still an important feature of Soviet economic planning. For example, the Food Production Plan for the period to 1990 and the measures taken for its realisation published in 1982, may be considered as an attempt to develop the food-producing sector of the economy, but close reading of the published document discloses that 'it is absolutely essential to reduce imports from capitalist countries who sometimes use it as an instrument of political pressure. We must have our own resources in order to make our situation secure in any eventuality' (Prodovolstvennaia programma, 1982). It echoes a similar opinion expressed by Stalin in his pre-election speech on 9 February 1946 when he unveiled plans for economic development which, as he said, 'will guarantee the security of our Motherland in any eventuality' (Stalin, 1967).

The conflict between national security considerations and economic benefits flowing from mutual trade presented the Soviet leadership with a dilemma on the question of economic relations with the West. Economic rationality would indicate obvious advantages from trading with the capitalist world, but political considerations and the ideological dogma concerning the nature of capitalism resulted in a suspicious attitude. Capitalist economic policies in relation to the USSR were seen as geared to achieve political rather than economic goals (Lebedev, 1978, p.144). 'The Soviet Union has rejected and will continue to reject in the future any attempts designed under the cover of economic cooperation...to shake the foundation of the socialist system' (Krylov 1979, p.223).

Contrasting such a view is the realisation by other Soviet analysts that without access to Western technology, economic growth, and by implication defence, might be impaired. According to the same source, 'no country can effectively develop the basic branches of production and science if it relies exclusively on its own assets and capabilities' (ibid., p.222).

The contradictory views regarding relations with the West encountered in the Soviet press, indicate the existence of a current of a pragmatic approach to questions of economic rationality – a current that runs counter to the conservative view on the necessity for economic independence. The influence of the new breed of economists is also reflected in the decisions taken by the Congresses of the CPSU since Stalin's death. They underline the 'need for mutually advantageous cooperation and exchanges of scientific achievements between countries...and...the role of external economic relations in tackling economic tasks and speeding up scientific and technological progress' (Sarkisiant, 1980, p.467).

The expansion of trade with capitalist countries which, according to Soviet data, in 1980 constituted 33.6 per cent of Soviet total foreign trade (Stepanov, 1981, p.41), but in absolute figures grew between 1975 and 1980 from 15.8 billion rubles to 31.6 billion rubles – more than double (same source) – was mainly concentrated in the acquisition of Western technology.[5]

But according to another Soviet source 'external economic ties with capitalist states are only an additional factor in the development of the Soviet economy because it relies first of all on its own resources'. Imports from the West amounted only to 1.5 per cent of GSP (Soviet equivalent of National Income), and the share of industrial equipment imported into the Soviet Union did not exceed 5–6 per cent of Soviet total investment in machinery (Stepanov, 1981, p.41). The stress on the minor importance of foreign economic relations appears to be based on the ideological ground of the superiority of the Soviet economic system, which does not have to rely on the capitalist world. In the words of one Soviet analyst: 'the countries of the socialist community rely primarily on their own resources and the advantages of the socialist system of production...they are technically and economically independent of the capitalist world' (Lebedev, 1978, pp.123–5). The confirmation of the superiority of a socialist system over capitalism is usually seen by Soviet theoreticians in the ability of the USSR to mobilise available resources for the purpose of maintaining a strong military power and economic growth simultaneously.

The apparent direct relationship between the growth of the Soviet economy and its military power has attracted much attention in the United States, particularly in those circles of American politicians and the military who saw Soviet military capabilities as dependent upon the growth of the Soviet economy. According to this view, Soviet economic achievements implied growing military power and were relevant to the US national security. Allan W. Dulles of the CIA expressed a concern in 1961 that 'if the Soviet industrial growth-rate persists at 8 or 9 percent per annum over the next decade, as was forecast, the gap between the two economies will be dangerously narrowed by 1970', which led one American strategic analyst to conclude that 'under these assumptions the military power of the Soviet Union and its bloc will exceed that of the United States and Western Allies by the 1970s' (Hardt, 1961, pp.4–5).

Although the pessimistic prognosis about the economic and military power of the USSR did not materialise by the 1970s and not even by 1980 or 1986, at least in the economic area, the tendency to view the relationship between Soviet economic performance and its military power as an important factor in Soviet strategic capabilities still persists today. (See, for example, a survey of the Soviet economy by the American Congress Joint Economic Committee, 'Soviet Economy in the 1980s, Problems and Prospects', Washington, Government Printing Office, 1983.)

THE SOVIET MILITARY – INDUSTRIAL COMPLEX

In the light of the American perception about the equation by the Soviets of their economic potential with military power, the question which is often raised and discussed as to whether a Soviet military–industrial complex exists requires some examination. As in other areas of investigation into the functioning of the Soviet system, the diversity of opinions on the subject of the Soviet military–industrial complex suggests the importance of the issue. It involves, in the first place, the decision-making process at the highest level of the Party hierarchy and, above all, the role of the military in that process. Is there such an institution as a separate military bureaucratic machine to which belongs effective power over political, economic and military decisions, as people like Vernon Aspaturian (1972) and Castoriadis (1981) would like us to believe?

There can be little doubt that the highly centralised economic and political system of the USSR has the advantage of being able to control the allocation of resources to the various branches of the economy as well as for defence. The Soviet leadership does not have to justify its military effort in order to obtain funds from the state budget, and the approval of its policy by the public is assumed. The concentration of political and economic power in the hands of the Communist Party is reflected in the integration of military expenditure within the overall economic planning and 'the requirements of military strategy are taken into account when formulating economic development plans' (Sokolovsky, 1963, p.31). According to one Soviet source, 'military development is a combination of economic, political and military measures, and the maintenance of a united political economic and military leadership is a function of the entire Soviet system of socialist social relations and the Soviet state system' (Grechko, 1977, p.35). A question therefore arises: what are the common interests, if any, of a Soviet social strata to qualify it as a military–industrial complex?

It is in the definition of the concept of a 'military–industrial complex' that we ought to search for the answer to the above questions. As is well known, the term 'military–industrial complex' has been coined by Eisenhower in order to indicate the existence of certain groups who would use all available economic and political means at their disposal, especially intensive lobbying, to influence political decisions favourable for the interests of the military sector of the economy. In a more limited sense it means an 'interlocking and interdependent structure of interests among military–industrial and political figures that enables them to behave as a distinctive political actor' (Aspaturian, 1972, p.1). Taking the above definition as a starting point in the investigation into a Soviet military–industrial complex, we are faced with the problem of a 'mirror-image' method of analysis, mentioned earlier, whereby by applying Western concepts to the Soviet system we arrive at conclusions which are at variance with Soviet reality.

Soviet realities are much more complex than they appear. First, the designation of a Soviet military–industrial complex assumes the existence of distinct social or political groups whose interest and influence would set them apart from the rest of the Soviet decision-making body. There is little evidence to indicate the existence of either. In fact the number of military figures in the Politburo was traditionally very small, and it is the nature of the system itself that precludes the existence of such groups. This is not to say that the influence of the military is negligible. There can be little doubt that decisions of military significance are always taken in consultation with the military, but this must be understood in the context of domestic as well as military policies in their totality.

Secondly, the concept of a Soviet military–industrial complex assumes the separation of the military sector of the economy from the civilian. The question of the two-sector economy will be examined in Chapter 6, but suffice to say at this stage that the dependence of military capabilities on economic resources and on the performance of the Soviet economy as a whole, makes such separation most unlikely. In view of the close link between the Soviet military effort and the economy, it would be more appropriate to see the USSR in its entirety, as one Western analyst observed, as a military–economic complex (Krylov, 1979, p.61). What can be said with some degree of certainty is that a compromise had been reached between the requirements of various branches of the armed forces, on the one hand, and the demands for resources by the economy and consumers, on the other (Goure *et al.*, 1974, p.13). One can also conclude that the decision about the share of the economic pie that is to be allocated for defence is taken by the Party's hierarchy in conjunction with the military.

> The question of improvement of weapon systems and war technology of every kind, as well as their equipment by the armed forces, are always in the center of attention of the Central Committee of the CPSU and the Soviet government. It is being resolved by the combined effort of the Ministry for Defence, the Ministries of the military branches of industry and many scientific establishments. (Ogarkov, 1981, p.88)

The above statement indicates that military planning and production are closely interwoven with the Soviet economy as a whole. Consequently, an attempt to separate or, for that matter, to define which branch of the Soviet industries works solely for the equipment of the army is subject to much guesswork and speculative suppositions. Add to this the Soviet principle that any branch of industry must have the potential of being able to switch to war production should the necessity arise, and one is faced with the almost impossible task of determining the extent of Soviet economic resources that are being channelled into its military effort.

CONCLUSION

The Reagan Administration has shown consistent interest in the implications of the Soviet economy as a factor linked to the arms race. Such interest was based on the assumption that the USSR could not sustain indefinitely a constant increase in its military expenditure, given the state of its economy and its poor performance in recent years. Viewed from this angle, the pursuit of political objectives through an intensified arms race meant the use of American economic power as an additional option in its policy *vis á vis* the USSR. Although President Reagan's public statement, that the United States will initiate an arms race 'which the Soviets will not be able to afford', may be considered as pure rhetoric, there are indications that alternative economic means of influencing Soviet policies were carefully examined (Feulner, 1978, p.32).

It had been suggested that 'the use of an economic strategy as an integral part of US national security policy must be endorsed at the highest decision-making level of the US government' (ibid., p.47).

At the conference at Versailles, in 1982, Reagan proposed stiff credit restrictions for the USSR which, he said, were needed in order to hamper the Soviet economy and the buildup of Soviet military strength (*New York Times*, 6 June, 1982). The still classified National Security Decision Directive 75 implied that an attempt will be made to make Soviet leadership more responsive to internal demands from the population and non-military sectors of the economy. This would make the Kremlin's choice between military and civilian spending more difficult. Some even saw the armament race cycle as an anti-Soviet weapon in itself. Their argument was that the West can 'bleed' the Soviet system by forcing it to keep up with the high level of US arms programmes, which presumably would strain the Soviet economy to breaking point (Kolkowicz, 1971, p.440). As the history of the Soviet Union shows, military related expenditure has always been at the expense of consumer-related sectors, but as the economic burden caused by defence spending will increase, so goes the argument, the pressure for a reduction in military expenditure will make the USSR more willing to offer concessions in any negotiations. This implied that the United States might be able to exert significant leverage at the negotiating table over political and military matters reflecting America's economic superiority.

The importance attributed to Soviet economic capacity and the attention devoted by Western analysts to the economic performance of the USSR in the context of the present arms race is reflected in the substantial volume of writing that appeared in the last two decades, and in the reports on the Soviet economy published from time to time by the US Congress Joint Economic Committee. It indicated American preoccupation with Soviet military policy as it impinges upon economic planning since, it had been suggested, the solution of Soviet domestic economic problems depended increasingly on lowering the level of military spending.

The suggestion made by many American political analysts, to use the economic option as an instrument of foreign policy whose objective would be to influence Soviet behaviour, was based on the perceived close link between Soviet military expenditure and the economy. The proposals for using American economic power as an additional lever in the relations between the superpowers also took into account the notion that there is a straight and direct correlation between defence expenditure and military power. The more the Soviets spend on armament the more powerful they become. It was the argument, used by Ronald Reagan, that Soviet military spending exceeded that of the United States, consequently making the USA militarily weaker, that was instrumental in increasing America's military budget. It was followed by the controversial SDI programme considered by some experts as the ultimate in defence, but by others as 'unaffordable, ineffective and destabilizing' (Valley, 1985, p.294). The question arises, therefore, whether by challenging the Soviets to initiate an SDI programme of their own, President Reagan genuinely believes in the possibility of rendering nuclear weapons obsolete, or are there other motives behind it?

If one looks at this question in the light of the analysis of the economic factor of the arms race, one would be justified to assume that by launching the SDI project, the United States hopes that the USSR will not be able to devote sufficient economic resources to match the new technological development. The mere fact that the Soviets have launched an intensive international propaganda campaign, and furthermore that they have agreed to continue disarmament negotiations after having walked out, indicates that the Soviets may not have the economic or technological resources to keep up with the race, although they may find other ways to counteract what they perceive as America's quest for a first-strike capability. The problem is one of the economy and technology – both interdependent.

The big question mark in this respect is whether the Soviets possess the economic capacity for increased military expenditure? The answer to this question lies obviously in the assessment of the Soviet economy and its resources. Thus the link between defence expenditure and the Soviet economy, the so-called 'defence burden', and the question of Soviet military spending as a determinant of its military power are important issues in need of examination; they are the subjects of the following chapter.

5 Assessing the Soviet Military Effort

INTRODUCTION

America's perception of Moscow's military capabilities in terms of defence expenditure acquired increasing importance over the years because it was generally assumed that military expenditure indicates trends in Soviet military policy and, as some analysts claimed, increased defence spending by the Soviets implied growing military capabilities (Burton, 1983, p.85). In that sense, Soviet defence budget impinged upon US decisions on defence expenditure. This had been reflected in the changing composition of Federal expenditure on defence, foreign policy considerations being only one of the factors which determined the American defence budget. For while US foreign policy always involved commitments for the defence of Europe and other areas of the world, American national security considerations also included an assessment of the military capabilities of a potential adversary – namely the USSR.

Budgetary decisions are still influenced, to a great extent, by the Soviet strategic buildup and by the level of funds which the USSR devotes to defence. Specific programmes as well as Soviet military expenditure and R&D activities are often seen as calling for countermeasures by the United States (Schultze et al., 1972, p.83). In a document published in 1984 (*Soviet Military Power,* 1984), the US government drew attention to the fact that during the period 1973 to 1982 the dollar cost of Soviet procurement of arms and other military items exceeded that of the United States by some 240 billion dollars (*Soviet Military Power*, 1984, p.99). It also claimed that the magnitude and growth of Soviet military spending provided an indication of the priorities that the Soviet leadership accords to the military. Although the document qualified the large investment of resources for military purposes as not necessarily equated with military capabilities, it nevertheless implied the necessity for an appropriate American response. This line of argument helped the US Administration to secure funds for defence and the approval by the Senate of an increased Defence Bill.[1]

A more recent document published by the US Department of Defence, in 1987, claims that the cumulative Soviet military costs from 1977 to 1986 greatly exceeded those of the United States. During this period, the estimated dollar cost of the total Soviet military programmme was 25 per cent higher than comparable US defence outlays, and the weapon procurement costs were 30 per cent higher.

Closely connected with the assessment of Soviet defence spending is the so called 'defence burden', or the impact of military spending on the Soviet economy. It is generally agreed that the performance of the Soviet economy as a whole, and of its civilian branch in particular, constitutes a certain restraint on Soviet military spending in that it imposes, at least in theory, a limit on resources allocated for military purposes. It is for this reason that the assessment of Soviet military expenditure is usually not limited to the specific items in the Soviet military budget, whether disclosed or hidden, but involves an analysis of Soviet economic and political considerations relating to the share of the GNP which the leadership decides to devote to the military effort. Thus estimating Soviet defence expenditure and measuring the burden of defence is not simply a matter of analysing the Soviet annual budget. It involves a number of assumptions and approaches which, as we shall see, lead to sharply contrasting conclusions. Furthermore, the methods used for the determination of the above are as varied as are their results. But the fact that the Soviet Union has been able to achieve rough strategic parity with the United States seems to indicate an increasing level of military spending, and possibly a rising economic burden – both difficult to quantify.

The assessment of Soviet military spending and the economic burden that it implies are two different, though closely related, subjects of study and serve two different purposes for American policy-makers. American estimates of Soviet military expenditure, as an indicator of the military effort and as a determinant of its military power (Becker, 1979), serves the purpose of intensifying US military response and to secure funds from Congress. The purpose of assessing the burden of defence and the Soviet economic potential lies in the assumption that increased defence expenditure may create internal political problems for the Soviet leadership; consequently, such a possibility must have some implications for US policy toward the USSR.

The position taken by the Administration on the question of the Soviet defence burden appears to support the opinion that 'Soviet leaders have been more willing to forgo economic growth and consumer satisfaction in favour of military power, and that there is no evidence of economic considerations deterring the Soviets from continuing the pace of their defence efforts' (CIA, 1976, p.2). The still classified 'National Security Directive 75' implies economic policies that will make the Soviet leadership responsive to internal demands, the idea being that economic pressure will make the choice between military and civilian spending much tougher for the Kremlin (*Los Angeles Times*, 16 March 1983). Another CIA document (1976a, p.16) drew attention to the concern expressed by Soviet leaders about the sacrifices in economic growth for the sake of defence. Noting that such concern is not reflected in Soviet military programmes, the document concluded that 'lagging economic growth will make rising defence costs a painful issue for the leadership'. A later document claimed that based on historical evidence, Soviet military-related effort in the area of industrial investment will remain substantial both in absolute terms and as a share of the Soviet budget (*Soviet Military Power*, 1984, p.101). In the 1987 edition, the United States asserted that the enormous expenditures for defence purposes have been a prime factor behind slowing economic growth rate and that military spending was at the expense of living standards.

SOURCES OF INFORMATION

A major source of information regarding Soviet military expenditure on which the Administration relies for the formulation of its defence policies, is the reports submitted from time to time by the CIA. Some of the reports have been unclassified and are accessible to political analysts interested in that area. Other sources of research and analysis are contained in contributions by individual political and economic analysts that can be found in the Reports of the Joint Economic Committee of the Congress, as well as in papers commissioned sometimes by the military and published by various research organisations.

But the use made by the Administration of these reports for the purpose of formulation of its policies and their implementation, is characterised by a certain degree of selectivity. The Administration appears to be careful not to endorse unconditionally all reports presented by either CIA or DIA, except those parts of a particular document or data which seem to support and justify its policies (see for example *Soviet Military Power*, 1982 to 1987, Department of Defence, US Government Printing Office, Washington DC). This is partly due to the fact that none of the reports is conclusive in their detailed analysis, except at the highest level of aggregation that indicates trends in Soviet military spending in very broad terms. Furthermore, due to new evidence that emerges from time to time, or some new information becoming available, the CIA has been forced to revise many times its assessment of Soviet defence spending, the trends in Soviet allocation for national security, as well as the evaluation of the performance of the Soviet economy and the defence burden.

A major revision of the estimates of Soviet defence spending by the Central Intelligence Agency occurred in May 1976, when in its report it has effectively doubled all previous estimates, increasing the defence burden of the Soviet Union from 6 to 8 percent of GNP to 11–13 per cent. In absolute figures the increase was in the order of 45–50 billion rubles in 1970, to about 55–60 billion rubles in 1975. This represented an average annual growth rate of 4–5 per cent over the period, rather than 3 per cent estimated previously. The CIA claimed that a reassessment was undertaken in view of an unusually large body of new information. The nature of the new information was not made clear in the document, but has been attributed to the new understanding of Soviet prices and costs. About 90 per cent of the increase in the new estimates was accounted for by such improved understanding according to the CIA. It is important to notice that despite the doubling of previous estimates of Soviet DE in rubles, the assessment in terms of dollars remained virtually unchanged (see, CIA Research Paper SR-76-10053, 'A Dollar Comparison of Soviet and US Defence Activities 1965–1975', Washington, DC, February 1976).

A further report by the CIA, published in January 1980, painted an even grimmer picture of the relative Soviet and US defence activities expressed in terms of a dollar comparison. (The problem of assessing Soviet defence spending in either dollars or rubles and its implications will be analysed in the later part of this chapter.) For the decade 1970-79, according to this document (CIA, 1980), the cumulative estimated dollar cost of Soviet defence activities exceeded US outlays by almost 30 per cent. Soviet defence expenditure grew at an average annual rate of 3 per cent (4–5 per cent when valued in rubles), catching up with American defence outlays in 1971 and exceeding them by a widening margin during the years to 1979. In 1979, the report claimed, the Soviets spent about 165 billion dollars compared to a US total of 108 billion dollars – approximately 50 per cent higher (ibid., p.3).

Reacting to these reports, the new Administration undertook an intensive programme of rearmament with a corresponding increase in defence outlays. However, a few years later, early in 1983, a dispute erupted among US intelligence analysts regarding Soviet military spending. Some specialists within the CIA asserted that the growth rate of Soviet defence activities for the past six years was grossly overstated and that the Soviet Union has been producing less military equipment than had been estimated. The rate of growth of Soviet defence expenditure was now estimated at no more than 2 per cent (*New York Times*, 3 March 1983). In June of the same year, the Defence Intelligence Agency released its own report in which it said that the actual rate of increase in Soviet defence procurements had slowed and might even have stopped (*Newsday*, 22 June 1983). But the CIA and DIA gave this new estimate a different interpretation. The USSR was spending as much as estimated but has been getting less for it due to higher prices of modern technology and because of the inefficiency of the Soviet system. This latest estimate has been officially confirmed by a CIA report released by the Congressional Joint Economic Committee in November 1983. According to this report on the basis of 'new information', the rate of growth of Soviet defence spending declined in the late 1970s and Soviet production of military hardware hardly grew at all. The new estimate indicated a 2 per cent annual increase, according to the CIA. However, even the new estimate put the dollar cost of all Soviet defence activities as being 45 per cent higher than US outlays. Although the new revised assessment of the Soviet military effort ran counter to the Pentagon's view of Soviet military buildup, the Administration still sought to justify its claims for an increased defence budget on the basis of its own perception of Soviet defence activities.

A wide range of variations in the estimates of Soviet defence spending can be found not only in the official reports of US Government agencies, but in various works by political and economic analysts who attempt to evaluate the Soviet military effort. Table 5.1 illustrates the wide margin of estimates, and if we add the revisions that took place from time to time, we can comprehend the uncertainty which such estimates must necessarily contain. The only common feature of these estimates is the conclusion that a sharp increase in the annual Soviet military expenditure has taken place since the early 1970s (Alexander *et al.*, 1979, p.v). But even the CIA admitted that a comparison between the Soviet and American defence activities based on costs that contribute directly to the military effort, are not necessarily indices of relative military capabilities (CIA, 1976a, p.2).

Table 5.1 Soviet defence expenditure estimates

	1970	*1975*	*1978*	*1979*	*1980*	*1970–8*	*1970–80*
	Billions of rubles					*Annual growth rate (%)*	
USSR(i)	17.9	17.4	17.2	17.2	17.1		0.4
CIA							
Original(ii)	24.0	25–28					
Revised(iii)	44–53	50–55	56–61	59–75	62–79	4.5	3.7
Lee(iii)	43–49	72–79	91–101	N/A	N/A	8–10	
Rosefielde(iii)	43.5			91			8.5
	Billions of Dollars						
CIA(iii)	105.0	120.0	145.0			4.5	
Lee(iii)	80–105	97–133	116–154			5.0	
Rosefielde(iii)	104.5			160.9			

Source: (i) Narkhoz, 1981; (ii) Lee, 1977; (iii) *Military Balance*, 1979–80, 1983–84.

The latter qualification about the relationship between military expenditure and military power begs an answer to a simple question about the utility of value measurement of military activities. After all, physical indicators of relative armed forces would be logically of much greater use to military planners than raw figures expressing costs, which in any case are subject to interpretation. The usual answer to this question is that military establishments of the USSR and the United States are very difficult to compare given their different structure and characteristics (CIA, 1980, p.1): 'physical units of heterogenous elements cannot be added or substracted unless converted to a common denominator. The most general of all metrics is money; therefore, the simplest mean of aggregating physical forces...is money prices' (Alexander *et al.*, 1979, p.3).

METHODS OF ASSESSMENT

But having a common denominator does not solve all the problems involved in assessing and comparing relative military efforts; on the contrary, it creates many more. To clarify the problems linked to the value measurement of defence activities of the USSR, we must now turn to the issue of alternative ways of measuring and estimating Soviet military expenditure. For in order to explain the wide range of estimates it is necessary to look at the different methods that are used for the various assessments.

There are basically two measures of Soviet defence spending which allow one to draw conclusions of political interest. One is a dollar valuation of Soviet military expenditure which can be used as an indicator of the size of the Soviet military establishment (but not necessarily its strength). Being expressed in dollars, in terms easily comprehended in the West, it also makes it possible to compare respective military efforts of the United States and the USSR. Also, along with the valuation of Soviet military expenditure in dollars for comparison with that of the United States, an assessment of US military expenditure in rubles for comparison with the respective Soviet outlays, is sometimes used (Alexander *et al.,* 1979, p.6). The purpose of such an approach was expressed by the former director of the CIA, Colby, as being helpful in the decision-making about the American military budget (JEC, 1976, p.24). The second measure is the value of Soviet defence expenditure expressed in rubles as a ratio of Soviet GNP, which would indicate the share of national output devoted to defence. This is the so-called 'burden of defence' and is calculated in rubles so as to reflect as closely as possible, using Soviet prices and other data, the opportunity cost – the alternatives forgone – of Soviet defence expenditure.

The attempts to estimate the above mentioned values can be broadly classified into three methods. The first method of assessing Soviet defence spending, one used mainly by the CIA, is what is commonly known as the Building Block method or technique. It begins with a detailed analysis of Soviet military activities, the physical size of Soviet armed forces, weapons inventory and mode of operation. It then estimates what it would cost to produce and operate a military force of similar size and composition in the United States using American dollar prices. The ruble valuation of Soviet defence spending follows a similar procedure. But whereas the dollar valuation is costed directly by applying known dollar prices, the alternative ruble assessment is arrived at by costing some items directly using available ruble prices, and others by converting one value base into the other. This is done through the application of dollar-to-ruble and, to a much more limited degree, ruble-to-dollar ratios, which are to reflect the estimated relative efficiencies of the USSR and the United States in a particular activity (CIA, 1976, p.5).

It is clear that such a complicated method of costing must necessarily rely on accurate information regarding the Soviet armed forces and weapons systems. Indeed, the CIA admitted that the reliability of such an assessment depends on the precision and accuracy of information supplied by military intelligence, but was confident that the probable error was unlikely to be more than 10 per cent in the current period (1979), or more than 15 per cent early in the decade (1970–9) – a rather wide margin (ibid., 1980, p.2). The CIA avoided using Soviet statistical data as much as possible, since it was not considered sufficiently precise, and was manipulated at will to suit Soviet political purposes. The CIA, nevertheless, had been using Soviet data to assess military related RDT&E costs. Although it considered such estimates to be less precise 'it is clear' – according to the CIA – 'that a substantial military RDT&E programme is included in the published Soviet statistics on science expenditure' (ibid., p.5). The CIA estimated that about two-thirds of Soviet expenditure on science is related to defence. The total obtained through this method is then converted into dollars using purchasing power parity (Cockle, 1978, p.214).[2]

The second method focuses on statistics of industrial production and attempts to locate the production of military hardware by various branches of Soviet industry, the so-called Hardware Approach. This method relies primarily on Soviet data and has limited itself in the past to the estimates of weapons' production. A more recent extension of this method is by William T.Lee, who claims that by adding the hardware estimates to the official defence budget and the estimated R&D, one can obtain a reasonably comprehensive assessment of Soviet defence expenditure. This

'Unconventional Method' of estimating Soviet National Security is based upon Soviet industrial production, budgetary data, labour force and national income (Lee, 1977, p.51). Three components constitute such an assessment: national security durables computed as a residual of the machine-building and metal-working sector of Soviet industry; defence expenditure in the Soviet budget which presumably includes pay, maintenance, operation and military construction; finally RDT&E and space, being the sum of inputs less the civilian share of the 'science expenditure' reported by the Soviets (ibid., p.54).

The starting point of the Hardware Approach is the Gross Value of Output of the MBMW industries. It is generally assumed that this industrial classification contains most of the weapons industries, and that by deducting all known civilian components one arrives at a residual which presumably contains the 'hidden' armament output. The Hardware Approach, as do other methods, involves the conversion of rubles into dollars; a major difficulty in the assessment of Soviet defence expenditure, to which reference will be made when dealing with various problems and difficulties in estimating Soviet military effort in monetary terms.

The third method is based on the analysis of the annually published state budget. It attempts to identify various sources within the budget which could possibly finance the Soviet military establishment. It is not a simple task, since defence expenditure is contained in a single line in the budget and shows a constant figure since the late 1960s. It had been argued that even allowing for the apparent very low rate of inflation in the USSR, it would have been impossible for the Soviets to build up their armed forces and to equip them with modern and costly technology using only the officially published funds. By comparing, for example, in index form the growth of men and equipment with the growth of the official defence budget (Cockle, 1978, p.211, table 1), one can see that to accommodate such growth in weaponry within a constant budget would have required a corresponding fall in other parts of the budget, or extreme efficiency and economies of production, which is not very likely. Furthermore, the constant figure of around 17 billion rubles per annum would indicate a constantly diminishing share of Soviet GNP devoted to defence – equally unlikely.[3]

This apparent inconsistency led to a search for other sources of financing Soviet defence expenditure which could conceivably be hidden among other items in the state budget, especially among resources provided by non-defence ministries, in support of military activities (Marshall, 1976, p.76). The search for hidden items of expenditure produced a number of tentative conclusions based on 'unexplained residuals' in the Soviet state budget, where the totals did not correspond to the sum of the particular items, and on articles and statements published in the Soviet press which sometimes throw some light on the question of defence expenditure.

One Soviet source states that the expenditure on the armed forces is financed from one source – the Union budget. It defines such expenditure as 'the provision of financial resources for the needs of the armed forces which are used in accordance with the estimates of the Ministry of Defence of the USSR' and include the following:

> payments for deliveries of armaments and other materiel, fuel and lubricants, food, uniforms and other goods and services; the financing of construction and of industrial enterprises, the repair and maintenance of armaments and other military property; the payments of allowances to servicemen and wages to workers and other employees of military establishments. (Zhlobin, 1975, p.199)

While it is clear from the above what is included in defence expenditure, it is not so obvious what the budgetary item does not contain. It is almost certain that R&D are excluded; one has only

Table 5.2 State and other expenditure on science and defence (billions of rubles)

	1965	*1970*	*1975*	*1980*	*1984*	*1985*	*1986*	*1987*
Science	6.9	11.7	17.4	21.3	27.6	N/A	29.0	30.8
Defence	12.8	17.9	17.4	17.1	17.1	19.063	19.063	20.2

Source: Narkhoz, 1981, pp.523–4; 1984, pp.573–575
The 1986 and 1987 expenditure on science is estimated on the basis of the report by the Soviet Minister of Finance regarding the 1987 State Budget (*Pravda*, 18 November 1986).
Note: The data contained in Table 5.2 shows a much faster increase in expenditure on science relative to defence spending. In 1975, expenditure on science equalled that on defence, but by 1984 it exceeded the latter by some 10 billion rubles or over 60 per cent.

to look at the item in the budget under the heading of science to see that, as some analysts claim, military related R&D is probably part of the expenditure on science, despite the assertion by the same Soviet source, that 'the total expenditure on the armed forces of the USSR is fixed annually by the Supreme Soviet as a special item in the State Budget of the USSR' (ibid.).[4]

PROBLEMS WITH ASSESSMENTS

Although the budgetary method is useful for the assessment of the defence burden as a share of the national product, since both are expressed in the domestic currency, it is also being used to estimate defence expenditure by itself. However, the latter involves currency conversion with all the associated problems and difficulties. But currency conversion is not the only problem facing political analysts. It is not surprising that none of the methods of assessing Soviet defence spending and defence burden is not without its critics who, when taking as their point of departure the analysis and assessment supplied by US government agencies, especially the CIA, point to a number of associated problems of such assessment. This led some analysts to consider the CIA assessment as either underestimating or overestimating Soviet defence expenditure. William T. Lee, mentioned earlier, saw Soviet defence spending growing much faster and taking a larger share of GNP than estimated by the CIA. Another critic of CIA estimates is Professor Steven Rosefielde, who puts his own dollar estimate of the Soviet arms procurements as being more than twice that perceived by the CIA. His estimates are based on putting what he considers to be the real price on advanced technology which, he claims, is more costly for the USSR. The problem of costing and generally pricing Soviet output is the main difficulty in this approach. Finally, one who considers the CIA assessments as much too high is Professor Franklyn Holzman (1982) who focuses on the so-called index-number effect. The problem of the index-number effect arises in all international comparisons due to the fact that countries have different relative scarcities and, therefore, different relative prices of goods and services. There is also the question of relative efficiencies, particularly the capability of absorption of new advanced technology by the Soviet military industrial sector. Here opinions are equally divided between those who consider the operation of the Soviet economy as a whole as being much less efficient and, consequently, more costly than that of the United States, and those who attempt to prove the existence of a two-sector economy – the highly efficient defence sector, and the civilian sector trailing far behind in efficiency.

Let us now proceed to a detailed analysis of the main problems and difficulties connected with the assessment of Soviet defence expenditure and the burden of defence.

All three methods – the Building Block Approach, the Hardware Approch and the Budgetary Approach – involve the conversion of one national currency (rubles) into another (dollars) and vice versa. Although the CIA Building Block method dispenses partly with the need for conversion – it prices Soviet production directly into dollars – it still requires the conversion into dollars of some items of Soviet defence spending, and more so for the purpose of estimating the burden of defence. The other two methods, which rely on Soviet statistical data, necessarily involve calculations which convert rubles into dollars.

The simplest method, one often used in international comparisons, would be to use the official rate of exchange. Unfortunately, this method, which may be more appropriate for a comparison between countries at a similar level of economic development, is not suitable for making a valid comparison between the USSR and the United States. The official Soviet exchange rate is set arbitrarily by the Soviet authorities and does not represent the relative purchasing power of the two currencies. Exchange rates are usually determined by international trade between countries and by international capital movement. In the case of the USSR, its currency is not convertible and does not represent purchasing power ratio. Thus it cannot be used as even a rough measure of relative purchasing power (Edwards *et al.,* 1979, p.373–4).

In view of the currency conversion problem, there were attempts to overcome it by calculating a purchasing power ratio, to establish a theoretical relation between two currencies that would represent the real respective purchasing power.[5]

The purchasing power of the ruble in the Soviet defence sector would then be expressed as a ratio of the dollar's purchasing power in the American defence sector. However, this type of solution of the conversion problem based on calculations of the purchasing power of a currency, is not satisfactory either since purchasing power varies widely between commodities, and no dollar–ruble purchasing power parity has yet been calculated for actual military hardware, due mainly to technological differences, production methods, and efficiency (Cockle, 1978, p.16).[6]

The best illustration of the currency conversion problem is that ruble and dollar comparisons yield different results, and neither provides a satisfactory measure of Soviet defence spending compared to that of the United States. As Table 5.3 shows, the results of the dollar comparison differ markedly from those in the ruble comparison

Table 5.3 Expenditure on defence and space in the USSR and the US

	1965	*1977*
Billion 1976 rubles		
USSR	38	64
United States	60	49
Billion 1976 dollars		
USSR	90	133
United States	108	92
USSR as a per cent of US		
Rubles	63	131
Dollars	83	145

Note: Different relativities when expressed in rubles or dollars. Of interest are the 1977 figures showing the USSR as exceeding US expenditure by 31 per cent in rubles and 45 per cent in dollars

The revision by the CIA of its estimates in rubles in 1976, mentioned earlier, is a further confirmation of the conversion difficulties. Since the revision did not come as a result of increased Soviet spending, but from a 'change in understanding' of ruble prices and costs, it meant that the CIA began to apply different purchasing-power ratios.

Closely linked to the currency conversion problem is what is known to economists as the index number problem, whose effects lead to different results depending on which country's prices are used. This problem springs from the fact that 'given different resources endowments and technologies, countries tend to use more of the resources that are relatively cheap, and less of those that are relatively expensive, for a given purpose' (CIA, 1980, p.3). The above principle, when applied to the comparison between the USSR and the United States, means that since the US has less labour and more capital than does the Soviet Union, labour-intensive commodities and services are relatively more expensive and capital intensive relatively cheaper in the United States than in the Soviet Union. Americans tend generally to produce and consume fewer labour-intensive and more capital-intensive products than does the Soviet Union (Holzman, 1982, p.79). As the former CIA Director, Admiral Turner, said: 'Military hardware is much more expensive than manpower in the USSR, while in the United States manpower is relatively more expensive than hardware' (ibid., p.82). Therefore, a comparison of Soviet and US defence expenditure expressed in dollars tends to overvalue the Soviet military effort because those things on which the Soviets spend a lot (e.g. manpower) are very expensive in dollars (the CIA when assessing Soviet defence expenditure in dollars applies American rates of pay to the cost of maintenance of the Soviet army personnel). By contrast, price comparison would overestimate US defence expenditure because American advanced high technology content of military equipment would make it very expensive in rubles. A critic of the CIA estimates of Soviet military expenditure, Professor Franklyn Holzman, presents the following figures in Table 5.4 to indicate the bias contained in the estimates by the CIA and calls on the Agency to provide US decision-makers with as accurate and unbiased estimates as are possible on such important subjects (ibid., p.101).

Table 5.4 Ruble and dollar comparisons of Soviet and US defence expenditure: USSR/US

	1974	*1976*	*1978*	*1980*
CIA estimate in:				
Dollar prices	1.20	1.40	1.45	1.50
Ruble prices	1.10	1.25	1.25	1.30
Index number spread (dollar/rubles)	9%	12%	16%	15%

Source: Holzman, 1982, p.92.

Defenders of the CIA estimates point out that, although the index number effect may be applicable to a comparison between economies, it may not work as well under arms race conditions as it does in competitive markets. Besides, whether a comparison is made in dollars or rubles, it shows that Soviet defence expenditure exceeds that of the US by a wide margin (Alexander *et al.*, 1979, p.vi).

The question of Soviet pricing of its resources and goods has long been recognised as important for the understanding of the operation of the Soviet economy. It became even more so not only for the purpose of comparison between the USSR and US military efforts, but for the calculation and measurement of the Soviet burden of defence. Whether or how the Soviet leadership evaluates the extent of the military drain on national resources and the alternatives forgone is not really known, but judging by the attention devoted to this question by US Government agencies (CIA, JEC), the measurement of the burden as a share of GNP devoted to defence and its economic effects on the USSR must have political implications for America's decision-makers. Clearly, dollar values would not be appropriate since they have no relation to the operation of the Soviet system. Only ruble prices would indicate the trade-off between military spending and civilian production foregone. But to use Soviet prices as a tool of analysis is not a satisfactory method because of the Soviet pricing system. As is well known, prices in the Soviet Union are administratively determined and do not reflect relative scarcities of resources as they do in market economies. It may well be that the Soviet budget indeed represents the actual outlay if some resources used in the production of weapons were given low, administratively determined prices, in other words, using a Western term, they were subsidised. That this may be so can be deduced from the decision made by the Soviet authorities in 1967 that all defence related industrial enterprises be converted to full economic accountability (*khozrashchot*). The steep increase in Soviet defence spending as expressed in the State Budget between 1965 and 1970 (Narkhoz, 1978, p.559) from 12.8 billion rubles to 17.9 billion rubles, may well be accounted for by the more realistic pricing and costing of military production rather than increased defence effort. The 1976 CIA report which mentioned a better understanding of Soviet practices may refer to the Soviet pricing system. It is quite conceivable that given the limitations related to the Soviet price factor, Soviet economic planners themselves do not really know the opportunity cost of the defence effort and the military are not really concerned.

The standard Soviet theoretical definition of the price of a commodity is 'the money expression of its value. It contains...the full cost of production and the value of the surplus product' (Zhlobin, 1975, p.123). But in practice, the determination of the real price of a commodity expressed in monetary terms – the price formation – 'has been, and remains, one of the chief problems of Soviet economic policy' (ibid., p.124).

An indication of an awareness of the problems created by the Soviet pricing system is the rather large volume of relatively recent Soviet economic literature devoted to the task of price determination that would reflect the real cost of production. One Soviet source strongly suggested the need to improve the price formation system in order to 'react more flexibly and rapidly to changes in new production requirements, while remaining centralised...free financing of capital construction must cease in the majority of cases' (Khachaturov, 1977, p.15). As can be seen from the above, at the time of writing (1977) the problem of unrealistic pricing still existed. But, as a survey of Soviet pricing practices and the periodical revisions of wholesale prices seem to indicate, the question of pricing has been under discussion for a long time.

The problem of price determination is still plaguing Soviet economists and planners. Since the revision of wholesale prices in 1967, the price structure became quite unbalanced; hence a new reform took place in 1979. The Central Committee and the Council of Ministers adopted a resolution in June 1979 on questions of improvement in planning, which again gave prominence to prices as indicators of performance and economic efficiency. 'As a reliable measure of performance and efficiency, prices play an important role. They allow, to a large degree, to measure expenditure and results' – wrote a Soviet economist. But he complained that very often prices of different goods diverge from costs, and that the attention given to the introduction of a new method of price-determination in 1968 has weakened considerably (Yakovetz, 1980, p.13–19). The most recent attempt to tackle the problem of pricing is contained in the economic reforms introduced under the leadership of Gorbachev. Esssentially, prices will still be determined by a higher authority and, where they may be fixed by the enterprise, will be subject to strict control (more about the new price determination in Chapter 10).

As we can see, the question of rationality of the Soviet pricing system still remains unresolved. It simply means that the relatively low figure for defence spending can be explained by administratively planned prices by which consumer goods are valued at a price that is higher than cost, while the armed forces purchase armaments at a price that does not cover full cost of production (Krylov, 1979, p.194).[7]

THE SOVIET BUDGET AND THE ALLOCATION OF RESOURCES

For those who attempt to estimate Soviet ME and try to determine the defence burden by analysing Soviet officially published data, the Annual State Budget of the USSR is particularly relevant. But even here there are a number of problems, not least being the contrasting role of the Soviet budget compared to that of a Western developed country.

The role of the budget in a market economy is mainly directed towards influencing business activities and, to a lesser extent, towards the distribution of national income. The size and composition of the budget and the way Western governments raise their incomes and change the pattern of government spending, whether a budget is in deficit or has a surplus, affects the level of economic activities, employment and the level of output. All the above objectives are irrelevant in the Soviet budget whose sole function is the allocation of resources and the distribution of national income produced (Schultze *et al.*, 1972, pp.2–3).

The Soviet budget itself is a rather simple document presenting the revenues and expenditure of the government. One Soviet source describes the Soviet budget as 'an efficient instrument of financial control', and as 'providing financial resources...for accelerating scientific and technological progress, and raising the material and cultural standards of the people. It is an instrument of control over the excercise of strict thrift in all the links of the economy, and for...utilising reserves within the economy' (Zhlobin, 1975, p.204). It is also supposed to influence money circulation and to facilitate the 'consolidation of the rate of the Soviet ruble'. (It is not clear whether this refers to foreign exchange.) The Soviet economist stresses the point that the issue of money in the USSR does not serve as a source for covering state expenditure but is determined by the needs of the growing exchange of goods.

It is for this reason that the Soviet budget is never in deficit.[8]

Budget revenue is subdivided into two main groups: receipt from the profits of enterprises, including turnover tax, and from the population in the form of income tax (a minor item of government revenue – about 8.5 per cent of total receipts). State expenditure is subdivided into four main categories: expenditure on the national economy, social and cultural funds, defence, and administration.

The attention of Western analysts has always been focused on the expenditure side of the budget, especially on the analysis of the distribution of the Soviet national income and its redistribution through the state budget. The state budget allocates funds for health, education, social services, science, defence, administration, and for the operation of the economy. According to Soviet classification, outlays on the economy include investments in means of production, building of new enterprises, maintenance of fixed assets, development of new technology and new items of production, as well as exploitation of natural resources (ibid., p.172).

It is on the aspect of resource allocation that the attention of some Western analysts has been concentrated in order to detect trends and possible changes in the allocation of resources that would indicate Soviet defence spending policy. The main direction of this approach was to analyse the budgetary allocation for investment and consumption, as well as economic growth, and at the same time to investigate whether the Soviet Union is able to sustain its military effort. Such investigation would reveal, at least in theory, whether DE takes place at the expense of investment, consumption or economic growth. Historically, the Soviet leadership always assigned the first priority to defence requirements while shifting priorities slightly between consumption goods and investment.

> The steeply accelerated development of heavy industry under the pre-war Five-Year plans required a greater share of the national income used for accumulation which, naturally, held back the growth of personal consumption. The CPSU consistently tackled these tasks...while facing the pressing need to quickly carry out technical re-equipment of the national economy and strengthen the country's defence capacity (Sarkisiant, 1980, p.55–6).

According to some Western analysts, since 1975 the Soviet policy shows increasing preference for arms over investment

(Rush, 1983). On at least three occasions since 1975 the USSR has made large cuts in the growth of investment, according to Myron Rush. This, he claimed, reflected Soviet determination to maintain rapid growth of defence spending despite the slowing down of economic growth. He concluded that an increasing share of the diminishing annual increment in national income is being allocated to defence; by the mid-1980s defence may receive more than half the increment, leaving little for additional civilian investment and consumption. In fact some investment funds were diverted to defence. This assessment of Soviet defence spending policy was based partly on the available Soviet statistical data, and partly on the assumption that increased military expenditure can only come at the expense of investment and/or consumption.

The Soviets themselves freely admitted the slowing down of the rate of investment, but justified this policy on the ground of 'improving production efficiency'. They appeared to be concerned by a trend of diminishing return on investment, and seemed to follow the Directives of the 24th Congress to reduce the number of enterprises and units being built simultaneously and to prevent an excessive number of uncompleted projects. The criterion of the general economic efficiency for the national economy was to be 'the increment of national income in relation to the investments which brought about this increase' – a clear indication of diminishing returns (Zhlobin, 1975, p.174–76).

The above analytical approach for the determination of the Soviet economic burden of defence takes as its point of departure the Soviet national income or GNP, which, in turn, leads to the question of establishing what the real Soviet GNP is. In addition, Soviet economic terms, definitions and concepts are different from those used by Western economists. The main difference lies in the definition of product and income concepts.

Gross social product is the Soviet definition of the 'total gross output of all branches of material production expressed in real prices including turnover tax' (Narkhoz, 1978, p.597). It is considered by Soviet economists as an indicator of the growth of the Soviet economy, but as it includes the cost of production of all intermediate goods as well as the cost of some services that are used in the intermediate stages of the production process, it is rather the net (*tchisty*) final product that is used. One Soviet economist complains that planning does not make allowances for economic measurement of the final net product, with the result that in many instances the total value of semi-finished goods is greater than that of finished goods; a case of double counting (Krasovski, 1975, p.102). As such, Gross Social Product is not of much use for a Western economist either.

Of more interest is the concept of national income produced which is 'that part of Gross Social Product which remains after deducting the cost of all means of production used in the production process (raw material, fuel, energy etc.). The national income is obtained as the total of net output (*tchisty produkt*) of all separate branches of material production' (Narkhoz, 1978, p.598). But since GSP is defined as the total of material and productive values produced, the value of certain 'unproductive' kinds of services is excluded. Defence, which is considered as an activity outside the sphere of material production is almost certainly not included, and, since defence activity does not add to the material product (or social welfare), the income generated in defence establishments does not constitute, according to the Soviet concept, part of national income (Becker, 1972, p.90).

It is clear that Soviet concepts and definition of national income creates difficulties for the analyst who attempts to assess the defence burden as a ratio of DE to GNP. To begin with, since services and defence production are excluded from Soviet national income, the real GNP must be necessarily estimated. Furthermore, since some output of the defence sector and the activity of labour engaged in production must presumably increase the GNP, it ought to be found in some categories of either investment or consumption – a task involving much guesswork.

An additional difficulty is the existence in the Soviet Union of a hidden economy whose output cannot be located in official data. The extent of illegal activities for private gain cannot even be estimated, but is said to add some output of goods and services to the Soviet economy. This factor would tend to underestimate Soviet GNP (Bergson, 1972, p.188).

Numerous attempts to estimate Soviet GNP have produced a range of different figures, and although there seems to be more of an agreement on the defence burden measured as a share of Soviet GNP – the estimates ranging between a low of 6 per cent and a high of 15 per cent – the ruble value of Soviet GNP itself is contested (Block, 1973, pp.176–7). Attempts to locate defence related output through budgetary and statistical analysis have equally led to different results.

CONCLUSION

The divisions of opinion among political and economic analysts about the significance of Soviet defence spending and the wide range of estimates are an indication of the considerable difficulties which Western observers have to face in their attempt to unravel the mysteries of the operation of the Soviet system.

This raises the question whether, in view of such difficulties, an accurate assesment of Soviet defence spending and the defence burden is possible and of its political utility. In fact the CIA analysis of Soviet defence expenditure has been questioned by a number of Western observers. Some consider the CIA assessment an 'exegesis of obscure tests, guesses at unexplained residues, hunt after analogues, and indulgence in assumptions. Research on Soviet defence is the feast of the assumptions' (Block, 1976, p.255). Given the reservations about the accuracy of the assessment of Soviet military spending, its value as a yardstick for the evaluation of the Soviet military effort would also remain in doubt.

> The noneconomist may wonder...whether the game is worth the candle. If ME has such qualified connection to military power, why bother with value measurement at all? Why not stick to physical indicators of force levels and power potential? (Alexander *et al.*, 1979, p.3)

An important and equally pertinent question may be asked as to whether the Soviet leaders themselves are aware of the real cost of the military effort and of the extent of the defence burden that these costs entail. This question may not be as far-fetched as it appears. While it is certain that Soviet planners and decision-makers have access to a great deal more information than does a Western analyst, they would almost certainly face similar problems of interpreting the data that is available to them. One could legitimately ask whether, in view of the arbitrary fashion in which the Soviet price system operates (prices do not reflect scarcities and alternative uses forgone) and the bureaucratic system which is based on a vertical flow of authority and information rather than horizontal cross-feed, Soviet planners draw the appropriate conclusions regarding the defence burden. For as long as economic plans are being fulfilled and the economy shows, at least on paper, positive economic growth, they may see no reason for changing the priorities. An earlier Western view that Soviet statistical data is 'doctored' and that there exists a second set of information, has been discarded by most analysts. If it were so, the task of Soviet economic planners would have been made practically impossible. The proliferation of economic literature in the Soviet Union reflects the necessity for planners to receive as much reliable data as possible.

This is not to say that the leadership is not concerned about defence spending and its impact on economic growth and general welfare. Frequent references to the sacrifices that Soviet citizens must face and the hardship that they are expected to endure for the sake of national security, is evidence of such concern. But the absence of any precise economic analysis that would quantify the opportunity cost of the Soviet military effort seems to indicate that the extent of the defence burden is not a political issue. The Soviets may be reinforced in their belief by looking at the raw statistical figures which still show a steady, even if slow, progress in general welfare.

Soviet statistical data and literature devoted to questions of economic growth and improvement in general welfare of the population, constantly stress the point that the satisfaction of consumer demand is an important objective of Soviet economic planning, second only, if not equal, to national security expenditure. It is into this aspect of Soviet policy that one must turn, and establish whether the level of general welfare is rising, decreasing or remains static. This is important within the context of the question of the Soviet burden of defence, for as long as it can be shown that Soviet economic growth is reflected in rising living standards – an easier task than to estimate military expenditure – the trade-off between military spending and civilian consumption may not be as vital for the Soviet leaders as is assumed in some American Administration circles. There is little evidence, so far, that the Kremlin finds the military burden too much to bear and although living standards have risen only marginally, there are no signs of serious public grievances.

The following chapter will focus on the domestic aspect of the Soviet military effort and on the analysis of the economic and social progress of the Soviet population. The domestic aspects of the Soviet defence burden is of particular significance and relevance to the question whether the USSR will be able to sustain its military effort and stay in the armament race on an equal footing with the United States. This question has obvious implications for

American defence policies and for the Soviet effort to retain the superpower status, which is, so far, based mainly on the achievements in the military field.

6 The Domestic Aspect and New Economic Realism

INTRODUCTION

There is a widely shared view among Western analysts that the poor economic conditions in the Soviet Union are mainly a result of government policies which allocate a large share of GNP to military purposes. Many analysts have been concentrating their efforts in the search for evidence to show how military expenditure affects the Soviet economy as a whole and the consumer sector in particular. However, given the uncertainties about Soviet military expenditure, examined in the preceding chapter, the extent to which the Soviet military effort is at the expense of economic progress remains uncertain. There is less uncertainty about the link between the future capacity of the USSR to continue building up its military potential and overall economic growth. Therefore, any forecast about East–West relations, particularly on the balance of power between the superpowers, necessarily requires consideration of Soviet economic performance and future economic prospects (The USSR in the 80's, 1978, p.4). For while Soviet international standing and its superpower status are determined mainly by its military power, the Soviet Union appears relatively weak in terms of economic power and productivity compared to the developed Western European countries and the United States.

The analysis of the economic potential of the USSR, as it relates to the military effort and the economic burden that this may entail, has been generally confined to the question about the extent to which Soviet expenditure is limited by the capacity of the economy as a whole in terms of human and material resources, and to a much lesser degree on the impact of the arms race on the civilian development and on the general welfare of the population. The latter aspect has not attracted sufficient attention despite the fact that the situation of the Soviet population in terms of real welfare has economic and political implications and, as can be deduced from Soviet sources, is the subject of constant attention by the leadership.

Economic difficulties that affect the population at large can and do have some influence upon domestic policies. Raising food prices sparked serious popular unrest in the early 1960s [in 1978 the government found it necessary to deny rumours about impending rises in food prices. (*Izvestia*, 23 March 1978)], and there were reports of strikes in 1980 caused by inadequate supplies and poor economic conditions in some areas of the USSR. Chronic shortages of essential goods also act as an inhibitor on the attempts by the leadership to mobilise the population to more efficient individual performance (JEC, 1983, part II, p.196). It is obviously in the interest of the government to make sure that – apart from ideological slogans which may no longer have the desired impact – tangible proof of progress in the satisfaction of consumer demand is ever present. It is true that the economic situation of the average Soviet citizen has greatly improved over time – people are better fed and dressed than they were a few decades earlier and their spending capacity has also increased – but the improvement in the standard of living and growing spending capacity of the population, as evidenced by the substantial growth in personal savings, created additional expectations.

The critical appraisal in the preceding chapter of the methods and criteria used for the assessment of the Soviet military effort in economic terms must be seen, therefore, in the wider context of Soviet economic development, especially in the civilian sector of the economy. This approach may be more useful in the attempt to find an answer to the question of whether the satisfaction of consumer demands and raising the level of general welfare act as a constraint upon Soviet military spending. It is with this question in mind that we shall proceed with a survey and analysis of the achievements, future prospects and problems in the civilian sector of the Soviet economy.

In a speech on 8 July 1961 Khrushchev made the famous prediction that by 1980 the Soviet Union would have reached the stage of true communism, having left behind 'in its economic development the major capitalist countries' including the United States (*Pravda* 15 January 1960 and 9 July 1961). He based his prediction on the assumption that Soviet industrial production would continue to grow at a rate of 10 per cent per annum, as it did for the previous sixteen years, and that of the US at 4.5 per cent. He made the same assessment in relation to Soviet agricultural production. At the same time, Khrushchev announced a temporary halt to the planned reduction of Soviet troops for 1961, and an increase in the military budget by 3.14 billion rubles to 12.4 billion rubles. Apparently, he believed that both objectives, increased military spending and economic growth, could be achieved.

Twenty years hence, in 1980, this goal was as elusive as ever. In fact, the USSR made little progress towards catching up with the West. Soviet statistics make no attempt to hide it (see Table 6.1).

Table 6.1 National income of the USSR as a percentage of the US

1960		58
1970	more than	65
1977		67
1980		67
1984		67

Source: Narkhoz, 1978, p.51, 1981, p.59, 1985, p.67

In the late 1970s it was estimated that the level of Soviet consumption per head of population was still about one-third of the US level and less than half of France and West Germany (Schroeder, 1983, p.367). Generally, the Soviet standard of living remained rather drab and primitive, particularly outside of the main cities, and did not compare favourably with Western standards. But to make a comparison between the Soviet and Western level of welfare and personal consumption is not as straightforward as it appears. Different priorities, different social benefits which contribute to welfare but are rather difficult to assess in monetary terms, sharp differences in the availability, convenience and quality of comparative goods and services, are some of the difficulties in assessing relative living standards. 'A full understanding of [Soviet] living standards requires knowledge about shortages and queues, shadow markets and the economics of favours' (Eberstadt, 1983, p.198).

It is for this reason that a direct comparison between the Soviet and Western living standards would not be appropriate. Intertemporal comparisons within the USSR, rather than international, would be more relevant because they are less subject to ambiguity and even if this approach presents both conceptual and statistical difficulties, it has at least the advantage of revealing trends in the level of satisfaction of consumer demand and general welfare.

HISTORICAL SURVEY

The performance of the Soviet civilian economy and the progress in welfare did not follow an even pattern but fluctuated between different periods, particularly in the post Second World War periods. The disruption of Soviet economic development caused by the war and the subsequent efforts to rebuild a shattered economy are reflected in Soviet statistical data, which indicate a substantial economic advance in the period immediately following the end of the war. Despite the maintenance of relatively large armed forces, a sustained high level of military spending and significant outlays on scientific research that enabled the Soviet Union to develop and test its first atom bomb in 1949, the civilian economy grew at a rapid pace and there was a marked improvement in living conditions. In the period 1945–50, Soviet GNP almost doubled, and the main economic indicators have all shown sustantial growth. Compared to 1945 total industrial output increased by 89 per cent, output of means of production (group B) by 82 per cent, and that of consumer goods nearly doubled. According to Soviet data, by 1950 Soviet national income produced (Soviet definition) exceeded its pre-war level in many branches of the economy, except in agricultural production where it was still lagging.

Table 6.2 Soviet economic growth, 1940–50
(1940=1)

	1945	*1950*
National income produced	0.8	1.6
Total industrial output	0.9	1.7
Output of means of production	1.1	2.0
Output of consumer goods	0.6	1.2
Gross agricultural output	0.6	0.99

Source: Narkhoz, 1981, p.57.

The rapid achievement of the pre-war level of the Soviet economy can be attributed mainly to the relatively massive infusion of capital and labour (Becker, 1977, p.76); to the redirection of those branches of the civilian economy that took up military production during the war to their former activities, and to the rapid increase in the workforce due to the partial demobilisation and the absorption of many housewives into the workforce (Sarkisiant, 1980, p.177). While the population as a whole decreased from 194.1 million in 1940 to 181.6 million in 1951, Soviet data show an increase in the labour force of about 50 per cent between 1945 and 1950 (*SSSR v tsifrakh,* 1980, pp.7, 39).

Productivity was only a minor factor in Soviet economic growth and this is borne out by the fact that once the absorption of the bulk of the demobilised workforce into civilian economy had been completed, and further addition reduced, economic growth began to slow down. The rapid growth observed in the immediate post-war period up to the early 1950s and the subsequent persistent reversal of the previous trend show a marked correlation with the slow growth of the population and the labour force. The slower rate of growth is evident in the major sectors of the Soviet economy.

Table 6.3 Rate of growth of the Soviet workforce and selected indicators of economic growth
(percentage increase over period)

	1965–70	1970–5	1975–80	1980–4
Number of persons in employment	17.0	11.1	10.0	3.0
National income produced	45.0	31.0	23.7	15.6
Total industrial output	52.0	41.6	23.5	14.3
Production of means of prod'n	66.7	43.8	26.0	13.8
Production of consumer goods	37.5	38.5	22.2	18.0
Gross agricultural output	22.2	4.5	8.7	8.0

Source: Narkhoz, 1981, p.37–8, 1985, p.36–7.

Demographic trends in the Soviet Union indicate that the sources of manpower necessary for sustained economic growth are severely limited at present by the low natural increase and the changing age structure of the population (Khachaturov, 1977, p.32). Consequently, improving the economic situation and increasing the supply of consumer goods could no longer come about by adding more to the labour force. This question figured prominently in the Report of the CC to the 25th Congress of the CPSU. Since, it was noted in the Report, additional labour sources have been exhausted, the number of workers can only increase in accordance with their natural growth. There will be, therefore, much less reliance on enlisting additional labour power (Documents and Resolutions 1978, p.5). 'At present there are considerably fewer opportunities for raising the population's real incomes by enlisting for special production, people engaged in personal subsidiary plots or housework' (Sarkisiant, 1980, p.183).

The depletion of human resources resulted in a shifting emphasis by Soviet economists from extensive to intensive development of production. While in the past the availability of labour allowed the commissioning of many new enterprises, the new situation was characterised by an attempt for the 'ever fuller utilisation of existing productive capacities' (ibid., p.43).

> A solution to the problem of labour resources must include the...intensification of exploitation of existing resources, an improvement in planning and in the methods of fixing monetary wages as a stimulus for increased production. (Pogosov, 1980, pp.81–2)

It was around 1970 that the Soviet economy began to run out of plentiful reserves of labour for industrialisation and modernisation (Connor, 1981, p.160). According to some Western calculations, Soviet GNP rate of growth shows a declining trend from 6.7 per cent per annum in the 1950s to 4.2 per cent per annum in the middle 1970s. Soviet data, although showing higher rates of growth, confirms a downward trend from 10.2 per cent to 5.7 per cent per annum (Levine, 1981, p.78).

As can be seen from Table 6.4, the greatest gains in per capita consumption have been made during the 1950s. After relatively low rates of growth during the early 1960s, per capita consumption rose in the late 1960s, to be followed by a slowdown in the early 1970s.

The last decade was characterised by a very slow gain for the consumer compared to previous periods. The average annual growth of real per capita consumption in the 1970s (2.6 per cent) was only half of the 1966–70 period, less than 2 per cent in 1981 and under 1 per cent in 1982. The fall in growth occurred in all

Table 6.4 Growth of per capita consumption in the USSR 1951-80
Average annual rates of growth

	1951–5	*1955–60*	*1961–5*	*1966–70*	*1971–5*	*1976–80*
Total consumption	5.3	4.2	2.5	4.7	3.2	2.4
Household goods	5.6	4.5	2.1	4.8	3.0	2.3
Food	4.7	2.8	2.0	3.5	2.1	1.3

Source: JEC, 1976, p.622; 1983, p.370.

categories of consumption, but the most noticeable slowdown was in the area of food supply. Some gains in per capita consumption of quality food – notably meat – took place in the middle 1970s, but no progress has been made since. Soviet data confirms this assessment (Narkhoz, 1981, p.406).

Poor harvests in 1980, 1981 and 1982 (see *Ekonomicheskaia gazeta*, no.5, January 1985 and *Pravda*, 26 January 1986) have no doubt contributed to the deteriorating situation, but because of widespread imbalances between the supply and demand of consumer goods generally, the prospects of any improvements were considered rather remote, according to most Western analysts. It was evident from Soviet sources that the government was contemplating relatively slow gains in per capita consumption, especially in food. The rather modest planned increase in production and consumption of basic food products for the decade 1980–90 was an indication of an awareness by the leadership of the problems and difficulties facing the economy.

Table 6.5 Planned consumption of major food items, 1980–90
(per capita per annum kg)

	1980	*1990*
Meat and meat products	58	70
Fish and fish products	17.6	19
Milk and milk products	314	330–340
Eggs(pieces)	239	260–266
Sugar	44.4	45.5
Vegetable oil	8.8	13.2
Fruit	38	66–70

Source: 'Prodovolstvennaia programma SSSR na period do 1990 goda i mery po eio realizatsii' (Krasnaia zvezda, Moscow, 1982).

While blaming poor harvests for the poor performance of the agricultural sector, the shortcomings in storage, transport, processing and methods of trading were also mentioned as contributing factors. Very often the bottlenecks were not in the production process itself but in storage and in the channels of supply to the consumer. The role of private subsidiary farms in the supply of food was promoted once more and a call made to offer them every assistance (Prodovolstvennaia programma, pp.8–12).

In 1982, an increase was also announced in prices for government purchases of a wide range of agricultural products, as well as extra additions to those paid for production under adverse conditions and for farms with low rentability. As a further incentive to enhance agricultural production, the government decided to write off 9.7 billion rubles in bank loans for collective farms, and allowed a postponement of payments of over 11 billion rubles (Prodovolstvennaia programma, pp.13–14). The main objective of incentives offered to the collective farms was not only to increase total production, but to enhance greater efficiency and productivity, and which, as we shall see, was also extended to the industrial sector.

INCENTIVES FOR GREATER EFFICIENCY

Soviet economists saw both factors, the satisfaction of consumers' demands and efficiency of production, as closely connected. They saw efficiency as depending to a considerable degree on a proper application of material incentives, particularly in the rational use of money wages (Khachaturov, 1977, p.38) and the supply of goods that can be purchased with their earnings by the working population. The importance of the human factor in the economic development of the Soviet Union is recognised by the leadership and is being constantly impressed upon the population, but mobilising the broad masses to more efficient individual performance without tangible incentives is a difficult task. It is clear that the question of motivation is no less important in a socialist than in a capitalist economy (Eberstadt, 1983, p.196), although according to ideological principles 'the Communist Party rejects outright a consumer interpretation of the socialist way of life' and emphasises the role of moral, rather than material, incentives and the 'cultivation of a communist attitude to labour' (Sarkisiant, 1980, p.58).[1]

The material incentives which the government offered to the working population were mainly in the form of money wages and, indeed, in the area of per capita earning, the Soviets show considerable growth. But despite a substantial increase in the purchasing power of the population caused by the growth of money income, remarkably little progress toward a more satisfactory – from the Soviet consumer point of view – pattern of supply has been made in recent decades. As we shall see, the imbalance between rising money incomes and the supply of consumer goods gave rise to considerable problems that cancelled out the potential benefits which monetary incentives may have presented.

Before proceeding with the analysis of the issues connected with the imbalances between income and supply of goods, it is necessary to examine the way incomes are distributed and the sources of income of the Soviet population. There are two basic categories of distribution of Soviet national income: remuneration for work expressed in monetary terms of wages and salaries and the social consumption fund (Rzhanitsyna, 1977, p.13), which is part of the state budget that allocates funds for social services supplied free (medical services, education, subsidised rent etc.), as well as pensions, family support funds and other assistance schemes. The proportion of the main categories of income distribution in the income of an individual industrial worker is shown in Table 6.6.

Table 6.6 Average monthly earnings, 1960–84 (rubles)

	Cash wages and benefits from social consumption fund	*Cash wages only*
1960	107.7	80.6
1970	164.5	122.0
1975	198.9	145.8
1980	232.7	168.9
1984	260.0	184.8

Source: Narkhoz, 1985, p.417.

The distribution of national income for a collective farmer is somewhat different in that part of his income is derived from his personal private plot – 'personal subsidiary farm' in Soviet terminology. A comparison between the income structure of an industrial worker family and that of a collective farmer reveals that a substantial proportion of a collective farmer's family income still comes from the private plot. About 53 per cent of income of the average family originates from the work done on the collective farm, 25.3 per cent from the private plot, the balance being derived from social consumption fund and other unspecified sources (Narkhoz, 1981, p.385). For the assessment of incomes derived from subsidiary farms in cash terms, the statistical practice, according to the Soviet source, is to evaluate the part of the production which is consumed by the family at state retail prices, and that sold on the collective farm market in actual prices obtained (Rzhanitsyna, 1977, p.103). Where no reliable statistics are available, it has been decided to fix a monthly cash income per family regardless of the size of the plot or the number of cattle owned. The latter is taken into consideration when establishing allowances for low-income families, which is based on the aggregate income including subsidiary farming.

It is interesting to notice that the Soviets have also established what they call the Material Welfare Minimum Budget – a concept similar to the Western poverty line – which is the minimum cash income necessary for the purchase of, among other things, 'more than 3000 calories worth of foodstuff a day' and other items of basic necessities. In 1975, 50 rubles per month per person, or 200 rubles per family, was considered the minimum necessary to cover such expenditure.

Table 6.7 Material Welfare Minimum budget (1975)

	monthly(rubles)	*per cent of total*
Food	115.0	56
Consumer goods	61.2	30
Sevices	29.4	14

Source: Rzhanitsyna, 1977, p.128.

The introduction of minimum wages for industrial workers and farmers together with low below-equilibrium prices had the same objective of ensuring a Minimum Material Welfare. The minimum wage level relative to the average wage increased considerably from 28 per cent in 1951–5 to about 45 per cent in the 1971–5 period.

Coupled with rising personal incomes, state retail prices for basic goods have been rather stable over the years. One Soviet source indicates a drop of 40 per cent in the average retail prices between 1947 and 1954. Subsequent years show a slight increase in prices with the retail price index in 1975 compared to 1950 at only 75. There was a relative stability of prices between 1965 and 1975, the state retail price index for all commodities being 99.3, including food at 101.2 – a slight rise (Sarkisiant, 1980, p.77). However, when we consider the increases in personal incomes and the stability of prices as an indication of growing purchasing power, we must also keep in mind the fact that a number of important items of consumption is covered by subsidies from the state budget.

The increasing emphasis on money income growth rather than a reduction in prices, which took place since the economic reforms of 1967, was justified by Soviet analysts on economic and social grounds. They saw that the main advantage of money income growth over massive price cuts was that 'in absolute terms the benefit of lower prices goes to the higher paid earners, while increased earnings are of greater benefit to the less well-off'. Secondly, wage rises are a powerful incentive to 'work more efficiently and to avoid excessive labour turnover' (Rzhanitsyna, 1977, p.36). Furthermore, the real incomes of the population, being a form in which national income is distributed, are an aggregate indicator of the standard of living, according to another Soviet economist (Sarkisiant, 1980, p.65).

In the area of individual money incomes, the Soviets can indeed claim substantial advances. Between 1966 and 1975 alone, real per capita money incomes have increased by 65 per cent, according to Soviet sources, and were to grow by another 21 per cent under the Tenth Five-Year Plan, doubling by 1980 the 1965 level of per capita income.

Table 6.8 Growth of wages of an industrial worker (percentage increase)

1956–60	12
1961–65	20
1966–70	26
1971–75	20
1976–80	18
1980–85	11

Source: Rzhanitsyna, 1977, p.42 and *Pravda*, 26 January 1986.

Impressive as these figures (indicating the growth of personal income and associated social benefits) may be, they only reveal the increase in the purchasing power of the population and do not necessarily signify a corresponding improvement in general welfare. The purchasing power of a consumer is usually associated with money incomes which theoretically determine the quantity of goods and services that can be bought, but under conditions of severe shortages and in the absence of market forces that would determine prices for goods in short supply, the usual criteria used for assessing the relative level of welfare are difficult to apply. The need to balance money incomes and expenditure of the population, the purchasing capacity and the availability of goods, appeared as a constant subject in Soviet publications. They reveal imbalances between the level of individual income and the possibilities to spend it. In that sense, notes a Soviet economist, the mere growth of the population's cash earnings does not yet mean a real rise in living standards (Sarkisiant, 1980, p.78). Consequently, money income as an indicator of welfare was less meaningful and the purchasing power of money earnings even more difficult to determine.

STATISTICAL SURVEYS IN THE USSR

In an attempt to determine the real level and movement in general welfare and living standards, periodical surveys of the pattern of family spending have been conducted in the USSR for a number of years by a specially established branch of Soviet statistics known as 'Budget Statistics' (Rzhanitsyna, 1977, p.90). The surveys were based on the use of the sampling method whereby every year about 62 000 families were surveyed and their budget closely studied. They were conducted every month in the course of one year and sometimes over a period of years (Narkhoz, 1978, p.409). It must be said that the data supplied by Soviet statisticians regarding the sources of income and the pattern of individual spending appear consistent, but the conclusions which the analysts drew from the statistics were clearly biased towards the official line imposed by the Party – they invariably pointed to the progress in general welfare and in living standards. The method used to indicate substantial improvements in living conditions of the average citizen were rather simple and lacked the sophistication of

Western analysis. By contrasting conditions over two widely separated time periods they were able to offer evidence of some considerable achievements. These, they said, were most noticeable from the changes in the pattern of consumption of food and manufactured goods.

The change in the food consumption pattern, to which Soviet sources refer, was a reduction in the consumption of staple food, like bread and potatoes, and an increase in the consumption of eggs, sugar, meat and fruit between 1951 and 1975. This trend, according to one Soviet source, reflected a qualitative improvement in the diet, which now has a high calorific content (more than 3000 calories per day per capita) and is in 'accordance with the physiological needs of the average person' (Prodovolstvennaia programma, p.7). A similar approach was adopted for the analysis of consumption of manufactured goods. However, in contrast to food which is available from government run outlets as well as from markets, the supply of manufactured consumer items is available practically only through the state trade network. This is why the sales structure of manufactured goods in state-run stores is a more accurate reflection of the pattern of their consumption. The change in the consumption structure of the latter was mainly in the increased sales of durables. Generally, the overall tendency in the changing structure of consumption is towards a faster growth in the purchases of manufactured items rather than food, and towards a higher consumption of quality foods (Sarkisiant, 1980, p.83).

When one compares the pattern of individual spending between 1945 and 1980, then it is obvious that significant improvements have occurred in all areas. The share of expenditure on food out of the aggregate income has fallen from 53.8 per cent to 32 per cent, whilst on consumer durables it increased from 15 per cent to 24.6 per cent. A shorter time span between 1965 and 1980 shows very little change (Narkhoz, 1981, p.383). This should be seen in the context of changes in money wages which have grown nearly sixfold since 1940, almost doubled between 1965 and 1980, and increased by 46 per cent since 1970. But it appears that a Soviet citizen still spends a relatively high share of his income on food. The share of the family budget going into purchase of food is still about one-third.

The changes in the pattern of food consumption and manufactured goods may well indicate an improvement in the living standard, but it must be borne in mind that these trends took place over a relatively long time span, between 1951 and 1975. An analysis of the general trend in consumption expressed in volume, or value, rather than in the structure of consumption, reveals a rather slow progress towards improved consumer satisfaction, especially since 1970. Yet, according to Soviet commentators, the steadily increasing aggregate production of specific items of manufactured goods suggests rising living standards, the assumption being that whatever is produced will necessarily be consumed.

> The steady growth of effective demand...is one of the best proofs of rising consumption level in the USSR. The Soviet Union is never faced with the problem inherent in capitalism of overstocking, of the antagonistic contradiction between production and consumption. (Rzhanitsyna, 1977, p.107)

This may have been a justified claim at a time of severe shortages of basic commodities, especially in a command economy where the planning authorities determine the needs of the population and where consumer sovereignty is quite restricted. But this situation has been changing over time into one where the consumer has at least the alternative of not buying what was available. Formerly, production was seen as being reflected in trade and in the turnover of goods. 'In its growth were reflected economic indicators – the relationship between accumulation and consumption, production of consumer goods and demand' (Orlov, 1969, p.52). However, the gradual increase in production of some consumer items that were in short supply, resulted in an ever increasing volume of unsold goods which remained in stores and warehouses. Soviet data reveal that stocks of goods held in retail stores at the end of the year increased by 80 per cent, from 26.4 billion rubles in 1965 to 48.7 billion rubles in 1977 (Narkhoz 1978, p.464).

PROBLEM OF SAVINGS

It would appear that to the extent to which increased earnings were meant to constitute an incentive for better production efficiency, they also created difficulties for the planners and negated their potential economic advantages. This is the problem of balancing incomes with the production of consumer goods. Despite the claim that 'the Tenth Five-Year Plan will balance out the population's income and spending', there is substantial evidence which indicates that the supply of some consumer goods lags behind the buying capacity of the population. Periodical shortages of certain items and even basic commodities are still the rule rather than the exception, and given the unfulfilled demand for some kinds of goods and the selectivity of Soviet consumers, there must be a certain part of the earned money income that cannot be spent (Table 6.9). This is indeed confirmed by the increase in the savings of the population, and it points to the shortcomings of Soviet economic planning rather than a rising standard of living.

Table 6.9 Growth of saving deposits

	1965	*1970*	*1975*	*1980*	*1984*
Billions of rubles	18.7	46.6	91.0	156.5	202.1
Percentage increase		149.0	95.0	72.0	29.0

Source: Narkhoz, 1981, p.408; 1985, p.462.
Note: The apparent slowdown in the rate of increase in personal savings is in line with a policy of reducing the rate of growth of average earnings (see Table 6.8). Nevertheless, savings are still on the increase. In 1985, they grew by 18.7 billion rubles (*Pravda,* 26 January 1986).

There was an apparent concern among Soviet economists about 'postponed demand', which made planning more complicated because of the uncertainty of how much was voluntary saving and how much was induced by unfulfilled demand. One estimate has put the total of saving deposits of 91 billion rubles in 1974 as being larger than the total retail sales of non-food goods (Schroeder and Severin, 1976, p.638), while in 1977 savings reached 131 billion rubles – 55 per cent of all retail sales (Khodzhaev, 1977, p.26).

The question of growing personal savings was a subject of much debate in the Soviet Union and not all economists were in agreement as to its meaning and causes. One Soviet economist saw the imbalance between the purchasing capacity of the population and the supply of goods and services as a major factor leading to the growth of savings (Pogosov, 1980, p.81). Another saw the problem of imbalance in terms of the relative level of stocks of goods and its movement. When the production of goods falls behind the increasing buying capacity, the market is quickly exhausted and shortages ('irregularities in supply') occur. On the other hand, large stocks do not indicate a saturation of the market, but lack of consumer satisfaction with the goods offered (Lokshin and Tyukov, 1976, pp.36-7).

Opinions were also divided between those that adopted an idealistic approach and considered the phenomenon of large savings as evidence of rising welfare, and those that explained it in terms of shortages of goods. There was, on the other hand, a more general agreement about the sources and causes of growing incomes, quite apart from the increase of money wages.

A major impact upon the growth of per capita income has been the decision by the government to monetarise the income of collective farmers and the introduction of the guaranteed minimum labour remuneration (Zhlobin, 1975, p.97). In addition, since 1965 collective farmers became eligible for pensions and other benefits similar to urban workers (Sarkisiant, 1980, p.76). There was also a gradual increase in procurement prices for agricultural products which contributed to a substantial and rapid rise of peasants' incomes. The disposable income of the working population also grew somewhat as a result of the abolition of compulsory purchases of government bonds in 1957.

The proponents of the view that increased savings were an indication of rising welfare appear to have followed the official line which favoured a positive opinion about the achievements of the socialist economy. They supported the view that interruptions in the supply and shortages of goods, although indicating that demand is still above the production level, are caused primarily by the increase in earnings, and, to a lesser degree, by changes in the structure of demand. For example, the provision by the government of paid services for annual vacation and the development of the vacation industry, induced the workers to save money for that purpose. Another example was the growing demand for durables which had to be bought for cash when available (Alexandrova and Fedorovskaia, 1978, p.69). A contributing factor to the growing demand, they said, was also the decreasing number of people employed in the agricultural sector and a corresponding increase in the number of town dwellers (presumably the urban population consuming more manufactured goods) and increased purchases of food-stuff by the country population (Prodovolstvennaia programma, p.7).

REFORMING THE ECONOMY

The Soviet Government was certainly not indifferent to the problem of imbalance between income and the supply of consumer goods. The mere fact that open debate on this question did take place is indicative of the concern about the situation and its potential consequences. A wide-ranging discussion on the subject of imbalances with the participation of the representatives of Gosplan, the Ministry of Trade and some light industry enterprises, took place in December 1976; a discussion that revealed the extent of difficulties facing the civilian economy arising from the imbalances.

The main criticism voiced during the debate was directed towards the deficiencies of planning. Theoretically, inconsistencies between income and expenditure by the population should not have existed for 'there are financial calculations which are supposed to coordinate turnover with money expenditure, but in practice there is no method of planning, organisation and coordination of production and sale of goods. There is no consumer demand research and no method of assessing the quality of consumer goods' (*Voprosy ekonomiki*, no.3, March 1977, p.31).

Faulty planning brought about a situation where industrial enterprises were, to a large extent, insulated from the suppliers of raw materials, on the one hand, and from the consumer, on the other. As a result, raw materials and components were directed towards areas remote from their place of production, while enterprises located in the vicinity experienced long delays in supply (Kurtchenko, *Pravda*, 6 May 1980). Similarly, shortages of consumer goods were very often caused not so much by an insufficient volume of production as by deficient distribution which lead to a glut of goods in some places while in others consumers had to queue up.

Since the production plan was only approximately according to demand, and responded only slowly to changes, more mistakes were made while the problem was studied, and the output of goods that nobody wanted continued. Very often they remained on the shelves for a long period of time until they become obsolete and useless (*Voprosy ekonomoki*, no.3 March 1977, p.22). Some enterprises were producing the same type of goods for decades – washing machines of 1950–2 models were still being produced, even if only a few were bought. 'One could ask a legitimate question: why are the unsalable goods kept by the stores and not by the enterprise that produced them? Why does not the store refuse to accept them?' The simple answer, as was revealed during the debate, was that since the store had a plan to fulfil, it feared that if it does not accept the goods, it may not receive any at all. A solution to this problem was nevertheless provided by Soviet planners in the form of an allowance for unsalable goods which allowed the store to clear them at much reduced prices. But, as was reported, after a certain period of time the same problem reoccured, for the goods were still being produced and the stores were forced to take them (ibid., p.43).

Other economists saw the phenomenon of accumulation of unwanted goods closely connected with the problem of pricing, of wholesale and retail prices, turnover tax and generally with the whole Soviet system of rebates, surcharges and pricing zones. Since prices did not represent either the quality or consumers' wishes, it would appear that in some cases the consumer was willing to pay a higher price for better quality goods on account of higher income, but they seem to have been in short supply.

Soviet authorities made numerous attempts to rectify the situation through the introduction of economic reforms that would make the distribution of goods more rational, and would, at the same time, speed up the turnover of goods in the stores. Prior to the economic reforms of 1965, the only criteria of assessment of the efficiency of domestic trade, was the fulfilment of the plan of sales, which was not very difficult given the acute shortages of goods. The introduction of two indicators of trade efficiency – turnover of goods and profitability – made the situation even more complicated. According to one Soviet economist:

> what happens now is that stores are interested to sell goods for which there is a greater demand. Under conditions of shortages one can play a game in the assortment field, and push sales of goods which offer greater scope for profit – especially spirits and vodka. (Orlov, 1969, p.55–6)

Another reform allowed some freedom in direct dealings between enterprises producing consumer goods and trading organisations, whereby a producer enters into a contractual agreement to supply goods (it was an attempt to widen horizontal links – a problem that will be discussed in Chapter 8). From 1 January 1978, the fulfilment of actual orders placed by the store according to the contract was to become, among other things, a new criteria of evaluation of results. Furthermore, the contractual obligation of the producing enterprise became subject to 'economic sanctions' in case of non-delivery or other failures. Apparently, little success has been achieved.

In the area of production of consumer goods, the difficulties for Soviet planners were even more acute, for in addition to anticipating public demand for specific items, they also had to overcome the inertia of production geared towards certain types of goods and the resistance from enterprises themselves to change their production pattern. The introduction of reforms offering greater flexibility and autonomy of operation for the managers exacerbated the problems of planning even more. While the objective of the reforms was to make production more efficient in terms of costs, it also gave the managers the possibility of selecting production of goods offering higher profitability. One Soviet source quoted as an example the reduced range of goods manufactured by some enterprises to the detriment of the consumer. In 1977, there was an acute shortage of small sizes of shoes and garments for children. It was found that to manufacture large sizes has been more convenient and profitable, because for only a small additional input of labour and material, relatively higher prices could be obtained. Ninety-three per cent of orders for small items of crockery were not fulfiled, while large pots were overproduced (Orlov, 1978, pp.6–7).

Linked to the objective of reaching the production target was the question of quality. In the pursuit of the fulfilment of production plans and profitability, the quality of consumer goods was generally neglected, which did not matter much as long as a particular item was in short supply. It has been reported that in 1977 about 80 per cent of cloth and clothing, over 90 per cent of knitted goods, and 70 per cent of shoes, that were rejected on account of inferior quality, have been subsequently repaired or downgraded (Orlov, 1978, p.60).

Servicing of goods bought by the consumer was another problem. Since Soviet-produced goods are generally of low quality, returns of faulty items are the rule rather than the exception. According to one Soviet estimate, about one million specialists are busy handling rejected goods. In addition, the lack of service facilities at the point of sale forces stores to send back faulty goods from remote places (e.g. Vladivostok) to the factory which may be located in Grodno (Lithuania), at a cost which was about half of the price of the product (Orlov, 1978, p.62). The economic cost of such practices cannot be estimated, but that the problem exists and is difficult to solve is evident from the many articles by Soviet economists offering a wide range of solutions. These vary from suggestions of greater incentives to the improvement of efficiency through better organisation of production and planning.

NEW ECONOMIC REALISM

The relatively recent realistic approach to problems of internal economic policies was concentrated mainly in the attempt to improve the efficiency of operation of the Soviet economy. However, while the theoretical ground was laid for the solution of economic difficulties, the practical implementation of the conclusions reached on the basis of quite realistic assumptions still appeared rather remote.

It was, nevertheless, a far cry from the strictly dogmatic attitudes adopted by Soviet economists only a decade earlier. The basic principle applied to economic theory and practice at the time was that 'Lenin's works supply to the Soviet economists an inexhaustible theoretical arsenal that allows to resolve successfully theoretical as well as practical goals and to constantly develop economic thought' (Levshin and Oreshkin, 1974, p.12). It appears that as early as 1968, following the Congress of the CPSU and the subsequent directives of the Central Committee about the development of social sciences, various trends emerged in the field of economic thought that were in variance with traditional Marxism–Leninism. Some economists began to apply Western economic concepts, while others stuck strictly to the Marxist determination of political economy.

The existence of such trends could be found in the harsh criticism to which some economic scientists were subjected by the dogmatists. The proponents of a pragmatic approach to economic theory were described as 'incompetent in Marxist–Leninist theory' and criticised for applying methods which 'open the way to the penetration of bourgeois methodology' (Fedoseev, 1974, p.61). Soviet economists were warned against the contamination by pseudo-scientific theories of 'convergence', 'pluralism', and 'free marketism' as purely subversive and as a form of anti-communist propaganda (Trapeznikov, S., 1974, p.13).

In view of the traditionally entrenched Marxist dogma among most economic scientists, the publication of the debates at a conference of economic scientists that took place, in 1983, in Prague deserves a special mention. Although the official subject of the conference was on 'Laws of economic development of socialism and the competition between the two world systems', the emphasis was on questions of improvement of the economic performance of a socialist economy at the present stage of its development within the context of Marxist theory. The conference devoted most of its time to a critical assessment of what was negative in the operation of the economy rather than to its positive achievements.

The question of successful fulfilment or overfulfilment of production targets has not been considered at all. 'The task of improving economic performance' has not been linked any more to 'quantitative increases of production', but to the problem of 'balancing the economy' (Mikulsky, 1984, p.5). There was general agreement that the Soviet economy was deeply unbalanced – the imbalance coming about as a result of past excessive emphasis on growth maximisation of leading industries at the expense of those considered less important. The emphasis on extensive sources of economic growth resulted also in a less than efficient exploitation of foreign economic relations, particularly in the reliance on credits that caused balance of payment problems for a number of socialist countries.

Another reason for economic imbalances was the rapid technological changes in production, changes in world markets, and the rise of consumers selectivity of demand. But the main cause of economic imbalances was found to be the deficiencies in the management of the national economies (ibid., p.39). Such a bold statement, however, must not be taken as an indictment of the Soviet economic system, for as was said at the conference, 'the existence of imbalances within a socialist economy does not indicate that it is caused by its social nature – imbalances are not inherent to a socialist system'. The above conclusions ought to be understood as an attempt to pinpoint the sources of the problems and as a search for remedies within the operation of thc system (we shall analyse this attempt within the context of the new economic reforms introduced under Gorbachev in Chapter 10).

The search for solutions began with the definition of what

constitutes an economic balance. This was defined as the 'relationship between economic resources and the satisfaction of planned demand for those resources'. In other words, planning must determine a level of demand for resources that corresponds to their availablity. The non-adherence to that principle was seen as the main cause of the imbalances in the economy and of the emergence of its main symptom – shortages of some resources needed for planned demand. This in turn caused the imbalance between production and consumer demand. To sum it all up: the causes of imbalances or, to be more precise, the non-availability of resources for planned production were attributed to unrealistic plans that did not take into account the real supply situation, plans that included production goals not covered by the availability of resources. For example, plans that relied on supply from new enterprises that were not yet put into operation. It all came down to the non-compliance or the physical impossibility to fulfil a certain plan. An enterprise which, according to the plan, was supposed to commence production of a certain component needed for the production process in another enterprise, did not come into full operation in time causing a break in the chain linking several enterprises and resulting in shortages of finished goods at their final destination – the retail outlets.

Similar problems of balance between the supply and demand of resources occurred in many sectors of the economy, including the labour sector. While in the past labour shortages were attributed to demographic causes, the problem was looked upon as one of imbalance. It had been noted that shortages of manpower became sharper in the USSR during the 1970s when there was an unprecedented growth in the labour force. What happened then was that the emphasis being on extensive development, more employment opportunities were created than the available manpower could satisfy. Consequently, a tendency emerged at the enterprise to increase the number of employees in order to fulfil the plan rather than invest in new equipment. This contributed to the creation of a large pool of hidden reserves and corresponding labour shortages. It created the impression that labour was 'cheap' relative to investment.

> At the present time, the prevailing practice is to request a larger than necessary quantity of resources in order to minimise the risk of the non-fulfilment of the plan. To create hidden reserves

> to be used in case of an unexpected change in the production process. (ibid., p.53)

As a result of this situation an attempt was being made by the enterprise to retain employees at any price. This was exploited by the workers through frequent changes of places of employment, leading to higher wages without a corresponding increase in productivity.

Some remedies offered at the conference were in terms of suggestions for legalising such practices in order to identify their extent. But, essentially, the remedies were mostly concerned with the creation of an effective economic mechanism that would enable the correct and timely supply of information about existing imbalaces, and would be able to react rapidly to changes occurring in the production process and technology.

Productivity of labour was also an important topic of discussion and, for the first time, the negative effects of full employment were mentioned.

> If the absence of unemployment is one of the main achievements of socialism in that it constitutes a social guarantee for the workers, labour shortages or full employment have a negative influence on the attitudes to work by the employees. It contributes to the feeling of dependence [on the state] and to excessive labour turnover. (ibid., p.105)

Some attention was devoted to unemployment as an option to solve the problem of excessive labour turnover and of low labour productivity. The question as to whether a low level of unemployment could be justified on account of its effect on work discipline has been resolved in the negative and rejected outright because 'the practice in a socialist country is based on the principle of full employment'. However, severe unemployment was rejected not on ideological grounds alone, but on account of its effect on the introduction of new technology that might be prevented by the workers themselves, if they would then consider it to be against their interests (ibid., p.46).[2]

A similarly pragmatic attitude was adopted at the conference regarding the Hungarian economy. Previously, references by Soviet leaders to the experiences of 'fraternal socialist countries' only implied the Hungarian experience with no direct implications to other socialist economies, certainly not the USSR. There was open debate about the lessons that could be learned from it. There were also frequent references to the role of small enterprises, mainly private, which contribute greatly to the supply of consumer goods in Hungary. Leasing of restaurants and small shops is allowed there, as are small private industrial enterprises where relatively little outside labour is required. 'Some economists consider the role of small and medium [private] enterprises in the production of some consumer goods to be unjustifiably underestimated' (ibid., p.244).

The debate about the role of private enterprise that was taking place among Soviet economists and its publication was an indication of a changing trend in Soviet economic management. There were signs that this may have been so because of purely practical expediency and on account of the gradual shedding of classical Marxist economics. According to Gorbachev: 'large scale economic experiments are under way. They are aimed essentially at developing a more efficient mechanism of management' (*Time,* 9 September 1985, p.12).

The Soviet press also reported another innovation in Soviet economic management whereby small state enterprises are 'contracted' to the working staff, and underlined the dramatic results achieved when the workers were given the right to purchase material and provide services to customers, while retaining the net profit for their personal use. In one particular instance, the service to the public by a repair shop for domestic appliances has improved to such an extent that the time usually taken for repairs has been reduced from over one month to just a few days with a much reduced staff (*Pravda*, 16 September 1985). Admittedly, this may have been an isolated case of an experiment promoted and assisted by the appropriate departments, but the fact that it was debated and widely publicised without any reference to Marxism–Leninism, suggested a new pragmatism in Soviet thinking (it became part of the economic reforms introduced by Gorbachev).

It may also have been designed to counteract the activities of the Soviet underground economy. While the existence of a 'second economy' was common knowledge, it was only in 1985 that it became a subject of open discussion. For the first time, a value has been put on the level of production of goods and services on the black market. According to the estimates by Soviet economists, sociologists and managers, some 17 to 20 million people were engaged in these activities and their earnings were estimated at 5 to 6 billion rubles (*Izvestia,* 19 August 1985). 'This trend cannot be diminished neither can it be controlled', but as we shall see in Chapter 10, the problem has been resolved through the Law of Individual Labour.

There remains one other area of Soviet economic policy where political rationality is increasingly getting the upper hand over ideological considerations. Foreign trade and imports of consumer goods and Western technology have been suggested by Soviet economists for some time in order to 'satisfy much better the direct demands of the population' (*Vneshnaia torgovlia* no.6, 1978, p.4). Although it is generally assumed in the West that the Soviet Union is mainly interested in importing advanced technology, Soviet data indicate that in 1981 over 40 per cent of imports were of manufactured goods, food products and raw material used in their production (ibid., p.18). As with all Soviet statistics, the above figures are rather incomplete, but they do allow confirmation of a conclusion by some Western analysts that imports have assisted the Soviet government to complement the supply of consumer goods and to reduce the imbalance between the population's purchasing power and consumption. One Soviet source stated that in recent years imports constituted more than 10 per cent of total retail trade (Schroeder, 1983, p.381). Imports have also contributed indirectly to consumption through imports of raw materials and machines for agriculture and other consumer-goods producing industries. However, since the introduction of new economic reforms in 1986 and 1987, there seems to be less emphasis on the significance of imports and more on sources of supply from either the USSR itself or the satellite countries. We shall come back to this question in Chapter 10.

CONCLUSION

The new economic realism to which reference was made in the latter part of this chapter is a significant development in the Soviet approach to matters of national importance. While in the past the exclusive emphasis on Marxism–Leninism as a guide to solutions of any economic, social, military or political problems did not take into account the existing reality – the changes taking place within Soviet society and on the international arena – the recent pragmatism heralds a different direction in Soviet domestic policies. This has important implications for East–West relations in connection with mutual trading relations. It raises a number of issues that impinge directly upon American foreign policy, especially on the question of strategic importance for the Soviet Union of imports generally and Western technology in particular. We shall now turn our attention to this aspect of Soviet economic and military policies.

7 Transfer of Technology

The link between the economic and political aspects in East–West relations can best be observed when examining mutual economic activitics between the two blocs. Mutual trade is affected to a large degree by the extreme caution exercised in its dealing with the USSR by the US, due to fears that trade, especially in the area of high technology, may assist the Soviets in their military efforts.

The Soviet position in this respect is equally subject to political considerations but for different reasons. Economic rationality would favour extensive trading links with developed capitalist countries as a source of supply of consumer goods and advanced technology needed in the civilian sector, as well as in the military area. On the other hand, increased commercial relations with the West represent the possibility of the USSR losing its economic independence – a feature of past Soviet economic policies. It would also entail increasing international contacts and their potential ideological consequences.

THE AMERICAN PERSPECTIVE

The United States always looked at East–West trade from a highly political point of view. The question of national security, the concern that trade will add to the military and economic power of the Soviet Union, arose from time to time resulting in severe export restrictions. In the words of the former Secretary of Defence, Haig: 'the United States would like to bring economic relations with the Soviets in line with political and security objectives'.

The main objection against unrestricted trade with the Soviet Union was, and still is, that it will contribute to the Soviet attempt to redirect resources to the military sector.

> the industrial assistance provided to the Soviet Union significantly helps its military effort, even if indirectly...Much of our Soviet sales and credits are for 'dual use' technology which can be applied to both civilian and military advantage. Western aid for the development of Soviet energy resources has had the added

> effect of providing the USSR with hard currency which its own economy cannot generate. (Kampelman, 1985, p.22)

For those supporting this point of view it meant that most of the hard currency obtained in this manner is spent on acquiring abroad equipment of some military application. While basic Soviet military hardware is of domestic manufacture, they would claim, the West and Japan have provided the Soviet war industry with advanced technology which the Soviets have integrated into their production (Pipes, 1984, p.28). In the run up to the Geneva meeting between Reagan and Gorbachev, the former US President Nixon warned against providing the USSR with high technology as long as it pursues policies that are opposed to American interests: 'for the U.S. to increase trade, which the Soviets need and want would be stupid and dangerous. No nation should subsidise its own destruction' (Nixon, 1985, p.8).

There was also a concern that closer economic ties would provide the Soviet Union with means of control over Western Europe. Such concern surfaced during the construction by the Soviet Union of the Trans-Siberian pipeline when the United States tried (unsuccessfully) to prevent the delivery of industrial equipment by Western European companies. According to a report, at the time, by the Institute of Studies of Conflict:

> the advantages to the Soviet government of increasing West European dependence on areas under Soviet control for essential raw materials, and more especially petroleum products and other forms of energy, would give the Soviet government a much more effective hold over the economy of Western Europe than Western Europeans could exercise over the Soviet economy, even if they could operate together. (Pinder and Pinder, 1976, p.270)

A different kind of objection against extensive trade with the USSR has political as well as military connotations. According to this view, Western technological and financial credit assistance to the Soviet Union helps to maintain the present economic and political regime. It is in the interest of the West that the USSR introduces reforms which will raise productivity by greater incentives and decentralised decision-making. In this way the economic and political power of the Party would be weakened. It comes down, once more, to economic pressure. For, while the supply of Western technology could make the system more efficient, it makes it possible for the regime to avoid the introduction of reforms (Pipes, 1984, p.30).

The extreme view that any trade with the Soviet Union is bound to assist its military effort and to retain its political and economic control is not entirely a matter of rhetoric. Proponents of the hard line in trading with the Soviets usually see such trading as benefiting the USSR more than it would the West. One example is the so-called 'compensation' deals under which thc USSR repays its debts incurred through loans for industrial projects not in cash but in goods which the projects will produce in the future. This method has been employed in financing the Siberian pipeline, the cost of which was to be recovered in deliveries of natural gas. After these costs have been repaid, the income generated by the sales of gas was to be used by the Soviet Union to buy imports from Western Europe, particularly from Germany. In the opinion of some political analysts, it was the desire to provide the USSR with the necessary funds for purchases from Germany, rather than the need to diversify energy supplies, that motivated the German government in particular. It meant enabling the USSR to acquire Western technology.

A further point was made that almost all the technology acquired by the Soviet Union is of 'dual use': it can be used for civilian purposes as well as for military. Some of the acquired technology can be immediately incorporated into the production of armaments. The Soviet Union has made significant purchases abroad of integrated-circuit technology, which is also of military significance in electronic warfare. It has purchased the equipment to produce high-grade specialised steel that can be used in tanks and submarine hulls, and a plant built by an American corporation to manufacture rock-drill bits can most likely be used for the production of anti-tank ammunition (Pipes, 1984, p.29).

An example of the contribution that Western supplied technology has made to Soviet military capabilities, often quoted by opponents of East–West trade, is the sale by the United States in the early 1970s of equipment to manufacture miniature ball bearings. These are a vital component for the missile guidance system and since the Soviet Union did not possess the machinery to manufacture large quantities of the miniature ball bearings, in 1961 it approached the only American firm that made such machinery, the Bryant Chucking Grinder Co. of Springfield, Vermont, to supply the necessary equipment. At first, the firm's application for a licence to sell the machinery to the Soviet Union met with an objection by the Defence Department, but in 1972, eleven years later, in the more favourable climate of *détente*, permission was granted. 'The accuracy of Soviet missiles is a contribution from American technology as a result of legally permitted sales of miniature ball bearings [equipment]' according to Max Kampelman (1985, p.22). Another example was the sale to the Soviet Union by the Japanese firm Toshiba of the technology which would enable the Soviets to produce silent submarines – thus difficult to detect.

Drawn to their logical conclusion, the latter opinions would imply a complete economic isolation of the Soviet Union, if it were possible. Professor Peter Wiles argued that even if access to Western advanced technology could be denied to the Soviets, the transfer of non-military technology from the West to the Soviet Union could have immediate, if indirect, effects on Soviet military capability, by making it possible to shift funds and resources resulting from these imports to defence purposes (Jacobs, 1978, p.201). According to Richard Pipes, this is due to the Soviet political and economic system where the line separating the military and the civilian economies is not very distinct: 'we are dealing here with a war economy operating on an intermediate level of mobilization'. It follows that the Soviet leadership views all industries in the context of their contribution to the war effort. Therefore, any contribution to the Soviet industrial potential must be viewed as a contribution to its war-making potential.

The United States has long perceived the necessity to withhold from the USSR and from countries likely to pass on to the Soviets, equipment incorporating advanced technology. The agency charged with monitoring technology transfer to the East is known as COCOM. It maintains a list of embargoed technology agreed upon by the NATO countries and it routinely processes and approves or rejects the sale of technology to the USSR. However, the effectiveness of COCOM controls over technology transfers is rather dubious on account of some neutral countries – Switzerland, Sweden and Austria – who are not bound by the COCOM rules and sell restricted material as well as providing transit facilities. Washington itself had difficulties in enforcing its restrictions on trade with the Soviet Union generally, and technological transfer in particular. Lack of coordination with other Western countries providing the Soviet Union with the possibility of substitute relations is one of the difficulties (Levine, 1981, p.197). Pressure from American domestic commercial interest, usually backed by the Department of State and Commerce, which argue that such restrictions serve only to divert Soviet business elsewhere, is another.

THE SOVIET VIEW

Objections to unlimited trade with the West are also voiced in the Soviet Union, but for different reasons. Concern about dependence on the West is one of them and has been reflected for a long time in the quest for self-sufficiency and economic independence. COMECON came into being as a means of diverting foreign commerce of the Soviet satellite states from the West, and the formation of the Council of Mutual Economic Assistance (CEMA) had as its main objective increased production specialisation. Economic interdependence within the Soviet bloc has been seen by the Soviets as security against separatism. It was only after Stalin's death that the Soviet intra-bloc trade began to decline somewhat and that with capitalist countries expanded (Pisar, 1970, p.15). Statistical evidence indicates that trade between the USSR and the West is increasing over time. This suggests that, despite political and ideological considerations, objectives of purely economic rationality seem to have prevailed, but considerations of military nature may also have played a role in changing Soviet attitude. This has taken the form of outright purchases of Western designed and built industrial plants, and 'new forms of economic ties-...like...compensation agreements between Western firms and Soviet enterprises, of wholly Soviet-owned enterprises set up in cooperation with foreign firms that provided credits, equipment and licences' (Lebedev, 1978, p.136).

The Soviet economist A.Dostal (1977) saw the main obstacle to more trade with the West in the limitation of credit facilities, particularly by the US Export-Import Bank. Consequently, more trade was going to Europe and Japan, and even some US enterprises were moving to Europe in order to be able to trade with the Soviet Union (ibid., p.21). He implicitly denied that the USSR has other than economic objectives in the development of foreign trade: 'the supporters of the Cold War are throwing doubts about the purely economic aims of securing more credits [from the US] and about the credit worthiness [of the USSR]'.

Although the Soviets saw sufficient benefits arising from foreign trade, not only in the area of high technology but as a source of supply of consumer goods, they usually expressed the reservation that 'economic relations between socialist and capitalist states must be established with a provision to counteract any attempts by capitalist states to use economic links as a means of political pressure' (Mikulsky, 1984, p.271). Despite the recognition that the acquisition of Western technology is beneficial for the Soviet economy and, most probably to the Soviet military effort, the Soviets strenuously rejected the assertion that 'Soviet technology has...in effect been Western technology as a result of aid, trade, credits and theft' (Kampelman, 1985, p.21). In an interview with *Time* magazine correspondents prior to the Geneva Summit, the new Soviet leader, Mikhail Gorbachev, flatly denied the idea that the 'USSR is being consumed with thirst for US technology' (*Time*, 9 September 1985, p.12). He affirmed that the Soviet Union became technologically independent after the Revolution, and pointed to Soviet achievements in space exploration and the acquisition of a reliable defence potential as evidence of technological self-sufficiency.

The above statement, which appears to be an assertion of the Soviet status as a superpower, is in sharp contrast with the reality one can clearly observe in the Soviet literature dealing with the role of foreign technology in the Soviet Union.

> The place and role of foreign economic relations in the structure of the Soviet economy is in the speedier solution of economic problems thanks to the exploitation of additional foreign resources and the realisation of the possibilities of scientific and technological progress. (Mikulsky, 1984, p.271)

Gorbachev's assertion is also contradicted by a number of resolutions adopted in the past by the CPSU. As early as 1965, Kosygin broke with previous policies in a speech to the Gosplan by launching a turn to Western technology. Later at the October 1976 Plenary Meeting of the Central Committee of CPSU, Brezhnev apparently gave the directives to trade increasingly with the West to obtain the latest technology for different branches of Soviet industry. At the 25th Congress of CPSU, in 1977, Brezhnev again underlined the importance and, indeed, the necessity of foreign trade relations for the development of Soviet economy:

> [I]t is rather difficult to find a branch in the economy that is not connected, in some way or another, with foreign trade; that does not receive from it effective help and practical cooperation in its further development. (*Vneshnaia torgovlia*, no.6, 1978, p.3)

N.S. Patolichev, the then Minister for Foreign Trade, expressed a similar opinion about the practical contribution of foreign trade to the Soviet economy which, he said, 'can in no way be compared with what was happening in the early stages of its development, say 15 to 20 years ago'.

Although the exact timing of the change in Soviet foreign economic policy cannot be determined with absolute certainty, it is quite clear that by the 1970s the Soviets were eager to widen commercial relations with the West as well as other economic ties with a number of uncommitted countries. The new course in foreign economic relations was reflected, as is usually the case, in Soviet economic literature and writings by political commentators.

THE 'NEW' THEORY OF FOREIGN TRADE RELATIONS

The more recent trend in Soviet theoretical analysis of foreign trade relations, especially with Western developed capitalist countries, shows a tendency to steer away from the Marxist–Leninist interpretation of Soviet economic problems and towards a more realistic approach to questions of foreign trade relations. Soviet economists are now more inclined to look at foreign trade, and at the benefits that could be derived from trading with the West, from a purely economic point of view little different from Western classical economic theories. The fundamental economic principle that governs trade between countries is the principle of comparative advantage. It is based, according to one Soviet economist, on the fact that there exist differences of methods of production of various goods in different countries. Given the natural–geographical and historical–economic causes, the cost of production of various goods in different countries are not identical. Consequently, each country has an interest to concentrate its efforts on the production of goods in which it has a comparative advantage and to exchange them for goods whose domestic production would be more costly. Thanks to foreign trade, countries may receive, either a larger quantity of goods for the same expenditure, or the same quantity of goods at a lesser cost (Akademia Nauk, 1977, p.261). To anyone familiar with basic economics this would appear as an excerpt from an elementary economic text book, but we have quoted the views of the Soviet economist expressed in familiar Western terms to underline the transformation in Soviet economic thinking and the adoption of Western terminology.

Once the principle of comparative advantage and the benefits of its exploitation had been adopted by Soviet economists, the next step was to determine the nature and extent of the benefits derived from foreign trade and the guiding rules that would determine the direction of foreign trade. 'The more we develop foreign economic relations, the more important becomes the question of their efficiency' (Savostianov, 1979, p.62). The evaluation of rentability of foreign trade is of particular significance in respect of imported machinery and equipment. It is linked to returns on investments and the problems of absorption of Western technology (discussed in the following chapter). The main problem with the methodology of determining rentability is the choice of criteria. This, according to the Soviet economist, can be expressed in the growth of national income which would come as a result of increased production through new technology, and partly in profits.

The difficulty in establishing the methodology of determining rentability of imported machinery and equipment, particularly its internal valuation in the Soviet Union, lies in the determination of prices. The capitalist market determines the value of machinery by its rentability based on capitalisation of early income. But as 'the aim of socialist production is the maximum satisfaction of the needs of society', rentability is only one factor that is taken into account when a decision is made to purchase foreign machinery (ibid., p.68). Its rentability also depends on local conditions. In some instances more labour is needed than originally planned, or there is a shortage of skilled labour with the resulting underuse of new equipment. Underutilisation of imported machinery and equipment appears to be an important issue, in view of the fact that the share of imports of machinery and industrial equipment constitutes over one-third of total imports and is close to one-third of investments in machines and equipment. This, adds the writer, is typical of an industrially developed country trading internationally.

BENEFITS AND PROBLEMS

The principle of comparative advantage, although generally recognised in the West as providing mutual benefits for the countries concerned, is not always adhered to because of interplay of domestic politics connected with interest groups whose influence bring about some undesirable, from an economic point of view, tendencies like protectionism. In respect of the USSR, the implementation of the principle of comparative advantage is just as complex but for quite different reasons. The stated objectives of foreign trade which, in theory, enables a particular country to obtain benefits in terms of goods and services, offers also additional benefits for the Soviet Union; benefits that are important for the economy as a whole, but at the same time presents problems which stem from the economic and political system of the USSR.

Soviet economists make a distinction between the direct and indirect effects of foreign trade relations. The direct effect is its contribution to the national income, which simply means that by importing goods that are more costly to produce domestically, and by exporting those in which the Soviet Union has a comparative advantage, the total national income is thereby increased for the benefit of the whole society, since it increases the availability of goods. Another direct effect is the contribution by foreign trade to the acceleration of economic growth through the use of the acquired modern technology. 'Foreign trade takes advantage of the international division of labour and contributes to the raising of productivity of labour' (Akademia Nauk, 1977, p.262). This is a clear indication that raising the efficiency of production is dependent upon the application of new technology and the updating of production methods in line with Western trends.

No less important for the Soviet economy are the indirect effects of foreign trade. These are broadly classified into three distinct categories: balancing the economy, more efficient exploitation of productive resources, and improved quality of goods produced.

Foreign trade as an instrument of balancing the economy means, in Soviet terms, a more appropriate structure of production in accordance with the needs of the economy as a whole and the consumer sector in particular. Although foreign trade is not considered as the main or the only means of balancing the economy, its use for that purpose has definite advantages. First, goods that are exported are those in which the Soviet Union has a comparative advantage; they are relatively cheaper to produce, while imported items would be more costly to manufacture domestically. Secondly, goods that are in short supply because of insufficient productive capacity are to be imported in exchange for goods that are in surplus. In this way, the internal balance between demand and supply of goods can be achieved much faster than through the growth of domestic production (at least in theory).

Foreign trade also assists the USSR, to a great extent, to overcome the limitations on capital investments, thereby enhancing the possibilities of exploitation of resources that would have been otherwise unused. This is done through the participation of countries interested in purchasing from the USSR raw materials, mainly minerals and energy, by way of compensation agreements. Such would be the case regarding commercial relations with developed capitalist countries in exploring natural resources. Although as one Soviet economist claims: 'historical experience, especially that of the last Five-Year Plans, has shown that from the point of view of science and technology our country is capable of independently mining useful minerals surveyed by geologists including in regions difficult to reach'. He admits, nevertheless, that foreign technological assistance allows the speeding up of the exploitation of these regions and, at the same time, economises on capital outlays essential for other purposes (Akademia Nauk, 1977, p.279). The Soviets refer also to the building of infrastructure, especically transport, that will enable it to shift bulky commodities like minerals and timber to Japan in exchange for industrial and mineral processing plants, much needed in the eastern regions of the USSR.

Another example of more efficient exploitation of economic resources through foreign trade was the agreement with Iran for the latter to supply the southern regions of the USSR with 13.4 billion cubic meters of gas. This allowed the Soviet Union to export an equal quantity of gas from its own sources to Austria, France, Germany and other Western European countries. Thus, according to the Soviets, the USSR was to receive from these countries about 150 million rubles annually in convertible currency (ibid., p.280).

Finally, the third indirect effect of foreign trade refers to the quality of Soviet-produced goods. This is an apparent admission that the opportunities for Soviet export to the West are severely limited due to the relatively low quality of Soviet goods. Referring to trading conditions in the capitalist world, the Soviet economist sees the consumer as one who ultimately influences the quality of goods. International trade stimulates improvements in the production methods and quality of merchandise because foreign markets are subject to fierce competition between producers. It is for this reason alone that in order to increase Soviet exports it will be necessary for enterprises that are geared for export production to 'show utmost concern about quality'. Because the Soviet Union is insulated from the influence of foreign markets, quality is not a prime consideration, although, as we shall see, the quality factor has much wider implications than just the supply to the domestic market.

> If we export goods of poor quality, obsolete equipment, badly selected minerals with a high level of humidity, sometimes contaminated with impurities, not well packed etc., the country loses currency to a much greater extent than it would cost to eliminate these defects. (Savostianov, 1979, p.63)

BALANCING FOREIGN TRADE

As we can see, on theoretical grounds and on practical considerations, the Soviet Union has a great interest in the promotion of foreign trade and commercial relations with developed capitalist countries who have the capacity to supply most of the goods needed to satisfy consumer demands, as well as the know-how and technology for the modernisation of the Soviet industry. But despite the call by the leadership for increased trading links with the West, the volume of foreign trade remains low relative to the size of the Soviet economy, and its share in world trade is equally low.

> One must take into account the fact that the share of the Soviet Union in world industrial production is about 20 per cent. This is much higher than its share in world trade. That does not mean that the two should be equal, but the optimum level of foreign trade is evidently much higher than is USSR's at present. (Akademia Nauk, 1977, p.276)

There are several reasons why the share of Soviet world trade remains low. According to one Soviet source, a significant factor that has a negative influence upon foreign trade, particularly on its balance, is the inefficient utilisation of foreign credits obtained for investments. Slow absorption of foreign know-how and licences, the excessively long time it takes to put into production foreign equipment, poor quality of goods produced by imported machinery, and the subsequent non-fulfilment of planned exports are some of the problems. Sometimes, the simple solution adopted to overcome these problems, was to limit the volume of imports, but this was done mainly at the expense of technical equipment that should have been imported, and this retarded, to some degree, modernisation (Mikulsky, 1984, p.278).

The extent to which foreign trade could be balanced is obviously dependent on the quality of the exported product compared to what is available on the world market. Very often, the main obstacle towards more export is not the high cost of Soviet domestic production, but the low prices that these goods can fetch on international markets because of their poor quality. Lower cost of production is a necessary but insufficient condition for balancing world trade. To quote a Soviet source: 'foreign trade has its own peculiarities that do not appear on the domestic market. International trade is characterised by a greater selection of goods of much better quality' (ibid., p.282–4).

The difference between domestic production and foreign trade is based mainly on the fact that the exchange of goods on the world market is determined by international prices. It follows that Soviet foreign trade depends, to a large degree, upon the domestic prices of imported and exported commodities. At the present, prices of imported goods are determined in accordance with prices of similar goods produced domestically, while export goods are supplied to foreign trade organisations at domestic prices less turnover tax. Because of this practice imports and exports expressed in foreign currency prices do not normally balance. It makes the task of determination of the effectiveness of foreign trade rather difficult. In the opinion of one Soviet economist, this area of Soviet economics requires further study. Soviet literature still devotes little attention to the question of methodology for accounting of the effects of foreign trade.

But, at the same time, it makes it necessary for the Soviet trading organisations to pay much more attention to the changes in the conditions of international trade. The effects of changes in world prices are generally measured in international statistics with the help of the index of 'terms of trade' (Table 7.1). Such an index is defined as the relationship between the export prices index and import prices index (according to Western economic terminology adopted by the Soviets).

Table 7.1 Index of world prices and terms of trade

(1965 = 100)	*1970*	*1971*	*1972*	*1973*	*1974*	*1975*
Export prices	97.1	101.6	100.9	110.0	127.8	143.5
Import prices	107.4	107.3	108.6	111.0	129.9	155.8
Terms of trade	90.4	94.7	92.9	99.1	98.4	92.1

Source: Akademia Nauk SSSR, 1977, p.272.

The improvement in the early 1970s of the Soviet position in terms of trade has been caused by the rise in energy and raw material prices. This changed, however, in 1975, when the majority of raw material prices decreased or remained unchanged, while prices for industrial goods, especially machinery and equipment, rose sharply. The rise in world prices affected the Soviet balance of payments which had to be compensated either by borrowing abroad or by increased exports. The latter meant shifting some internal resources for export which in turn affected the internal balance between demand and supply of goods (Mikulsky, 1984, p.272). Between 1976 and 1980 the terms of trade with capitalists worsened even further and it became necessary to increase the volume of export goods for each unit of imports. But despite the deterioration in the terms of trade, Soviet trade kept growing at an increasing rate, indicating the importance of foreign trade for the Soviet economy. Since 1955, according to Soviet data, when the total turnover in foreign trade (import plus export) totalled only 5.8 billion rubles, it had been almost doubling every five years (Table 7.2).

What is peculiar about trade relations between the USSR and the United States is the enormous imbalance of trade in favour of the United States. In the two years 1980 and 1981, for example, imports from the United States to the Soviet Union increased from 1351.5 million rubles to 1662.0 million – an increase of about 23 per cent. In the same period, exports from the USSR to the United States were only 151.0 and 183.4 million rubles respectively. On the other hand, the share of total imports from all

Table 7.2 Soviet foreign trade, 1955–84
(billions of rubles)

Year	*Total turnover*	*Export*	*Import*
1955	5.8	3.1	2.7
1960	10.1	5.0	5.1
1965	14.6	7.4	7.2
1970	22.1	11.5	10.6
1975	50.7	24.0	26.7
1980	94.1	49.6	44.5
1984	139.7	74.4	65.3

Source: '*Vneshnaia torgovlia SSSR* v 1981 g.', 1982, p.6; Narkhoz 1985, p.586

developed capitalist countries was only 8.6 and 9.1 per cent respectively (*Vneshnaia torgovlia*, 1982, p.14). The relatively low level of mutual trade points to the restrictions placed by the American Administration on trading generally, and on the provision of credits in particular. This would explain the huge imbalance in trade between the superpowers. The Soviets have to pay for their purchases in hard currency and are not able to offer suitable finished goods or other commodities for export to the United States.

From the data supplied by Soviet statisticians, it would appear that the Soviets are careful to maintain an equal balance between imports and exports (see Table 7.2). This may indicate that Soviet planning authorities would prefer to rely on exports as a source of financing imports rather than borrowing in order to avoid the problems of foreign debts incurred by some of its allies. The fact that the Soviets have a complete monopoly over trade makes the task of managing foreign trade much easier, in that it allows it to solve the problem of its balance of payments by keeping foreign trade at a desired level. Therefore, foreign trade does not have any direct influence on domestic prices nor on the rate of exchange.

SOURCES OF FINANCING IMPORTS

A question that must be asked is whether the Soviet Union has the capacity to export sufficient goods and services to obtain the necessary hard currency to cover payments for imported goods?

Soviet statistical data offer a partial answer to the latter question. A survey of the structure of Soviet exports shows that the main commodities exported from the USSR were energy, minerals, some chemicals, timber, raw materials and some foodstuff – mostly unprocessed. From Table 7.3 it can be seen that the bulk of Soviet exports, about two-thirds of the total, consisted of energy and minerals, while machinery and consumer goods accounted for only 18 per cent in 1980 and 15.5 per cent in 1981. It confirms the assertion that the Soviet Union has a distinct comparative disadvantage in industrial products and an advantage in unprocessed raw materials and energy.

Table 7.3 Structure of exports from the USSR
(Percentage of total exports)

	1980	*1981*	*1984*
Energy	46.9	50.2	54.4
Minerals	8.8	8.0	7.2
Chemicals	3.3	3.5	3.5
Timber	4.1	3.3	2.8
Semi-finished textile and raw material	1.9	2.0	1.2
Food	1.9	2.0	1.5
Consumer goods	2.5	1.8	1.8
Machinery and transport	15.8	13.7	12.5

Source: '*Vneshnaia torgovlia SSSR* v 1981 g.',p.18; Narkhoz 1985, p.589.

There are also other sources of financing imports which do not normally appear in Soviet statistics. One of them is foreign trade in services, considered by the Soviets as an important component of foreign revenue. According to one Soviet source, tourism, trade in licences, technical assistance, transport and cultural relations constitute an increasing share in the balance of payment. Trade in these services is one of the sources of foreign currency. Other items that do not appear in the statistics of Soviet exports are the sale of gold and diamonds – always considered an important source of hard currency – and the sale of armaments. The latter has not only economic implications but political as well.

The political rationale for sales of arms has been mainly in the objective of the supplier gaining influence over the recipient nation. It was for this reason that the Soviet Union has transferred arms to Arab states and to national liberation movements, and also as a demonstration of support for their cause. It has also sold weapons to Peru on a long-term, low-interest basis in order to establish a base of influence in South America (this has shifted to Nicaragua).

A further incentive for the sale of arms has also been the economic advantages that arms transfer is thought to bring. Arms sales are sometimes an important earner of foreign exchange and a contributor to the balance of payment for any country that has the potential of becoming a supplier. The Soviet Union is certainly no exception and in view of its needs for imports from the West, the economic incentives are all the more important (JEC, 1976, p.236). Traditionally, the USSR has been following for many years a policy of granting long-term, low-interest loans to purchasers of arms for political rather than economic gains. But more recently the Soviets have been selling arms at higher prices to countries that could only pay cash from oil revenues, principally Libya and Iran. As the Soviet Union has sought hard currencies to pay for imports of Western technology and grain, it relied increasingly on revenues from sales of weapons (Pierre, 1982, p.27). According to the CIA, Soviet military deliveries to the Third World were less than 1 billion dollars per year prior to 1970, but have ranged between 2 and 3.8 billion dollars between 1970 and 1978 (ibid., p.74). The Soviet Union is considered to be the second largest supplier of arms in the world with approximately 30 per cent of the total.

The increased emphasis on arms sales as a source of revenue, rather than for political considerations, came about in the 1970s when the Soviet Union experienced an unprecedented hard-currency trade deficit because of its crop failure and the need to import grain, as well as its desire to acquire Western technology. Terms for arms sales toughened and some of the largest sales were to oil-rich countries that could pay in Western currencies. The earnings from arms exports were instrumental in helping the USSR pay for the imports of Western technology.

What also needs to be said is that the USSR's ability to sell big quantities of arms is determined, to a great extent, by the large quantity of surplus equipment. The Soviet Union stocks reserve arms in far greater quantities than does the West. The Soviet defence industry usually overproduces with potential sales in mind (ibid., p.77).

But while the political and economic considerations of foreign trade, particularly in the area of arms sales and general economic assistance, clash with each other, there are indications that the Soviets are becoming much more businesslike in their dealings with client-states, and that economic rather than political considerations are the more prevalent criteria. Exports are at present subject to evaluation as to their economic efficiency rather than political benefits. Until very recently, according to one Soviet economist, economic and technological assistance to some countries led to a situation where the cost of supplying complete industrial plants was higher than the payment received in foreign exchange. However, according to the same source, this situation has vastly improved in the last decade thanks to the limitation of credit facilities offered to the recipient states and the 'increased foreign exchange efficiency of export operations' (Zhukov, 1983, p.158).

EFFICIENCY OF TECHNOLOGICAL TRANSFER

Based on the evidence presented in this chapter, one can assume that the relatively new trend in Soviet thinking on trade relations with the capitalist world is still in the process of being developed into some guiding principles that would direct future Soviet commercial relations with the West.

> The evaluation of foreign trade relations is a very complicated and complex problem. The question...of the political consequences of economic and technological cooperation between the USSR and foreign countries has not yet been sufficiently studied on both theoretical as well as on the practical levels. (ibid., p.159)

Extensive trade with the West has, as we have pointed out earlier, economic as well as political implications. The willingness to entertain extensive trading relations with the West is certainly motivated by economic rationality. The dual purpose of imports: the modernisation of the industry through the application of new technology and the satisfaction of consumer demand from foreign sources, would require further development of foreign trade. But the concern about economic dependence on the West and the imposed restrictions on export of goods of military or 'dual' use are powerful inhibiting factors of East–West trade.

The question whether the acquisition by the Soviets of Western technology is geared mainly for military use is an important one in the context of the arms race and the East–West conflict. There are, indeed, some indications that advanced Western type technology has been incorporated in the latest Soviet military equipment, but whether it has been acquired from the West or came about as a result of indigenous research and development is not so clear.

Although legal imports can easily be defined and quantified, they do not point to specific military use. Soviet statistical data indicate a substantial part of imports as machinery and industrial equipment: 33.9 per cent and 30.2 per cent in 1980–1 respectively, but the far greater share of imported items consists of food and finished consumer goods (*Vneshnaia torgovlia*, 1982, p.18). Nevertheless, the possibility of 'dual use' of imported technology cannot be entirely ruled out. One Soviet source reports examples of the type of equipment and plant bought by the Soviets in the period 1970–5: iron casting equipment from West Germany, agricultural technology from Harvester International, a plant for the manufacture of cans from the American Can Co., equipment for the manufacture of azot fertilisers subject to a compensation agreement of repaying the loan by export of fertilisers, a plant to manufacture low pressure polyethylene from Britain and others (Dostal, 1977, p.21) that may have a 'dual use'.

While it may be correct to say, and there is evidence to confirm it, that some Western technology has been obtained by illegal means, and that some of the legally obtained equipment has military use, the extent to which imported Western technology has contributed to the Soviet military power cannot be assessed with great accuracy.

Available evidence from other sources, captured Soviet military hardware, intelligence, etc., confirm the opinion that it takes the Soviets quite some time to incorporate the acquired technology into their weaponry. The fact, mentioned earlier, that it took the Soviets eleven years to obtain from the United States the equipment to manufacture ball bearings is a clear indication that Soviet technology has not been able to develop, let alone build, such equipment over a relatively long period, by which time the American technology must have advanced even further.

There is less uncertainty about the impact of Western technology on the Soviet economy as a whole. Still, the contribution of imported technology to the rate of growth of the Soviet economy is subject to widely differing estimates, ranging from 1.1 per cent in the short run and 2.5 per cent in the long run using production function estimates, to 0.5 per cent using direct calculations of productivity gains (Jacobs, 1978, p.202). Others claim that the overall impact of imported technology is likely to be relatively small given the size of the Soviet economy. Hence, domestic technology is the main determinant of economic growth. Furthermore, because of the inherent characteristics of the Soviet economic system – the general level of technological and managerial skills – the imported know-how and technology is unlikely to operate at a level of productivity comparable to the exporting country. In fact the Soviets have primarily imported foreign technology for domestic growth purposes rather than for exports that would have to be competitive (Levine, 1981, p.186). Finally, due to the long lead time in absorbing new technology, the equipment and its products have already begun to become obsolescent. The acquisition of Western know-how in order to enhance efficiency of production is not reflected in the overall operation of the Soviet economy, at least for the time being, and there is little evidence to show that the efficiency factor is instrumental in economic growth.

There still remains the hypothesis of the 'two sector economy', the inefficient civilian one where imported technology is not being used to its optimum capacity, and the military sector that operates at a relatively high level of efficiency. The question of efficient absorption of Western know-how within the Soviet military effort is an important issue which requires an extensive examination, for the question of technological transfer is linked not only to East–West trading relations in general, but to American political and strategic considerations as well. It is also closely connected to the question of the Soviet 'defence burden' and the possible trade-off between military expenditure and the civilian economy. The latter issues will be the subject of the next chapter.

Appendix

Because of the diversity of commercial activities between the USSR and foreign countries, the coordination of exports and imports is a very long and complex task that involves a number of ministries and departments. Foreign trade activities are conducted by trade organisations of the Ministry of Foreign Trade. These include not only export and import of goods and services, but scientific and technological cooperation through the exchange of licences, patents, technical information, and the introduction of advanced technology.

The State Committee of the USSR for Science and Technology has the special task of organising and directing the exchange of specialists in the field of science and technology, as well as conducting joint scientific research and experiments. It can be safely assumed that it is through the activities of the latter that the Soviet Union finds its access to the latest technology – not necessarily by illegal means. What is rather significant in this respect is the guiding principle that 'what is bought overseas, whether raw material or equipment, must be of the latest design and conform to the level of world technology; as a rule it should have been tested in real production'. This approach to the selection of technology suitable to be imported is in accordance with the Soviet reluctance for taking risks, and it has the disadvantage that the imported technology will become more quickly out of date.

Another department which is involved in economic and technological cooperation with foreign countries is one under the direction of the State Committee for Foreign Economic Relations established in 1957. It includes a subcommittee which formulates the foreign exchange plan and controls the use of foreign currency to avoid excessive expenditure in foreign reserves. Receipts and payments in all foreign exchange transactions are planned in rubles. The conversion of foreign currency into rubles is affected according to the official rate of exchange fixed by the State Bank of the USSR (Gosbank) operative at the time when currency plan is formulated.

Source: Zhukov, L.M. 'Ekonomicheskoe i tekhnicheskoe sotrudnichestvo s zarubezhnymi stranami', *Mezhdunarodnye otnosheniia*, Moscow, 1983.

8 The 'Defence Burden' or the 'Burden of Inefficiency'

The difficulties experienced by the Soviet civilian economy which have been examined in the previous chapters are by no means exhaustive. But even those that were mentioned earlier indicate that consumer satisfaction and living standards in the USSR are very much dependent upon the efficiency of the economy as a whole. It is not the lack of resources that creates economic problems as the way they are utilised. This problem is an important aspect of the analysis of the Soviet military effort, for it is linked to the question whether the demand by the population for a better supply of consumer goods constitutes a constraint on Soviet military spending and whether the poor state of the Soviet economy is due to excessive military expenditure – the Soviets devoting too great a share of GNP for the armed forces. It is also relevant to the question of the trade-off between defence spending and the civilian economy. It may well be that the inefficiencies inherent in the operation of the Soviet economic system are affecting the growth of the civilian economy more than does military expenditure. If this were the case, even a substantial reduction in the defence budget would have a lesser impact on economic growth than would a modest increase in productivity through improved efficiency.

Under the latter assumption, the most pressing task for the Soviets would be to improve the efficiency of operation of the Soviet economy and to raise the level of productivity. There are good reasons to believe that this is indeed foremost on the mind of the leadership and that the problem of efficiency is perceived as being at the core of the shortcomings in the economy as a whole, including the defence sector. The debate on the question of efficiency and productivity which has continued among Soviet economists for quite some time, suggested a necessity for economic reforms as a means of overcoming the difficulties besetting the economy and for achieving satisfactory economic growth. But it also suggested that there are powerful forces within the Soviet system which would oppose such reforms because of their potential impact on the political power of the Communist Party. An analysis of the interrelationship between the civilian and defence sectors within the context of the functioning of the Soviet economic system and the interaction of the system with political control is the subject of the present chapter.

The awareness by the Soviet leadership of the basic causes of economic difficulties and their possible solution was openly expressed by the late General Secretary of the Party, Andropov, in a speech in November 1982. Contrary to the traditional practice of praising the achievements of the Soviet economy, Andropov devoted his speech to a sharp criticism of the performance of the Soviet economy. In a rare reference to the defence sector he criticised the quality of production, not only in the light and local industries, but also of items produced by the enterprises of the heavy and defence industries (*Ekonomicheskaia gazeta,* no.48, November 1982, p.3). This would suggest that the operation of the defence sector is not as efficient as is sometimes thought in the West, and that the efficiency factor is as important for the defence industries as it is for civilian enterprises. He also referred to the high cost of production which presumably was also applicable to the military.

However, if we accept the proposition that the inefficiency and the unsatisfactory rate of growth in productivity of the Soviet economy in its totality is also affecting the defence sector, then a number of questions arise. First, can Soviet defence spending be equated with military capability? In other words, is defence expenditure automatically translated into military capability in proportion to the size of military spending? Secondly, if the Soviet economy is only half as large, or even slightly more, as is that of the USA how can the Soviets spend on defence 50 per cent more than does America (according to the Pentagon) and still devote only 15 per cent of their GNP for defence, unless the Soviets were far more efficient than is generally thought? Yet, when in 1976 the CIA doubled its estimates of Soviet defence spending without a corresponding increase in the military capability of the USSR, it has downgraded considerably the estimate of Soviet military productivity (Alexander, Becker and Hoehn, 1979, p.23). The CIA claimed that increased ruble estimates did not represent a change in the assessment of Soviet defence activities but a better understanding of their efficiency of production. In other words, being less efficient it costs the Soviets much more to produce the necessary military hardware (JEC, 1977, pp.17–18). The revision by the CIA of the Soviet defence budget did not mean that the Soviets were stronger than previously thought – the Soviet arsenal remained the same – only that the cost was much higher (Prados, 1982, p.247). A third question can be asked: why does the USSR need foreign assistance to build a motor car plant or Pepsi-Cola plant, or drilling equipment, while at the same time being able to achieve military parity with, if not some superiority to, the United States?

One hypothesis put forward by some Western analyst is that the Soviet economy actually consists of two parallel economies: one producing consumer goods and one producing weapons and military equipment which is much more efficient compared to the former. One Western analyst goes as far as to say that the army is the only modern and efficient sector of the Russian society (Castoriadis, 1981, p.28). Proponents of this view claim that the military industrial sector has been insulated from the civilian economy by a number of methods which include priorities over material, equipment and personnel. It is most certainly protected from shortages experienced by the rest of the economy and does not have to compete for scarce resources because it is assured of automatic priority (Cockburn, 1983, p.78). A further point being made is that, apart from the quantitative aspect of such priorities – the organisation of supplies operating in favour of the military – there is also a qualitative one as well in the selection of raw material and personnel for the army establishments. 'It is not that so many engineers are absorbed into military production, but so many of the best' (Castoriadis, 1981, p.23). It is probably for this reason that defence-related items are of better quality than are consumer goods, and also, no doubt, because of the much stricter quality control than that applied to civilian production (Krylov, 1979, p.118).

The assertion about the existence of two parallel economies with different degrees of efficiency is not universally accepted. Opponents of the two-economies hypothesis, although in agreement that the military sector is being favoured over the civilian, argue that the former cannot avoid the inefficiencies of the rest of the economy. The increasing complexity of modern weapons systems calls for a broader range of inputs and technologies which makes the military increasingly dependent on the rest of the economy.

A further point can be made that if cost of production is, to a large extent, determined by the productivity of a given resource and by the efficiency of production methods or, putting it in simple terms, if efficient production implies *least-cost* (when economic units such as industrial enterprises combine various factors of production – labour, capital and land – in such a way as to minimise costs and maximise profits. While profits may not be necessarily a prime objective in Soviet military economic planning, minimum costs certainly is) then there is a sound reason to doubt whether the productivity and efficiency of the Soviet defence sector is that much superior to the civilian, as many Western analysts believe. It is reasonable to assume that the policy of favouring the military-production sector imposes higher costs, not only on the Soviet production of military hardware, but also on the economy as a whole – costs that are not detectable from official accounts. For the priorities in the supply of material and human resources accorded to the defence sector must also entail an opportunity cost of lost productive capacity in the civilian economy.

THE INTERACTION BETWEEN THE DEFENCE SECTOR AND THE REST OF THE ECONOMY

The extent to which this policy affects the production of consumer-related goods is difficult to estimate, but there are indications that because the defence sector has priority in the supply of plant and equipment, it has also spare productive capacity which Soviet planners attempt to use for the production of consumer goods. This is revealed in a number of articles that appear from time to time in the Soviet press, and they suggest that the inefficiency and wastefulness of resources which characterises the civilian sector of the economy also exists in enterprises which produce both consumer goods and defence related items.

Mixed production of defence and consumer items by the same enterprises seems to be quite widespread and in some cases constitutes a substantial part of their overall output. One Soviet source reports that in 1970 the production of consumer goods in the heavy-industry sector constituted 10 per cent of total production and 12.4 per cent in 1975. Other branches of the defence sector show a much higher share with enterprises of the ministries of instrument-making, automation and control systems showing a contribution to the production of consumer goods of over 30 per cent (Orlov, 1976, p.51). Other ministries involved in the production of consumer related goods include the ministries of ferrous metals, aviation, communication, electronics and machine building (ibid., p.52).

Despite the apparent contribution by the enterprises of the defence sector to the production of civilian related goods, the problems besetting the general civilian production sector, mentioned earlier, are just as prevalent here. The same Soviet source reporting about the production of consumer goods by the enterprises of the heavy industry, analyses the problems connected with their production and they appear rather similar to those in the rest of the economy.

Some of these enterprises have confined their production of consumer goods to quantitative output without bothering about quality and assortment. Factories where the production of the main items is mechanised are reluctant to produce labour-intensive consumer goods as this could reflect on their overall productivity, and when they are forced to do so, they are in a worse position than those that don't produce them at all. The reluctance by some enterprises to incorporate the production of consumer goods into their activities results in a disproportionate supply of closely related items of domestic use – in a greater output of less labour intensive articles while the production of 'unprofitable' items is severely curtailed. The Ministry for Defence Industries, for example, planned to produce 11.2 million stainless steel spoons and only 1.8 million forks and knives. In 1975, factories of the Machine-building Ministry were supposed to produce 5.4 million pieces of mixed cutlery, but produced only spoons. The imbalances in production are also due, to a great extent, to the fact that, according to the instructions of the Gosplan of the USSR about the order of planning, there exist a classification of 'basic' and 'non-basic', 'important' and 'non-important' goods and a division of 'privileged' goods, which enables the head of an enterprise to decide the order of priority of production (ibid., pp.54–8).

It is clear that in order to supplement the supply of consumer goods for which there is lack of production facilities, some spare capacity of the defence industry is being used. But the basic difficulties in planning and production characteristic of the Soviet system seem to prevail even here. The above examples indicate an overlapping of the respective production activities in some areas where the distinction between the purely military type of production becomes rather blurred.

DISSEMINATION OF TECHNOLOGY AND THE QUESTION OF TECHNOLOGICAL SPINOFF

None the less, it is beyond doubt that there exists a number of enterprises which are geared solely for the production of military hardware, particularly where advanced technology is involved. These are the so-called 'closed' establishments offering higher than average remuneration and generally better conditions and access to privileged sources of supply of consumer goods. The existence of 'closed' enterprises is confirmed by the fact that there is very little technological spin-off from the Soviet military to the civilian. This is rather surprising given the emphasis by the Soviets on intensive rather than extensive economic planning and on the role of technology in this process.

A direct reference to the problem of technological transfer from defence to the consumer sector is to be found in a speech by Brezhnev, in October 1980:

> Apart from the Academy of Science, I also have in mind scientists and designers working in the defence branches. I think that their contribution to the development of the national economy could be much greater and wider. It is, therefore, necessary to charge the Council of Ministers, together with some specialists, with the task of determining precisely which defence-industry scientific and design collective could give active assistance to certain types of civilian machine-building, give assistance in developing highly efficient and better quality models of machines and also render assistance in formulating specific programmes and targets. (*Pravda*, 22 October 1980)

Such were the intentions of the Soviet leadership expressed by Brezhnev at the Plenary Meeting of the CPSU in 1980. But there is little evidence to show that these directives were put into practice. Western research in the area of technology transfer from the military to the civilian sector of the Soviet economy does not reveal much evidence of this taking place. The main reason given for the lack or low level of technological and managerial spillover from one sector to the other is that 'it seems to have been very difficult for the Russians to identify innovations in the military area and bring them to the attention of an authority able to cut across the secrecy barrier and get them transferred to the civilian sector' (Campbell, 1972, p.607).

Logical as this assumption may be, it does not offer an entirely satisfactory explanation. While it is true that the Soviets have had successes in meeting demands for innovations in the military sector in contrast to the civilian, this cannot be ascribed solely to the inherent secrecy of the former. Theoretical writings by Soviet economists in which the question of transferability and dissemination of know-how between different branches of the Soviet economy is being discussed, suggests that the problem is far more general, embracing the whole Soviet economic system.

The operation of the Soviet system as a command economy is based on the principle of vertical coordination. Plans formulated at the highest level of the economic hierarchy flow down the line to the production units whose task is to put the plan into operation. Very little horizontal links between different enterprises exist, with the result that there is little dissemination of technological know-how not only from the military to the civilian but from one enterprise to another.

The question of horizontal links is one on which some attention has been focused in the USSR in recent times. The improvement of horizontal links between organisations operating on the same level – branch to branch, enterprise to enterprise, producer to user – was being considered for some time as a significant factor of improving the management of the Soviet economy (Pavlichenko, 1980, p.14). The inefficiencies and shortcomings in the operation of the present system of horizontal links is looked upon as one of the main obstacles to increased economic efficiency, and scientific–technological advance, according to one Soviet economist. 'The negative influence of barriers of knowledge on the scientific and technological progress is well known. It prevents the solution of inter-branch problems...and is causing trends toward economic autarky' (ibid., p.15).

To indentify the problem is one thing, to find a proper solution is quite another. There was little suggestion at the time of how to overcome the difficulties in technological transfer within the operation of the system apart from an appeal to management 'not to be selfish and share their knowledge and experience, and render assistance to those enterprises that attempt to apply new technology' (ibid., p.24).[1]

This throws some light on the question put earlier, why the USSR needs Western assistance and technology to build industrial plants. It is much easier and probably less costly for the Soviets to acquire a plant from the West, relying on the commercial motivation of a capitalist firm, than to rely on indigeneous technology which may be available but is dispersed among many Soviet enterprises.

The acquisition of Western-built plants is well known and importing Western technical ideas is also a well-established Soviet practice. All Western technical publications are closely scrutinised, particularly those dealing with defence technology. The extent to which they have been able to acquire and absorb advanced technology into their military sector is difficult to determine, but whether the Soviets have been successful in the efficient absorption and practical application of the newly acquired technology into the civilian economy can be more readily ascertained.

A QUESTION OF EFFICIENCY

Soviet literature abounds with examples of the difficulties experienced by Soviet industrial enterprises in the absorption and operation of plants supplied to the Soviet Union by Western companies. This is usually discussed in the context of efficiency of investment, but some particular examples are often critically analysed. They invariably indicate gross inefficiencies in running the newly received plants. One Soviet economist, who deals specifically with the problem of absorption of Western technology, made a bold comparison between the efficiency of operation of an identical industrial plant in the USSR and in a capitalist country. In one Soviet chemical enterprise where the plant had been built in conjunction with a foreign firm, it became necessary to increase the total number of auxiliary workers employed at the plant from 91 to 430 men, 'but in actual fact' – claimed one economist – '723 people were recruited or eight times as many as originally planned and as many times as were employed by the foreign firm on a similar plant. At the same time, the technical and other personnel exceeded the corresponding number in foreign firms by a margin of 3.5:1'. At the Shchekinsky chemical plant supplied entirely by a

Dutch and Italian firms, 806 persons were employed in running the plant instead of 278, complained the economist (Manevich, 1973, p.34). This was, according to the author of the article, contrary to the principle of technological progress which should diminish the number of workers in order to transfer those dispensed with to other places. While it is generally known that overemployment in Soviet industry is a widespread practice, as well as the creation of spare 'insurance' stocks of material assets because it assists Soviet managers to fulfil their plans, the economic consequences in higher cost of production and the opportunity cost in the waste of human and material resources must be considerable. Such practice was openly criticised by N.A.Tikhonov, Chairman of the Council of Ministers in his report to the XXVI Congress: 'we cannot reconcile ourselves to the fact that many enterprises hoard equipment, raw material...and other resources in excess of quotas, while others experience shortages in them' (Tikhonov, 1981, p.21). An additional problem which seems to be common in Soviet industry, is the reluctance of some managers to apply new technology because in the initial period of its application some additional costs necessarily occur and very often losses. This puts a brake on the introduction of new technology (Pavlichenko, 1980, p.24).

In the same context of efficiency of investment, another Soviet economist criticised the high prices of new equipment built by Soviet industrial enterprises, and also the fact that their prices do not bear any relationship with its quality and production capacity (Krasovsky, 1975, p.110). He particularly compared the increase in prices of Soviet-built machinery, which were in the range of 10 to 25 per cent in the last fifteen years, with those 'in the United States where real prices actually fell'. It is interesting to notice that the reason for the fall in prices offered by the economist was international competition and the availability of choice for the buyer: 'some US firms are prepared to supply equipment without payment until the user is satisfied with its performance' (ibid., p.108). The question of rising costs of investments and the problem of modernisation of fixed assets was raised again at the XXVI Congress of the CPSU.

> Newly introduced equipment, while being more expensive, in some cases differs little in technical and economic features from the old one. Because of poor operation, maintenance and storage, machinery at times becomes quickly unserviceable and

is written off before its rated service life has expired. (Tikhonov, 1981, p.21)

Within the discussion on the question of efficiency of investment, a rather pessimistic view has been expressed by one Soviet economist who saw the contemporary economic development of the USSR rapidly approaching a situation when the increase of the share of industrial accumulation in the national income may not compensate the resulting decreasing efficiency of new investment – a case of diminishing returns. This in turn may have a negative impact on the rate of growth of the standard of living. The slow-down in the rate of growth of the national income was seen as a result of the reduction of the volume of investment on the one hand, and the decreasing rate of growth of efficiency of new investments on the other (Shatalin, 1980, pp.6–7). Much has been made in the West of the reduction in the growth rate of investments in the Soviet economy since 1975. Some considered the reduction in investment as a result of Soviet determination to maintain rapid growth of defence spending (Rush, 1983). But there is much evidence to suggest that diminishing returns from new investments rather than additional defence spending may be the cause.

However, what stands out clearly is the emphasis on the growth of productivity as a source of economic growth, on introduction of new technology, and on efficient management. But in view of the problems and difficulties that the Soviet economy as a whole must overcome to attain this objective, it is difficult to accept the assertion that the military sector does not experience similar problems. Taking into account the apparent inefficient use of resources in the USSR and the difficulties in absorbing new technology, it is also difficult to reconcile Western estimates of Soviet defence spending with the perceived growth of Soviet military strength. 'Perhaps the Soviet Union's relative standing in...military strength is now less directly related to spending on procurement of weapon's systems' (Campbell *et al.*, 1973, p.139).

A Rand Corporation Note (Alexander *et al.*, 1979) prepared for the US Air Force which raises the question of efficiency of Soviet weapons acquisition, offers a plausible explanation of this apparent enigma. What emerges from the analysis of Soviet military production contained in the Note is that although the efficiency of production itself cannot be really ascertained, the use of financial resources is probably subject to much closer scrutiny than is generally believed. The Soviets seem to utilise the available funds in a more selective way than does the United States. It would appear that they are directing the allocated funds to the most essential, from their national security consideration point of view, military hardware and weapons system. The result is a military machine that disposes of relatively less sophisticated armoury than does the US, but of sufficient quality and in quantities that makes the Soviet military power appear at least equal to that of the United States.

Captured Soviet military equipment indicates that the Soviets are spreading their designs across very different types of weapons systems. The outstanding feature of this approach is relative simplicity of equipment, common use of subsystems, components and parts, but limited performance and mission capabilities (ibid., p.26). Soviet tanks, for example, have cramped interiors and Soviet designers have no consideration for the crew's comfort. The American military writer S.L.A. Marshall described the interior of an American tank as being 'unequal in space and comfort' but, compared to the Soviet T-62, of 'ballroom proportions' (quoted in Cockburn, 1983, p.118). Similar comparable features were found in other Soviet equipment. In general, Soviet hardware is uncomplicated compared to similar Western equipment, with the result that it costs less to produce – for example, the T-62 tank perhaps cost one-third to one-half less than an American equivalent, the M60A1 (ibid., p.28).

The principle of using the same designs, components and parts is also applied by the Soviets to technological changes and improvements of weapons. Rather than develop a new one, Soviet designers prefer to use proven components – designs with no known antecedents are rare (ibid., p.28). [2]

Another advantage, one that makes Soviet weapons acquisition more efficient, is the absence of fragmentation of power in a proliferation of agencies that is usual in the United States. The Note concludes that because of the mix of positive and negative forces on Soviet costs of its military effort analysed above, the efficiency of Soviet weapons acquisition is rather uncertain. The analysis nevertheless throws some light on the puzzling question of how the Soviets have achieved the status of a military superpower with the resources at their disposal. It also suggests that the problem of efficiency of operation (not to be confused with efficiency of acquisition) and productivity are equally relevant to the defence sector as they are to the civilian economy.

The issue of transferability of resources is an important one for the analysis of the Soviet defence effort, but in view of the qualitative differences between defence and civilian resources it is rather difficult to quantify the trade-off relationship between the growth of defence and that of consumption. Are defence resources more productive than those available to the civilian economy on account of qualitative priorities, and if so, would these resources retain their productivity if they were shifted to the civilian economy? These questions need to be answered before one can come to a definite conclusion. But even if the inefficiences and wastefulness in the civilian sector, which Soviet sources themselves reveal, are not as serious in the military sector, it is doubtful whether shifting resources from one to the other would produce tangible results, even if it were possible to do so. First, since both sectors, the civilian and defence, operate under different sets of rules and at a different technological level, examined earlier, this prevents any possible technological spin-off and makes the shifting of resources between the two sectors extremely difficult (Campbell *et el.*, 1973, p.136). Secondly, if one accepts the assumption that the defence sector is relatively more efficient, then a change in priorities and moving resources from the military into the less efficient civilian sector will yield less output and will only waste them.

The issue of transferability of resources in the Soviet economy and that of the defence burden have been much debated in the West, but the potential impact of transferability on Soviet economic performance still remains highly speculative (Hilderbrandt, 1983, p.334). There is more general agreement on the question of efficiency and productivity as factors of Soviet economic growth, and there are clear indications that efficiency and productivity of resources is a major concern for the leadership. Numerous articles in the Soviet press discussing these problems, and appeals for greater efficiency, suggest that productivity growth is perceived by the Soviets as a solution to the inadequate supply of consumer goods and as a condition for satisfactory economc growth.

PRODUCTIVITY AND ECONOMIC GROWTH

It is generally recognised among Western economists that an increasing factor-productivity is an important source of economic growth (see Appendix). There is little doubt that the enormous increase in the material standard of living of the typical family in the industrialised countries has been due to the introduction of new, improved ways of making products. This caused an increase in output per unit of input employed and is referred to as an increase in productivity. Richard Lipsey, a well-known economist, calculated that even a small increase in productivity has a substantial impact on total output over time. Between 1945 and 1970, the UK showed a productivity growth of about 3 per cent per year. Such rate of growth in productivity, according to Lipsey, doubles output every 23.5 years. Other countries show a much higher rate, with Japan, for example, where productivity has been increasing at a rate of about 10 per cent per annum. At that rate output doubles approximately every seven years (Lipsey, 1975, p.238). It is clear from the above calculation that the effects of increased productivity on the total output of goods and services in the USSR would be quite substantial.

However, Western calculations and Soviet data indicate a decrease in the rate of growth of factor-productivity over time, and this must be a matter of great concern for Soviet planners. Although it is usual for Soviet economic analysts to boast that 'the level of labour productivity grew in all sectors of the economy', the data presented in support of that statement clearly show a steeply declining trend as can be seen from Table 8.1.[3]

Table 8.1 Rate of growth of labour productivity (as percentage of previous period)

	1970–5	1975–9	1983–4	1984–5
Industry	134	114	103.8	103.5
Agriculture	122	116	101.0	101.4
Construction	129	110		
Railway transport	124	100.5		

Source: Sarkisiant, 1980, p.329; *Ekonomicheskaia gazeta*, no.5, January 1985.

The same source reveals that the output of one Soviet worker is still only about 55 per cent of the output of his American counterpart. This means that not only is the output of a Soviet worker slightly more than half of the American, but that in order to narrow the economic gap with the West, the Soviets would need to more than double that output. Various Western calculations show different values of productivity growth, but confirm a similar decreasing trend (see, for example, Greenslade, 1976, p.279 and Levine, 1981, p.178). Soviet data clearly indicate the correlation between economic growth and productivity as can be seen from Table 8.2. Not only was there little contribution to economic growth by productivity, but that decreasing factor-productivity was a major cause of the slowdown in the rate of economic growth.

Table 8.2 Rates of growth of national income and productivity (average percentage per year)

	National income produced	*Productivity of social labour*
1960–70	9.8	8.5
1970–75	6.2	4.9
1975–80	4.7	3.5
1980–84	3.9	3.2

Source: Narkhoz, 1985, pp.36–7.

This problem and the resulting economic difficulties were openly revealed at the XXVI Congress of the CPSU in its 'Guidelines for the Economic and Social Development of the USSR for 1981–1985 and the Period Ending in 1990':

> [W]e did not succeed in solving...the task of boosting labour productivity, accelerated development of certain branches of the national economy, and of putting an end to the scattering of capital investments...we have not entirely done away with the force of inertia, traditions and habits. (Tikhonov, 1981, p.11)

As a solution to the above mentioned difficulties, the Guidelines included a rather ambitious productivity growth projection, which if achieved would improve the economic situation in the USSR. The emphasis was to be on tangible economic results, as compared with increases in manpower and material expenditure, including capital investments, taking place earlier. The projected productivity growth in a few selected sectors of the Soviet economy was to be:

Industry	23–25 per cent
Agriculture	22–24 per cent
Construction	15–17 per cent
Railway	10–12 per cent (up from 0.5 per cent)

The Guidelines did not spell out clearly how these targets are to be attained, but it is certain that barring a dramatic upsurge in productivity, slow economic growth seems inevitable. According to one Western assessment:

> [T]he 1980s will be a period of austerity, but not serious privation of consumers, whose expectations...have been adjusted downward as a result of the events of the past 7 years. People will simply have to endure, having no real alternative...living standards would stagnate at best. (Schroeder, 1983, p.385)

So far the extensive reporting on the massive disequilibrium in the civilian sector and the views expressed by Soviet analysts were concentrated mainly on the potential and sometimes real damage that such desequilibrium is causing to the efficacy of incentives and labour productivity. Some were alarmed by the state of affairs in the consumer sector as a serious threat to the prospect of increased productivity. Some suggested a higher rate of investment and mechanisation which would create an additional source for raising labour productivity, since it would sharply reduce fluctuations in manpower caused by the discontent over working conditions and pay; while others saw in the latter solution the problem of diminishing returns from further investments. Very few voices were raised in favour of tackling the source of the difficulties – the problem of dysfunction of the Soviet economic system – and when they were raised they expressed their views in very general terms.

> For this decade, the development of economic planning was typified by...a search for the forms and methods for managing and organising production that best met the task of intensifying and increasing the efficiency of the economy. (Sarkisiant, 1980, p.244)

ECONOMIC REFORMS AND POLITICAL CONTROL

There were several attempts to reform the economic system but, so far, none of them resulted in any material change in the operation of the economy. Forces of inertia and, most important, political implications of a significant change in the economic system were much too powerful to allow for a new direction to take place. The interaction between the Soviet economic system with political power which claims its legitimacy from Marxist theory and communist ideology, makes a rational solution to economic problems difficult to achieve. Soviet leaders face the choice between meeting the demands of Soviet consumers through bold steps which would allow market forces to determine the composition of production, and an improvement by means of more bureaucratic control.

The latter had been tried on many occasions without much success, while the former confronts the leadership with a dilemma concerning the essence of Marxism–Leninism and indeed the role of the Communist Party. Economic reforms which would give freedom to forces other than socialist planners would put in jeopardy the role of the Party as a vanguard of the proletariat leading the masses to socialism. What is perceived as being at stake is nothing less than the traditional place of the Party in Soviet society (Rigby and Miller, 1976, p.244). The most pressing task facing the Soviets is to find ways to stimulate the economy through the introduction of new rules without, at the same time, unduly diminishing the dominance of the Party over society, and without eroding its controlling power (this will be discussed in Chapter 10 in the context of the economic reforms introduced in 1986–7).

Historically, the present system of rigidly centralised planning came as a result of the practical task of political control introduced by Lenin and Stalin. It was imposed by the internal economic situation and by the attempt to reach a high level of military power within the shortest possible time. While the Soviet Union was under the rule of Stalin, no deviation from his ideas and no discussion on economic matters were permitted. But the need to reform the Soviet economy had been recognised by Soviet economists and by the leadership since the beginning of the process of de-Stalinisation. A change took place particularly after the June 1955 Plenum of the Central Committee which led to different trends in Soviet economic thought and policies. The application of economic–mathematical methods, economic modelling, optimal planning, the introduction of automated systems of management etc. are but a few examples of new theoretical principles which Soviet economists attempted to apply to the analysis of the operation of the Soviet economy and on which they hoped to base economic reforms. For economists like Liberman, Kantorovich, Veinstein and others it was a most difficult task, for they were obliged to eliminate (at least in theory) any contradictions between the new approach to economic problems and Marxist principles (Katsenelinboigen, 1980, p.39).

On the practical level, the reforms which Khrushchev tried to introduce reflected the recognition that the relationship between the political system and the society had become an obstacle to economic development. However, the process of de-Stalinisation and the resulting economic reforms confront the leadership with a dilemma because the application of economic rationality within a planned economy, which meant a degree of decentralisation, was in conflict with strict Party control essential for the preservation of its power.

At the 22nd Party Congress, in 1961, a new programme of the Party was announced. It contained the ambitious 'economic task-...to create the material and technical base for Communism within two decades' (Hodnet, 1974, vol.4, p.215). The new programme also emphasised the principle of profitability and incentives through a more realistic approach to pricing and a somewhat larger role of the market. Following the Congress there were attempts at experimentation in some enterprises, (the Bolshevichka–Mayak experiment in 1964, for example) but these were later abandoned. The reforms had very little effect on the system as a whole because the experiments were conducted on a small scale and decentralisation had been limited to a few selected areas only.

There were two main reasons for this failure. First, the conflict between the centralised decision-making power of the Party and the economic objectives of efficient production was difficult to reconcile within the Soviet economic and political system. Secondly, the resistance of the entrenched bureaucracy in the planning institutions, who saw the new measures as a direct threat to its position, made the implementation of the reforms very difficult. Both factors – fear of losing its exclusive control over the economy, which in the long-run may have involved a threat to its political power, and the opposition to the reforms by the mass of ideologically uncommitted officials and administrators – diminished the scope of application of the reforms. Those introduced by Kosygin in 1965 were equally ineffective due to the necessity of extensive limitations of the role of the Party.

More recent attempts at reforming the economy through the introduction of different criteria of assessment of economic performance by enterprises (Sarkisiant, 1980, chapter 8.3) do not seem to have made any appreciable impact. But discussions about the problems facing the economy and their solutions continue with undiminished vigour. However, they were limited in their scope by the need to conform to the basic tenets of Marxism and the Party line. The latest trend in Soviet economic thought is to interpret Marxism in a way that would make the accommodation of economic reforms easier to accept by the Party ideologues.

One Soviet economist, for example, referring to Marx and to his analysis in *Das Kapital* of the role of competition under capitalism, particularly the role of prices, attempted to adapt the Marxist analysis to a socialist economy. While, according to the economist, the relationship between demand and supply under socialism is regulated by state planning, there is a pressing need to adopt other means of balancing demand and supply. To achieve this balance it is necessary to utilise the price mechanism the way it operates under capitalism, through systematic revisions of prices for specific goods and services. This would not contradict Marxist economics for

> there exists an empirical law which states that when prices rise then, all other conditions remaining the same, demand for goods falls and vice versa. This peculiarity of prices under capitalism makes it an automatic regulator of demand and supply, while under socialism it can become a potential instrument for planned management of demand. (Mayer, 1981, p.62)

The attempts at a Marxist interpretation of the role of prices under socialism is only one example of the obstacles that lay in the way of effective reforms and to the solution of Soviet economic problems. 'To think that the change in planning will greatly improve the economic mechanism within the existing political system is unrealistic; social and political factors affecting the effectiveness of this mechanism are still too great' (Katsenelinboigen, 1980, p.152). Yet the possibility of radical reforms must not be discarded. As Soviet history indicates, pressing economic problems sometimes led the Soviet leadership to non-Marxist solutions. The New Economic Policy introduced in 1921 is one example of a radical step taken by the Soviets to overcome economic difficulties. Admittedly, the serious and many-sided retreat from communist objectives, although temporary, was essential for the survival of the regime – a situation unlikely to arise in the foreseeable future, and the possibility of another Kronstadt is rather remote. None the less, the search for acceptable solutions to economic problems continues. Andropov himself, while pointing to the unsatisfactory growth in productivity and to the absence of improvement in the efficacy of utilisation of resources, admitted that he did not have 'ready made prescriptions', but remarked that economic problems cannot be solved through slogans alone. 'We must proceed', he said, 'with caution. We must conduct experiments, if necessary, and take into account and evaluate the experience of fraternal countries...[as well as] world experience' (Andropov, 1982). Whether the 1986–7 reforms are an experiment conducted on a gigantic scale or a permanent feature of the Soviet economic system depends to a great extent on its achievements and its implications for the power of the Party.

CONCLUSION

The call for greater efficiency and frequent references to the advantages of a socialist economy in this respect are often taken by Western observers as empty ideologically motivated slogans. However, a close look at the problems confronting the Soviet economy suggests that the solution to economic difficulties may indeed lie in the improvement of its operation. It would certainly appear that what the Soviets perceive as a major problem is the 'burden of inefficiency' rather than a 'burden of defence'. Consequently, the trade-off between defence and consumption may be less relevant for the Soviets than increased productivity and improved efficiency which would benefit the civilian as well as the defence sector. Writings by Soviet military economists seem to confirm the latter assumption. One Soviet source referred to the military sector and its connection to the problems of the rest of the economy in the following terms:

> The material and technical endowment of the armed forces is closely connected with the solution of a wide range of problems. One of these problems is related to the development and improvement of the structure of the national economy as a whole and of the defence industry in particular. Other problems

requiring appropriate solutions are in the area of exploitation of human, material and financial resources that are directly diverted to the armed forces. (Gurov, 1982)

It would appear that adequate management of the economy rather than a reduction in defence spending is the key issue for the Soviets. This may be the reason why one finds little reference to the 'defence burden' in Soviet writings. The emphasis is on raising productivity and efficiency as a solution to economic difficulties. A deteriorating situation in the industrial and agricultural sectors may have become the catalyst for forcing the leadership to make difficult decisions regarding the mode of operation of the economic system and for the introduction of radical reforms.

The new economic realism, to which reference was made in the preceding chapter, is still to be implemented in practice. It is probably a matter of time before the resistance of forces opposing these changes is overcome. There are two reasons for this to happen. The first and foremost is based on economic rationality. This suggests that unless adequate supplies of consumer goods rather than just monetary rewards are offered as incentives, there is little chance of raising productivity. The second reason is of a social and political nature – one of domestic pressure. While in the past Soviet domestic policies as a function of centralised planning did not take into account the social and political consequences of the economic situation, there appears to be a growing trend in Soviet political literature to investigate the factors which may influence the mood and attitude of the population, including research in public opinion. Contrary to the widely shared view that Soviet public opinion has little political significance for the regime, there is increasing evidence to suggest that this may not be so.

A number of economists have come to recognise that the domestic economic situation, the satisfaction of consumer demand, has a powerful influence upon the general attitude to work. Indicative of this trend is the assessment of the causes of upheavals in East Germany, Hungary, Czechoslovakia and Poland by a Soviet commentator: 'It was not the counterrevolutionary, reactionary and foreign elements that have artificially brought about the upheavals which took place at different periods, but the economic conditions' (Ambartsumov, 1984, p.17).

The relatively new pragmatism in approaching political and ideological questions is now being openly expressed by Soviet economists, who no longer hide economic problems and their impact on public opinion. They began to recognise that the consciousness of the individual and his worldview are being formed not only by the 'objective' development of society but also by 'subjective' factors that operate in his daily life – his economic situation. Furthermore, increased contacts with the West and the growing application of modern means of communication offer the Soviet population the opportunity to compare the respective economic conditions in the USSR and the West. The latter is perceived by the Party as threatening the stability of the regime, and this has become in recent years the centre of attention by the leadership.

Appendix

Productivity is not the only source of economic growth. The growth rate actually achieved is due to many other sources such as allocation of resources and gains from the application to production of advanced technology. But the growth of labour productivity is considered by many economists as the most appropriate criteria that can be applied to evaluate the performance of an economy and its development over time (Bergson, 1978). This is usually represented by the national income or output per worker. As indicated elsewhere in this book, productivity as defined by Soviet economists is essentially similar to the Western concept – it is derived from dividing the national income by the number of workers. But even when we take into account the somehow different Soviet interpretation of national income, we can still establish an approximate rate of growth in Soviet labour productivity by surveying the performance of the Soviet economy over time.

The present study does not attempt a detailed analysis of all the sources of economic growth in the Soviet Union, neither does it try to explore the question of the possible link between the Soviet system and productivity – whether a social system may promote growth of output per worker through its positive impact on the quality of labour, on worker's attitudes and skills and on technological progress. It may be appropriate to mention in this connection the familiar contention that one system may be inherently more favourable than another to workers' attitudes. In the case of technological progress, this may well be so because of the different incentives offered. Admittedly, these are important questions but for the purpose of this study we shall only consider the productivity factor as a prime source of economic growth – one to which the Soviets are devoting much attention.

By 'source of growth' we mean the changes that cause national income to increase over time. These can be divided broadly between changes in the resources used to produce the national product (changes in factor inputs – labour, capital, and land used in production) and changes that affect output per unit of input. Output per unit of input changes, among other reasons, because of advances in technological and managerial knowledge and the way resources are allocated in order to yield a maximum national product.

Productivity per person employed is the most significant indicator of the source of growth because labour is the largest economic resource of any developed country. Labour earns 70 to 80 per cent of national income in most developed countries (Denison, 1967). It is this aspect of economic growth that appears to be of a major concern to the Soviet leadership. This is not surprising and springs from the fact that the political system has almost total control over economic activities and that the sources of economic growth are subject to centralised planning. Ultimately, greater productivity depends on the policies adopted by the government in relation to various sources of economic growth over which it has exclusive control (allocation of resources, technological progress etc). But if one takes into account the fact that the conditions in the USSR are most conducive to a high level of economic growth due to the full utilisation of resources (full employment, etc.), the productivity factor is of even greater importance for the USSR than it is for the West.

Consequently, a direct comparison of the sources of economic growth in the USSR and the West is not appropriate, given the totally different methods of allocation of resources. It is also not appropriate because in a market economy the chief task of an entrepreneur or manager is to maximise profit by finding the best combination of factors of production which will result in least-cost, while in a planned economy profit may not be of prime consideration – the manager striving foremost to fulfil the plan. Although there has been for some time a trend in Soviet planning to introduce the profit factor within production activities, it has not led, so far, to any increase in productivity. Soviet statistical data confirm the latter contention and indicate, at the same time, a direct relationship between productivity and economic growth – both have been declining over the period 1960–84 (see Table 8.2).

The growing emphasis on productivity as the main source of economic growth is also due to the fact that a major source – labour – has been by and large exhausted through demographic causes and full employment (if we disregard the question of overemployment). Another source of potential economic growth – reallocation of resources – does not seem to be a viable option at the present time because it would lead to increased investments at the expence of consumption. As we have indicated in this book, increased investments have also been rejected by Soviet planners on account of diminishing returns.

9 War of Ideologies – the Propaganda War

As we have indicated earlier, in the context of the relations between the Soviet Union and the United States and of the ongoing arms race, the economic factor is seen by the Soviets as an instrument of American foreign policy in its offensive against the USSR. There is also another factor:

> While the first and foremost objective of the US is to achieve military superiority, they have also initiated an economic war whose aim is to weaken the Soviet economy, and, at the same time, have also launched an ideological and psychological war to undermine the social, political and ideological unity of Soviet society. (Volkogonov, 1983, pp.5–6)

While the economic situation and the internal problems besetting the Soviet Union have acquired some importance for American foreign policy in its efforts to exploit the weaknesses of the Soviet economy, ideological propaganda aimed at discrediting the Soviet system and directed toward the population of the USSR, have become part of American foreign strategy – a fact not much publicised in the West. The implications of the so-called 'ideological and psychological war' and its ramifications for the Soviet Union will be examined in this chapter.

The concept of ideological war is not a new one in Soviet political terminology, but for some time has been given a prominent place in the works of Soviet ideologues and political analysts. There is renewed emphasis on the importance of ideological propaganda and educational indoctrination as weapons to be used in the ideological confrontation between the two opposing world-views. Political propaganda, although rooted in the old notion of capitalist encirclement, reflects another facet of the conflict between the superpowers which has assumed increased significance.

Propaganda as an instrument of foreign policy, whose objective was to exert political and ideological influence on the public at large, was not confined to the Soviet Union alone. It has also acquired an important role in American foreign policy. This was expressed in the Reagan Administration's declaration of a 'crusade' against the Soviet Union and in the general ideological offensive against communism.

One of the reasons for this relatively new trend in East–West relations appears to be the perception that the arms race has reached a point where an all-out thermonuclear war is becoming impracticable as a means of achieving political objectives (Arbatov, G., 1973, p.58). This does not mean that the arms race has lost its impetus towards building more sophisticated weapons, but since political objectives may not be attainable in the immediate future, the conflict has taken on the form of a propaganda war between the two adversaries which highlights their contrasting ideologies. It is being perceived by the Soviet Union as a battle for the 'minds of billions of people on this planet' (Zamyatin, 1985, p.117). In the Soviet view, along with the attempt by the United States to achieve military superiority, there is also an all-out effort to attain superiority in the field of ideology and ideological propaganda. This, they say, became necessary because United States' foreign policy, which is based on the principle of diplomacy from a position of strength, is steadily losing the confidence of world opinion.

In the Soviet view, the American ideological offensive has been caused by the failure of past policies and strategies. 'Containment of Communism' failed and led to a policy of 'softening up' and 'bridge-building' whose aim was to 'choke socialism in the embrace of *détente*'. Since neither the Cold War nor *détente* succeeded in their objectives, the United States embarked upon an ideological war with the ultimate goal of penetrating the Soviet fortress in order to weaken it from inside, to undermine the social, political and ideological unity of Soviet society. The objectives of this war are to be achieved through intensive propaganda that will exert 'demoralising influences' on the minds of the Soviet people (Volkogonov, 1983, p.6).

Both terms, ideological confrontation and psychological war, are being currently used in Soviet political literature as evidence of a new form of the class-conflict between the two systems. The difference between the two concepts being that a confrontation between two opposing ideologies uses, at least in theory, means of persuasion, while the main method in a psychological war is the contamination of the minds of the people through an imposition of views and opinions using propaganda as its instrument. Accordingly, it is nothing else but a system of subversion not dissimilar in its objectives from foreign territorial intervention at the time of the Civil War, but in the spiritual sphere.

Ideological subversion by the United States is viewed by the Soviets as acting not only in the sphere of theoretical ideological concepts, but also in the field of social psychology; the effort being concentrated on the young as a social group of the population that has the least social experience, on the intelligentsia, and lately on the Soviet army personnel (Volkogonov, 1983, p.7). According to L.M. Zamyatin (1985, p.92), the former Soviet propaganda expert, the psychological war exploits the natural desire of the people of one society to become acquainted with the way of life and thought of citizens of another socio-political system, and the desire to understand the domestic and foreign policy of that system. This implies that the United States tries to satisfy this desire by supplying false information and misleading views to the Soviet people. It also suggests that the only source of objective information is the Soviet Union.

> The strategy of world bourgeoisie in its attempt to save the sinking ship of capitalism consists in concentrating all its means and powers in the field of propaganda and information. It does everything possible to create confusion in the minds of the peoples of socialist countries; in the first place the Soviet people. (Toshchenko, 1984, p.22)

In its concrete forms, the ideological war is seen by the Soviets as pursuing a number of clearly defined objectives:

1. to introduce doubts about the correctness of the foreign policies of the Soviet government;
2. to influence people to commit anti-social acts that are considered by the Soviets as being against socialist democratic and lawful standards (e.g. dissidents);
3. to awaken and stimulate nationalistic prejudices,
4. to create doubts about the spiritual values of socialism; its culture, ethics and ideology;
5. to encourage the emergence of private-ownership psychology and consumerism;
6. to induce people to leave the Soviet Union or to defect.

The listing of the alleged objectives of the American ideological offensive may be taken as an indication that such negative (from the Soviet point of view) trends do exist, as we shall see in the later part of this chapter, and are taken quite seriously. The perceived dangers of the ideological confrontation are summarised in the words of one Soviet commentator: 'the present struggle between the opposing ideologies may well determine the future of the USSR and the fate of socialism' (Babosov, 1984, p.163). Today, along with the attention devoted by the Soviets to the armed forces, few activities are more important to the Kremlin than propaganda. The USSR is estimated to be spending 3 billion dollars annually on it.

According to one Soviet source, propaganda and counter-propaganda is to concentrate on the following: first, it must study the content, methods, and means of Western propaganda; secondly, it must determine the ideological and socio-psychological preparedness of the population and its willingness to counteract foreign influence; thirdly, it must not be confined to the population of the Soviet Union, but must also take place on the international arena (ibid., p.116).

Soviet propaganda, therefore, is to act on two fronts: internally as a means of neutralising foreign influence; externally as a powerful tool in the global propaganda struggle between the United States and the Soviet Union. The emphasis on the global propaganda is to present the United States as the chief culprit in the present conflict while proclaiming the peaceful intentions of the Soviet Union, and, at the same time, to highlight its achievements in the social and economic sphere as a model for the developing countries. The Soviets have made some advances in Europe, particularly within the anti-nuclear movement and in some Third-World countries, and Soviet propaganda is becoming more pervasive and sophisticated.

AMERICA'S IDEOLOGICAL OFFENSIVE

Propaganda originating from the Soviet Union is not a new phenomenon and had not been ignored in the past. At the time of the Revolution there were fears in the West that revolutionary movements might spread accross Western Europe. The Brest–Litovsk Peace treaty signed on 15 December 1917, clearly reflected these fears. Among the conditions of the Treaty was an agreement that 'the contracting Parties will refrain from agitation and propaganda against the government or public institutions of the other

Party' (Degras, 1961, vol.I, pp.52–3). Russia was to put an end to all agitation or propaganda against the government or the public institutions of the Ukraine Republic. Clearly, the new regime in Russia considered propaganda as an instrument for spreading communist ideas. The signing of the treaty did not prevent, only a few days later, the People's Commissariat for Foreign Affairs from sending an appeal to the 'toiling, oppressed and exhausted peoples of Europe', assuring them that 'the Soviet government will...use all the means at its disposal to help the working class in all lands to overthrow the rule of capital and to seize political power' (ibid., p.19).

The perception of the dangers of communist ideological influence diminished somewhat after the failure of communist inspired revolutions in some European countries. Nevertheless, as late as 1933 on the establishment of diplomatic relations with the United States, the Soviet Union undertook

> to refrain and restrain all persons or organisations over which the Soviet Union has direct or indirect control...from any acts tending to...the bringing about by force of a change in the political or social order...of the United States. Not to permit the formation or residence on [Soviet] territory and to prevent the activity...of any organisation which has as its aim the subversion of the American political order. (ibid., vol.III, p.36)

When only two years later the Americans protested against the intervention by the Comintern in the internal affairs of the United States, the Soviet Government declined responsibility over the action of the Comintern. In its reply to the American protest the Soviet Government said: 'It is certainly not new to the government of the United States that the...USSR cannot take upon itself and has not taken upon itself any kind of obligations with regard to the Communist International' (ibid., p.39).

At the time the Soviets certainly had the advantage of being able to isolate Russia from foreign influence due to the technological constraint on communication, especially radio broadcasts, while spreading their propaganda through all the affiliated Comintern communist parties across the globe. Even so, communist propaganda had not been really considered as having an appreciable impact in the United States and counter-propaganda had not been an issue in American foreign policy.

The situation has changed drastically since the end of the Second

World War. With the advent of the Cold War and the growing role of the USSR in world affairs, the question of propaganda became an important issue for both superpowers. The advance in communication technology presented the United States with an opportunity to reach directly the population of the Soviet Union. The power of words as a means to send messages across national boundaries was reflected in the 1945 American proposal for a 'free and unlimited dissemination of ideas in the world'. The Soviets had certainly valid reasons to fear such proposals coming on the heels of the personal experiences of the capitalist way of life by millions of Soviet citizens under German occupation. The United States, where communist propaganda had not been very effective, had much less concern. The proposals were rejected by the Soviets for 'it became clear from its inception that this concept foresaw the freedom of anti-communist propaganda' (Volkogonov, 1983, p.138).

Further developments of mass media technology, creating the possibility of reaching the Soviet population through radio broadcasts and telecasts via satellites, have begun to be viewed by the Soviets with increasing concern as potential weapons in the attempt to influence Soviet public opinion. The launching of the first American communication satellite Echo-1, early in the 1960s, indicated to the Soviets that the United States had begun working seriously on plans for direct transmissions of television programmes to other countries, including the USSR. This was followed in 1969 with the launching of four INTELSAT-3 satellites, each of which had the capacity to transmit simultaneously four television programmes.

With the change of the American Administration in 1980, the issue of propaganda as an instrument of American foreign policy assumed much greater importance than is generally realised. Propaganda began to be directed towards counteracting Soviet influence in international affairs and, more importantly, to get messages across to the Soviet population explaining America's position within the East–West conflict, emphasising the negative aspects of Soviet foreign as well as domestic policies. The ultimate aim of this new trend in American foreign policy was to change Soviet behaviour by influencing public opinion in the USSR.

Soviet concern about American propaganda efforts became particularly evident after the address by President Reagan to the British Parliament on 8 June 1982. In his speech he denounced the

Soviet regime as an 'evil empire', called for the West to consign Soviet communism 'to the ash heap of history', and for a 'global campaign for democracy' as a means for achieving the above objective (Caldwell, 1985, p.8).

By challenging the Soviets to an ideological confrontation, Reagan touched upon a raw nerve – a most sensitive area of the Soviet political doctrine. Public statements by members of the new Administration, and practical measures to implement the new direction in American foreign policy, were perceived by Moscow as containing the seeds of a threat to the internal stability of the regime. While in the past the rigid and dogmatic approach to questions of ideology, based on the notion that the ideas of Marxism–Leninism are sufficiently ingrained in the consciousness of the Soviet people, enabled the leadership to be constantly on the offensive on the ideological front, it was suddenly confronted with a situation where the propaganda attack by the United States against Soviet communism brought out some doubts in the minds of the men in the Kremlin about the invulnerability of the Soviet society from foreign influence.

On the American side, the new political course appeared also as a response to Soviet ideological propaganda that had begun to show some successes in Western Europe and already had a record in some developing countries. Until recently, discussions about Marxist ideology and about the concept of democracy belonged mostly to the domain of academic polemics and had little political significance, but the new direction in America's policy endowed the ideological confrontation with a political legitimacy which it did not possess previously; it became, in fact, part of the United States' foreign policy (Berger, 1983, p.31).

Among the measures adopted by the new Administration was a five year academic research project into how the Soviet system works, financed to the tune of 9 million dollars by the Defence Department, the CIA and the State Department (*New York Times*, 3 October 1983). Another project was to create a National Endowment for Democracy, a new institution that would allocate funds to assist and advise democratic parties and movements abroad, especially in the Third World. At the same time, The United States Information Agency (USIA) has been directed to intensify its presentation of democratic ideas and realities to the world, including the population of the USSR. There were also voices advocating an additional effort in the area of ideological propaganda, directed not only to the Soviet Union but to the home front as well through a 'National Endowment for Democracy at Home'. The aims of such Endowment was to be a programme of study of the basic elements of a free society and to make the programme a part of instruction on every educational level (Hook, 1984, p.21). The justification for such a proposal, which might have been construed as a variant of propaganda and indoctrination practised in the USSR, was that 'truth sometimes needs propaganda', an argument always put forward by the Soviets regarding the dissemination of communist 'truth'.

More concrete measures were adopted by the US International Communication Agency, which runs Voice of America with a staff of 7500 and an annual budget of 489 million dollars. Voice of America together with Radio Free Europe and Radio Liberty were to be additional means of spreading Western information through intensive broadcasts beamed towards the USSR and Eastern Europe. Radio Free Europe and Radio Liberty have operated previously as independent bodies, although financed by the United States, but as a result of the introduction of the 'Pell Amendment' and its subsequent passing by the House of Representatives in 1982, both came under the control of the Administration. Following the restructuring of the control over the radio stations, additional funds were allocated to strengthen their power of transmission. Finally, the building of the giant relay station in the Arava, Israel – designed to allow VOA to counter Soviet jamming and boost American transmissions to the Soviet Union – was agreed on in principle between Israel and the US in July 1986 (but shelved in 1987).

In August 1981, the President launched 'Project Truth' whose objective was to refute 'misleading Soviet propaganda and disinformation', to underline America's commitment to peace, and to present the Soviet Union as a threat to world security. Since Charles Wick became the director of USIA, a more aggressive policy of propaganda has been adopted by the Administration. In the words of Charles Wick (1985, p.519): 'The craft of statesmanship may well depend on the extent to which you can use and master the tools of mass communication...Telecommunication has now made it possible for governments to speak directly to people in other countries.' President Reagan voiced a similar opinion in his 27 January 1987, State of the Union message to Congress. 'Peace and progress', he said, 'depend on much more than a sound military balance...The United States must be able to communicate information and ideas on a worldwide basis. Ongoing expansion of America's international broadcasting capability – the Voice of America, Radio Free Europe/Radio Liberty, and Radio Marti – must therefore continue' (USIS, 29 January 1987).

The objective of the new course in US foreign policy was to initiate and develop the flow of information destined for audiences in the USSR and its allies. The technological advance in global telecommunication, especially the capability to broadcast television programmes worldwide via satellites under the control of WORLDNET, the USIA's global television satellite service, was to be an additional tool to reach the above goal.

Thus propaganda became an additional feature of American foreign policy whose aim was to change Soviet behaviour through influencing Soviet public opinion. The effectiveness of this latter course of action cannot be ascertained as long as there is no feedback from the people to whom the propaganda is directed, and its effect on Soviet behaviour also remains in doubt. However, what can be said is that the possibility, even if remote, of American messages reaching Soviet society and the potential consequences that this may bring about, appears to have been taken with the utmost seriousness by the Soviet leadership.

IDEOLOGICAL PROPAGANDA AND THE NEW SOVIET MAN

The reasons why the Communist Party devotes so much attention to the question of ideological education and propaganda are connected with the awareness by Soviet leaders of the state of Soviet society. There is the realisation that the Soviet society is far from the idealised picture painted in the past by Party ideologues; 'drunkenness, hooliganism, parasitism, speculation, bribery, narrow-minded materialism' are some of the attributes often quoted as evidence by Party ideologues and other Soviet sources. It indicates, at least to some extent, the failure of the attempt to form a New Soviet Man (Babosov, 1984, p.45).

A second reason is the perception of a potential threat to the authority and influence of the Party over Soviet society due to the flow of information and ideas emanating from the West.

By means of ideological subversion our adversaries are attempting to revive in the minds of some politically immature individuals bourgeois views...to arouse hostile attidudes toward the socialist system and way of life. (Shcherbitsky, 1977, p.247)

Events outside of the USSR, particularly in Poland, have shown that forty years of communist rule did not mean that the society is immune from ideological contamination. In the Soviet view, the attempt to use propaganda as an instrument of American foreign policy almost succeeded in Poland; in their view Poland was chosen as an 'experimental field' by Western propaganda (ibid., p.26–7). Closer to home, the emergence of 'slanderers and renegades, the so-called in the West dissidents', the relative increase in defections and the voices of people allowed to emigrate expressing criticism of the Soviet system, were a clear indication that all is not well.

While it is true that in the USSR production, national and social relations, the way of life and culture, have created a socialist type of man with a high degree of collectivism, humanism, Soviet patriotism – a man dedicated to communist ideals – it is undeniable that in some individuals there still remain antisocial tendencies. (Volkogonov, 1983, p.35)

Soviet confidence in the Soviet society has always been based on the premise that socialism will enable it to develop the creative potentials of men for the benefit of society as a whole. But a revolutionary transformation of society had been considered impossible without the transformation of man himself. The formation of a new man – a Soviet Man – 'was not only a major objective, but an indispensible condition for building a communist society' (*Kommunist*, no.9, June 1983, p.17).

Such a belief was justified on theoretical as well as pragmatic considerations; the former linked to 'objective' factors, the latter to more practical 'subjective' influences. The concept of 'objective' laws meant that society develops according to some immutable laws and that natural–historical changes take place 'objectively' regardless of the will of individuals or governments (Arbatov, G., 1973, p.37). These were the laws of economic determinism put forward by Marx and Engels. According to these laws, the changes that are taking place in society are also instrumental in forming the social consciousness of its members. Accordingly, social consciousness represents the totality of ideas and views at a given period and reflects, therefore, social reality. It follows, that in the Soviet

Union, the country of developed socialism, the social consciousness of the individual cannot be anything else but socialist. Hence, Soviet society must necessarily be united and monolithic in its views. It is only in 'a socialist society where a complete unity of moral, political and spiritual values is possible' (Volkogonov, 1983, p.15). Western assertions that public opinion in the West does not accept communist ideas or that it shows support of bourgeois government policies is devoid of any scientific reasoning – these are subjective judgements. Even if opinion polls appear to support Western assertions, they are only the result of 'subjective' factors such as the powerful bourgeois propaganda. The social consciousness of the working class under capitalism has been deformed by such propaganda so as to conform to the interests of the bourgeoisie.

This is not to say that 'subjective' factors do not operate in the Soviet society; it is precisely for that reason that ideological education and propaganda are so important for the Party: 'The basic function of ideological activity under socialism consists in the formation of a conscious, ideologically convinced, socially active personality' (Babosov, 1984, p.41).

Propaganda as a means for spreading Marxist–Leninist ideas and as an instrument of communist power has been a distinctive feature of the Soviet regime since the Revolution and has its historical sources in the writings of Lenin. Lenin perceived the power of communication and propaganda in spreading the message of class struggle, not only within the Soviet Union but to the working classes abroad, well before the Bolsheviks took over the state power. He established a tradition of 'professional revolutionaries' who later became Party functionaries at home and abroad, and who employed communication techniques to propagate the socialist ideology and the policies of the USSR (Schultz and Gordon, 1984, p.34).

The leadership of the Soviet Union has always shared Lenin's views regarding the significance of propaganda as a political instrument, and used the same brand of propaganda that has been employed since Lenin pioneered it during the Bolshevik Revolution. Its objective was to programme people's minds into accepting unconditionally the Soviet model of state and society (Wettig, 1977, p.2). Propaganda in the Soviet Union is therefore inseparable from politics; it is a special means of political activity (Toshchenko, 1984, p.21). What facilitated in the past the implementation of the objective of propaganda was the complete monopoly of the state over the mass media and the resulting, almost total, isolation of Soviet society from the outside world.

Lenin in the early days of Soviet power, was fully aware of the role and importance of mass information. He perceived the power of information as a political power (Lenin, 1964–5, vol.41, p.399) which under socialism 'will serve to clean the consciousness of the workers from bourgeois-ideological admixture' (ibid., vol.24, p.340). The latter role of propaganda has become even more vital than in the past on account of the alleged infiltration of foreign ideas into the consciousness of Soviet citizens.

> Communist propaganda must at present wage a decisive struggle against the recurrence of middle-class psychology, manifestation of individualism in the form of consumerism, money-grabbing mentality; striving to live at the expense of society, and most important, against tendencies toward the so-called 'absolute freedom'. (Toshchenko, 1984, p.23)

The belief that Soviet social consciousness has been 'objectively' formed according to the laws of social transformation and the conviction that the ideological activities of the Party – the 'subjective' factor – succeeded in the formation of a 'fully developed, spiritually rich personality whose ideological attitudes coincide with the social and political strategy of the Party' (Babosov, 1984, p.125), is being increasingly questioned by some Soviet political analysts in terms that would have been unthinkable a couple of decades ago.

The question why after nearly seven decades of socialism in the USSR the problem of socialist consciousness should still arise, is clearly a matter of concern for Soviet ideologues –

> taking on the struggle with the negative manifestations in economic practices and in the psychology of [Soviet] men, one may legitimately search for an answer to the question whether a contradiction exists between the occurrencies of these negative trends and the maturity of socialism. (Toshchenko, 1984, p.38)

Although this appears to be a rhetorical question about the compatibility of socialism with its demand on the individual, it does point to the existence of a more realistic approach to the question of ideology and to the possibility of different views regarding the source of the problem and its solution: 'there is no secret that there are differences of opinions among communists on some concrete political and ideological questions' (XXV Siezd KPPS 1978, p.323).

One Soviet source quotes N. Stepanov, a member of the Central Committee of the Bulgarian Communist Party, as saying that the occurrence of a non-socialist consciousness among some individuals is caused by some errors and failures in internal policies. 'Socialism' – says Stepanov – 'does not guarantee the absence of mistakes. One must take into account that socialism is historically young and that Soviet society does not yet possess sufficient experience in order to consciously regulate all ongoing processes of its development' (*Mir i sotsialism*, no.5, 1983, p.35). A similar opinion has been expressed by Mikhail Gorbachev.

Others attributed the apparent failure to achieve the goal of forming a New Soviet Man to a number of more concrete 'subjective' factors operating within Soviet society. First, there still exist remnants of historically preserved relations, especially within the family where bourgeois morality may still survive and be transmitted through the following generations, over which the control of the Party is still limited. A contributing factor in this respect were the consequences of the Second World War. During the war tens of millions of Soviet citizens found themselves on the territory occupied by the Germans. Others were sent to Germany as slave labour and many Soviet citizens finished as prisoners of war. Millions of Soviet army personnel spent some time in European countries in the last stages of the war and many have done their military service immediately after the war as part of troops stationed abroad. According to one Soviet source, all Soviet citizens who were abroad or under occupation have been subjected to the influence of fascist ideology and, generally, to Western ideas. Although the majority did resist such influences, the source commented, some have succumbed to the influence of foreign ideology and morality. They have accepted 'uncritically the outside gloss of capitalist reality' (Epishev, 1983, p.228).[1]

Secondly, negative symptoms in Soviet society have arisen as a result of foreign propaganda which exploited the increased level of personal contacts, scientific, technological and cultural exchanges, particularly during the period of *détente* (Volkogonov, 1983, p.78). Despite the liberalisation of Soviet policy in the area of international personal exchanges, Soviet ideological propaganda on the domestic front did not slacken. It was still presenting the capitalist

West, especially the United States, as determined to destroy socialism by means of ideological subversion. 'In the final analysis, the adoption of anti-communism as the ideological platform of American foreign policy, comes down to the fact that it does not rely any longer on the overthrow of communism by force, but on its 'erosion'' (Migin *et al.*, 1978, p.140).

The Soviet perception of any relaxation of tension between the superpowers as an illusory state of affairs without any prospects for permanent reconciliation is based on the notion that capitalism, by its very nature, makes the conflict between the two opposing systems unavoidable, since the ideological struggle objectively reflects the confrontation between two contrasting worldviews and social systems. 'It cannot be otherwise', maintains Leonid Zamyatin, 'because the world outlook and class objectives of socialism and capitalism are diametrically opposed and irreconcilable' (Zamyatin, 1985, p.58).

This view about the irreconcilability between socialism and capitalism, about the 'objective' factors of the ideological struggle, makes the Soviet assertions that there is no contradiction between the latter and peaceful coexistence appear ambiguous, to say the least. But what it does reflect is an inner conflict between Soviet pragmatists who see economic and political benefits from improved relations with the West, and the conservatives who warn constantly about the dangers of reconciliation. Among the latter is the well known Georgi Arbatov who never ceased to point to the dangers that *détente* presents for the Soviet Union: 'the ideological struggle, the battle for people's minds, remains one of the principal bridgeheads of the struggle against imperialism...[it] remains acute in spite of the relaxation of international tension' (Arbatov G., 1973, p.8).

It must be clear to any Marxist–Leninist, according to Arbatov, that Western powers cannot be expected to have a different, friendly, policy towards socialism. The principle of peaceful coexistence does not in any way presuppose the cessation of the inevitable struggle between the two systems, but only implies the exclusion of military means. Hence, when the Soviets analyse American foreign policy, an assessment whether such policy is 'friendly' or 'hostile' cannot be used as a valid criterion; any US policy must be by definition inherently anti-socialist. Consequently, from the Soviet point of view, the dangers emanating from closer economic and cultural relations between the USSR and the West lie in the presumable exploitation of *détente* for the purpose of ideological subversion. To quote Georgi Arbatov once more:

> Propositions by the proponents of the 'bridge-building' doctrine to promote economic, scientific and technological contacts, conceal its real significance. The knowledge of how effectively these elements of the new policy can be used to prejudice socialism, is becoming the only criterion. In this context even good words about negotiations, trade and other contacts, acquire the form of ill-concealed subversive activity. (Arbatov, G., 1973, p.8)

The uncompromising attitude of Soviet ideologues towards the West in general, and the United States in particular, seems to imply that the contradiction between the principle of peaceful coexistence and ideological militancy might preclude any meaningful economic and cultural ties between the Soviet Union and the West. Thus, practical considerations and pure economic rationality seem to be in direct conflict with the ideological approach that could lead to further isolation of the Soviet Union. After all, the threat of ideological contamination, although perceived as originating mainly from abroad, was an internal problem linked to a number of 'subjective' factors analysed earlier, and required, therefore, 'subjective' solutions.

THE SOVIET RESPONSE

In response to the perceived threat of Western influence, the Soviet Government initiated a concerted effort on the domestic front as well as on the international arena, through propaganda and counter-propaganda, to counteract foreign ideas' penetration. A symposium of Eastern European socialist countries in early 1969 was devoted to 'problems of psychological warfare' waged against the socialist states by the capitalist mass media. It called for a vigorous campaign against the penetration of Western influences. Of particular concern was the potential impact of direct telecast via satellites to the USSR and its allies. This has been taken as 'an attempt to convert television broadcasting into means of meddling into the affairs of other states and subversive activities' (Zamyatin, 1985, p.112). The Soviets saw the potential threat of direct telecast in the possibility of receiving programmes directly on the TV screen with the help of relatively simple modifications to the set and special antennas.

In order to prevent direct telecast via satellites, the Soviet bloc countries, supported by some Third-World and non-aligned countries, have made strenuous efforts to influence various international agencies, like UNESCO and the International Communication Union, to adopt principles that would not permit such practices. The Soviet Union has been particularly active in the attempt to establish international laws that would limit the activities of governments in the use of satellites for communication and telecast. The Soviets always objected to the position of the American delegation to the various agencies who 'under the pretext of free flow of information' have resisted Soviet proposals for the establishment of appropriate conventions (Zamyatin, 1985, p.116). In August 1972, the Soviet Union submitted a proposal to the General Assembly of the United Nations for a convention concerning the use of satellites. 'The relaying of TV programmes via satellites to other sovereign states without their agreement' was to be regarded as illegal. There were other attempts to limit the use of communication satellites in UNESCO since 1974. It was done under the assertion that Western type of information was merely an instrument of propaganda in an attempt to gain 'ideological superiority' over the socialist countries. None of the proposals gained the approval of the majority.

At home, the subject of ideological counter-propaganda came up as one of the main topics at the Plenary Meeting of the CPSU Central Committee in June 1983. The meeting considered the implications of the new direction in US foreign policy, which was seen as geared to influence Soviet public opinion. In his speech the then General Secretary, Andropov, underlined again the importance of ideological education and propaganda through the press, radio, television, as well as oral propaganda as means of preventing the emergence of 'bourgeois-reformist tendencies within Soviet society' (*Kommunist*, no.9, June 1983, p.5). The recommendation adopted by the meeting spoke of the strengthening of ideological propaganda in the context of the ideological war between the two opposing systems. However, it also became clear that Marxist education and ideological indoctrination, no matter how vigorously applied, could not be considered effective unless the extent of the negative tendencies was known and the effects of propaganda and education researched rather than being taken for granted – 'the results of [ideological] propaganda must not be judged by the number of measures carried out, but by the real influence that such measures have on the consciousness and mood of the Soviet people' (*Pravda*, 16 September 1985).

The new direction in Soviet propaganda required, therefore, a more pragmatic approach to the analysis of social processes within the Soviet society. It implied a much greater emphasis on social sciences and on their practical application rather than on their theoretical Marxist interpretation. The July 1983 Plenary Meeting of the Central Committee sharply criticised past failures to develop social sciences: 'we have not, to this very day, sufficiently studied the society in which we live and work...For this reason we are forced to act, shall we say, irrationally by ways of experiments and errors'. The Plenum decided to raise the role of social sciences and to widen considerably the scope of social research. Empirical research was to use quantitative analysis, mathematical and statistical methods, model building, etc. It was to apply methods of opinion polls and interviews which were to supply information about the situation in various social groups, their activities, value judgements, motives and expectations. It requested that Soviet scientists should not become detached from the realities of life, not idealise what has been achieved, to abandon the practice of an abstract approach to concrete problems and to avoid dealing with 'contradictions'. Research in the area of social sciences was to be based on 'existing realities with all their pluses and minuses' (Rogovin, 1984, p.15). According to one Soviet commentator, the development of social sciences in the USSR and the implementation of the practical recommendations that would come as a result of scientific research were no less important than the exploitation of the achievements of science and technology in material production (Toshchenko, 1984, p.19).

PROPAGANDA AND PUBLIC OPINION IN THE USSR

The most revealing evidence of the implementation of the new recommendations adopted by the Party can be noticed in the field of study in Soviet public opinion. Research in this area is a relatively new branch of social science and if at the early stage it was concentrated on questions of little political significance, it has become, over time, much broader in its scope and tackles now some sensitive issues such as political attitudes of the population. Although the Soviet Constitution explicitly states that one of the features of 'the political system of Soviet society is a constant responsiveness to public opinion' (Article 9), this had no real meaning, for Soviet public opinion had been considered as 'objectively' united behind the ideology of the Party and there was no neccessity to conduct research or opinion polls.

A slow change began taking place since Stalin's death and the analysis of social processes within Soviet society became much more pragmatic. Prior to Khrushchev, the population had been held at some distance from public affairs and the leaders had only a limited knowledge about the mood of the people in different regions of the country. Khrushchev decided to open the gates of information and to encourage 'mass participation' in public life (Mendras, 1981–2, p.282). However, progress in the field of research in public opinion in a Western sense, was rather slow and very limited. The themes of research were confined to those that presented little risk of being criticised as deviationist from Marxist principles, and scientific writing on the subject had a neutral character.

The resolution by the Central Committee on 26 April 1979, about 'improvement in ideological work and political education' emphasised the role of public opinion. But public opinion was not defined by the official circles as being 'spontaneous opinion', but as 'formed opinion'. Consequently, the exchange between the population and the leadership was essentially in the direction from the government to the governed rather than the other way. This is illustrated in the following example:

Question: In which foreign country
A: has the economy progressed most remarkably after the Second World War?
B: is the standard of living the highest ?
C: is democracy most developed ?
D: is political activity of the masses particularly sensitive ?
E: is political freedom most cruelly suppressed ?

Source: Grouchine, B.A. and Onikov, L.A., 1980, 'Massovaia informatsia v sovetskom promyshlennom gorode', Politizdat, Moscow, p.312.

It is not known when the poll was taken, but the answers indicate that it took place before 1968 as Czechoslovakia was shown in a positive light in the answers to questions A, B, and C. Another poll on public interest indicated a preference for international affairs and least for the theories of Marxism–Leninism

(Tchernakova, 1979, pp.17–27). The importance of public opinion in the USSR and its role was also mentioned by Brezhnev in his report to the 26th Congress and in the resolutions by the Central Committee.

A number of more recent publications dealing with questions of public opinion reveal the increasing importance attributed to this branch of political science.

> Under mature socialism, public opinion reflects and expresses social demands and interests of various groups and strata of the population. It is also an indicator of the degree of development of mass consciousness, mood and attitudes of the workers toward various facts and events. It is one of the important channels that supply general and specific social information and, finally, it reflects the attitude of the masses toward the policies of the Party and Party line. (Gantchev, 1983, p.33)

The views expressed in the above statement clearly question the earlier promoted idea about the ideological monolicity of Soviet society in its support of Soviet policies. It points, at the same time, to a relatively new trend; a more practical appraisal of trends within Soviet society. One Soviet source advocated that problems which are subject to public opinion should be researched and analysed realistically, accurately and objectively. They should be looked upon as 'they really are not as the researcher would like to see them' (ibid., p.49).

There can be little doubt that the more pragmatic approach to the role of public opinion came partly as a result of the increased flow of information from the West that had been reaching the population outside Soviet official channels. The Soviets began looking with some concern at this latter development and initiated measures to find out whether foreign information and propaganda has any appreciable influence on the views of the ordinary citizen, and if so to what extent. Opinion polls were apparently carried out in 1966–8 and their results have convinced the Soviet leadership that the growing influence of Western-based radio information services was beginning to affect the credibility of official domestic news and general information services in the eyes of the Soviet population (Wettig, 1977, p.7).

One of the first measures taken by the Soviets to investigate and eventually counteract foreign influence was the directive by the CPSU to its regional branches, in 1979, to establish centres for study of public opinion. Their responsibility was to analyse the signals emanating from the population. At the same time, the regional branches of the Party propaganda together with the Institute of Social Research at the Academy of Science of the USSR and other academic centres were to conduct regular opinion polls among the population and to present periodical analytical reports about the state of public opinion. Such polls were to reveal with 'sufficient objectivity trends and various changes taking place in the societal consciousness'. The method to be used in the polls, called in Soviet terminology 'proportional mechanical choice' was similar to the Western Random Sampling method. A significant feature of the method to be applied was that the 'anonymity of those questioned will be guaranteed' (Toshchenko, 1984, pp.174–5). The importance of such research did not lie exclusively in its objective to find out opinions held by the population and the extent of foreign influence, but also in the measures to be adopted to counteract the propaganda that originates abroad.[2]

THE MURMANSK EXPERIENCE AND THE CASE OF CZECHOSLOVAKIA

The region where such research was to be concentrated, and where polls were to be conducted, was located where there was close proximity of borders with capitalist states, for example, that with Finland and Norway. Out of all the Soviet western regions where propaganda could relatively easy reach the population, the experience of the Murmansk region has been singled out as one presenting ideal conditions for research and study of the extent of Western influence. Apparently, having a relatively large traffic of foreign visitors, it was chosen as an ideal location for the investigation, not only of radio and television broadcasts coming from across the border, but also the consequences of the relatively free movement of people across state boundaries. According to one Soviet source, the region is being visited by thousands of foreign sailors, tourists, and members of various delegations from capitalist countries. Equally, thousands of workers, employees, students, and school children on visits abroad as tourists, are themselves experiencing the direct effects of Western propaganda. In addition, the influx of imported goods raised the possibility for the Soviet population to make comparisons between the standard of living and the way of life in the Soviet Union and the capitalist world (Rogovin, 1984, p.53). The pressure of Western propaganda and bourgeois ideology, states another Soviet source, is at present a real factor in the everyday life of a Soviet citizen. This fact, taken in the context of the ongoing conflict, means that 'the frontline between the fighting forces in the psychological war has crossed state boundaries and is now situated within the respective societies' (Toshchenko, 1984, p.166).

As the first step in their investigation, local Party organisations began to devote their attention to sounding out the population about the extent of foreign penetration through opinion polls. The results of this investigation are very revealing in their openness and in their findings. A significant feature of one particular poll was the suggestion to indicate whether the subject of the poll listens to Western radio broadcasts and if so the frequency of listening and the motives behind it. It was found that preference was given to foreign radio programmes because Soviet radio, television and press supply incomplete and mostly outdated information and news. Another reason, indicated by some, was the interest about life in other countries. The same poll revealed that among 1500 persons questioned, 36.4 per cent had visited capitalist countries. But what proved to be a matter of concern for the Party organisations was the fact that many of those who went abroad expressed admiration for the standard of living generally, and in particular that of services, choice and quality of goods. It also became clear that many Soviet citizens made 'unrealistic comparisons between prices of goods abroad and in the Soviet Union', and indicated a tendency for the 'idealisation of the superficial attributes of bourgeois way of life' (Toshchenko, 1984, p.177).

Following these findings, the regional office of the Party established a Council for Counter-propaganda. Its staff consisted of Party activists, managers of the media and propaganda, leading members of trade unions and other bodies responsible for the development of foreign tourism and for the reception of foreign citizens. It would appear that initially the Party experienced an acute shortage of trained cadres, which made the task of conducting successful polemics and argumentation with foreign visitors very difficult and sometimes embarrassing. Subsequently, the regional branches of the Party resolved to create a special section for training cadres in the art of free conversation without recourse to standard, ready-made formulas. Students of these courses were sent abroad as members of Soviet tourist groups and delegations so that they 'would personally experience and acquire impressions about the capitalist society', and, one would assume, to keep an eye on the behaviour of the others. At the same time, Party and trade union organisations that usually decide who is to travel abroad have become much stricter in their selection of prospective tourists and prepared them 'ideologically through improved political information' (ibid., p.178)

Another area of potential foreign influence considered by the Party organisation was the projection of Western-produced films depicting the bourgeois way of life. A survey of cinema attendances has found that although the share of foreign films allowed into the USSR was only 10 per cent of all films projected on Soviet screens, the percentage of viewers of foreign films bore no relation to their numbers. According to the Soviet source, foreign films attracted more than one-third of the general viewing public, and were projected for a much longer period. The obvious alternative to forbid their projection, which has been apparently considered, has not been adopted on account of contractual obligations linked to cultural exchanges, but their 'negative' influence has been curtailed by limiting the period of projection and by an appropriate selection of subjects suitable for Soviet audiences. Additional counter-propaganda measures were: increased promotion of home produced films; a vigorous propaganda campaign through a critical evaluation of foreign films in the local press, and the introduction of short lectures in the cinema hall by a competent specialist prior to the projection, explaining the negative features of capitalist life depicted in these films.

The publication of the Murmansk experiment in the study of public opinion is indicative of the concern about the potential effects of Western influence. Such concern is not limited to the territory of the Soviet Union. It appears to be just as vital regarding foreign influence among the populations of the Warsaw Pact allies. The case of Poland – where, in the Soviet view, Western propaganda succeeded in influencing internal policies – has been mentioned earlier. Another country which has become the subject of Soviet attention regarding Western propaganda, is Czechoslovakia. Of all the countries belonging to the Warsaw Pact, Czechoslovakia may be considered as one that has copied the Soviet model and follows faithfully the Moscow line. Not surprisingly, Czechoslovakia has echoed similar fears and voiced its concern about the dangers of ideological contamination in identical terms. These fears are reinforced by the fact that her geographical location, with direct borders with Germany and Austria, present a suitable target for Western propaganda. Almost one-third of her territory is covered by television signals from those two neighbours, and radio broadcasts in Czech and Slovak languages are beamed towards Czechoslovakia from eleven foreign radio stations. Nekola Ivzhi, a Czech political analyst, considered that the radio stations The Voice of America, Radio Liberty and Radio Free Europe were centres of ideological subversion whose ultimate objective is the destruction of the socialist system.

> Television broadcasts from West Germany and Austria take advantage of the fact that a relatively large percentage of the population speaks German. There are now plans to use satellites that will make it possible to cover the whole territory of the CzSSR. Information is already being broadcast how to tune-in a television set and how to modify it in order to be able to receive foreign programmes. (Toshchenko, 1984, p.285)[3]

The propaganda material beamed to Czechoslovakia, according to a Czech political writer, exploited recent economic difficulties in that country and concentrated on the assertion that the Soviet model is not suitable for Czechoslovakia and is unworkable. Western propaganda was also alleged to assert that it is the Party who is responsible for shortages experienced in the economy. The idea of 'free enterprise' was being promoted as a condition for successful economic development. This was considered nothing else but an attempt 'to exploit the still existing influence of the overthrown bourgeoisie...strong traditions of middle-class ideology, social democracy, Masaryk ideology and nationalism'.

PROPAGANDA AND THE SOVIET ARMED FORCES

The admission by the Soviets themselves about the extent of foreign propaganda and the readiness of Soviet citizens to listen to foreign broadcasts indicates that the Soviet leadership found itself confronted with a situation in which the monopoly of information, previously in the hand of the government, was being slowly eroded. Thus every item of information that reached the population outside Soviet control was felt to be potentially damaging.

Although the findings of recent surveys were confined to limited areas of the Soviet Union, their significance lies in the possibility that if transposed on a much larger scale they might reveal negative tendencies and foreign influence in other regions of the USSR, and within various strata of Soviet society, especially in that strata on which rests the prestige of the USSR as a superpower – the armed forces of the Soviet Union.

However, it would be wrong to assume that the military leadership is as much concerned about foreign influence among army personnel as the Party is about Soviet society as a whole. Given the technological limitations in reaching the military personnel through radio, television or press, there appears little danger of ideological contamination within the armed forces. Nevertheless, there are indications that the possibility of alien influence filtering through the armed forces is on the mind of the military, and counter-propaganda is an important feature of the Soviet military doctrine. 'The Party's directive that not one soldier should be left out from constant political influence, must be strictly observed' (*KPSS o vooruzhonnykh silakh Sovetskovo Soyuza*, 1981. Moscow: Voenizdat, p.448).

In the past, the leadership appeared to be convinced that 'the moral-political and psychological characteristics of the army personnel gives the assurance of its conduct in war times. These traits being a result of deeply rooted consciousness of the socially just cause and the absolute certainty about the final victory over the enemy' (Volkogonov, 1983, p.250). But together with the firm conviction about the ideological reliability of the Soviet soldier, some doubts began to be expressed on the idealised image of the armed forces:

> [H]istorical war experience shows that in some instances even in a socialist army there exist the possibility of negative spiritual conditions...it is, therefore, of utmost importance to psychologically immunise the armed forces, in the course of military, political, and psychological training in peace time, against such influence. (Ibid., p.251)

Although the precise nature of the historical war experience – 'the negative spiritual conditions and influence' – were not made clear, it would be safe to assume that it referred to the defections of some Soviet units under General Vlasov during the Second World War, and to the past contacts between the Soviet army and

Western forces. The consequences of foreign contacts during the war and at any other times are being thoroughly investigated.

The role of the armed forces in counter-propaganda activities is mostly confined to visits of Soviet warships to foreign ports, presumably to the less developed countries, where the Soviets can demonstrate the 'high level of Soviet military technology'. But, at the same time, such visits present the opportunity for foreign propagandists. Soviet ships stopping in foreign ports are sometimes open to many visitors. Some visitors, reports one Soviet commentator, attempt to 'forget' and to leave on the ship anti-communist publications. 'This is being practised with great zeal by Zionists and members of White emigree organizations'.

As in other areas of ideological activities, the military leadership views the period of *détente* as having been exploited by the West to undermine the ideological unity of the Soviet armed forces – 'détente required additional measures to explain to the army personnel that in the ideological struggle there is no peaceful coexistence, that under détente such struggle becomes even more fierce (Epishev, 1983, p.285).

Although the Soviet approach to the role of ideological education and propaganda is identical whether it is applied to the Soviet society as a whole or to the armed forces as a section of that society, there is a different emphasis on the methods to be used in both cases, and the problems encountered are not the same either. This stems from the fact that the armed forces represent a cross-section of Soviet society with their different features and characteristics. Therefore, the Soviets cannot apply uniform propaganda methods within the armed forces but take on a 'differential approach'. This approach assumes the existence of various categories of military personnel with their different ethnic background, level of education, etc.

The theoretical basis for the differential approach to ideological indocrination is the fact that although the Soviet Union is 'a classless society', it is not a 'uniform society'. In the last decade, according to one analyst, the social structure of Soviet society underwent a deep transformation. The working class proper became far greater in numbers as did the number of city dwellers. There was also an enormous increase in the size of the intelligentsia which is now exceeding that of the peasantry. The more the class differences become diffused, the more there appear differences of another kind: inner-class, regional, demographic, and national (Toshchenko, 1984, p.49).

The existence of national differences – which, as the Soviets say, remain much longer than expected – is of particular concern for the Soviet military. Indeed, the Party devotes much attention to the 'contradictions' that have arisen in the relations of Soviet nationalities. These are caused by the peculiarities of national psychology and culture. The most obvious difference in the social structure and way of life are those between the indigenous population of Central Asian republics and the rest of the Union. These are closely linked with their socio-ethnical features, particularly in family relations. Traditionally they have more children, retain to a large extent some religious practices and express themselves in their native language (Rogovin, 1984, p.53). The Soviets seem to be most concerned with the latter aspect, for it directly affects the armed forces. While the Soviets can wage a counter-propaganda campaign of their own to counteract foreign broadcasts beamed towards Central Asia in ethnic languages of the region, they find it more difficult to be effective on the conscripts coming from those regions. The main difficulty is the low mastery of the Russian language by a substantial part of soldiers conscripted from Central Asia and other areas where Russian is not widely spoken. The teaching of Russian in national schools is considered not to be everywhere at the desired level. This makes the task of ideological education in the armed forces and the fight against all 'manifestations of remnants of nationalism and chauvinism' extremely complicated.

Another problem is the difference in the educational level of army personnel, which prevents uniformity in ideological propaganda and makes it a weak instrument of indoctrination. According to Soviet data, 50 per cent of army personnel possess secondary or higher education, and with the introduction of compulsory secondary education it is expected that all army personnel will have secondary or higher education in the near future. But the quality of ideological education in the armed forces does not always correspond to the educational and cultural level of the conscript. The Soviet source complains that ideological propaganda is being expressed in very simplistic terms and is not sufficiently sophisticated and convincing (Epishev, 1983, p.294).

The question of the standard of ideological propaganda in the armed forces was raised at the XXVI Congress of the CPSU. Attention was drawn to the shortcomings in the field of application of social sciences, especially in that sphere of military theory which is linked to the changes taking place in the social structure of Soviet society. It was pointed out that 'taking into account the rising level of education and culture, it is necessary to achieve within propaganda activities, a higher level of persuasion, argumentation and realism'.

The same source reported that social research has shown that listeners with higher education demand from the political lecturer a much deeper analysis of the presented subject than do those with only primary education. This puts additional pressure to raise the level of theoretical knowledge and the 'methodological mastery of political activists'.

The Congress directed those responsible for propaganda in the armed forces to carry out 'serious improvements in the content, forms and methods of ideological training of soldiers'. The Party has apparently embarked upon a concerted effort to overcome the serious shortcomings in the area of indoctrination through a 'mass study of Marxism–Leninism – an important factor in the development of social consciousness'. Between 1965 and 1975 the number of PhD graduates in social sciences who have obtained their degrees in military academies has increased three and a half times (*Krasnaia zvezda*, 16 October 1976). A conference of social scientists of the commanding staff of the Navy took place, in early 1981, to discuss ways of further improvement in the political and psychological training, especially on ships operating in far away regions from the USSR (Epishev, 1983, p.323).

The new Programme of the CPSU announced at the XXVII Congress also devoted significant attention to the 'struggle against bourgeois ideology'. It called for incessant action in the area of communist education which, it said, is closely linked to the 'battle against the appearance of foreign ideology and morality, against all remnants of the past in the consciousness of the people' (Pravda, 7 March 1986, p.6). It was followed by articles in the press discussing the issue of propaganda in East–West relations.

In April 1987, the Central Committee of the CPSU anounced a programme of ideological education which was aimed at reshaping the minds of the Soviet people to bring them into line with the reforms. Education courses at all enterprises would be restructured to raise the awareness of the workers about their new social and economic tasks. Consequently, universities teaching Marxism–Leninism would also be restructured. Faculties of ideological education were to be transformed into faculties of propaganda and mass-political activity. Graduates of these faculties would become professional propagandists with much authority. They would be required to possess the ability to think in a non-standard fashion and to argue effectively about communist ideals. They would also have to combat alien ideology and morality – the latter task on account of the intensified ideological confrontation between the two world systems (*Pravda,* 15 April 1987).

CONCLUSION

The apparent concern about the effectiveness of American propaganda and the danger of foreign ideological contamination suggests that the wall of isolation which the Party has built since coming to power is being slowly breached. Charles Wick, the Director of USIA, may not have been wrong in saying that 'it is not Western military power that [the USSR] fears so much as the penetration into their societies of...ideas. Lenin himself once said: ideas are more fatal than guns' (Wick 1985, p.521). One Soviet analyst indeed expressed an almost identical opinion:

> The 'Star War' between East and West will be a war of images whose main weapons are audio-visual means. They might be more effective than nuclear weapons...Incessant propaganda and psychological attacks are a special kind of aggression by imperialists. The 'Star Wars' of information is waged through communication satellites, television and radio, such as Voice of America, BBC, Radio Free Europe/Liberty. (*Pravda,* 20 April 1987)

The long-term effect of the direct access to the Soviet population by means of radio broadcasts and communication satellite television transmissions are difficult to predict, and its immediate effects on the political views of those who are interested to listen cannot be determined. What can be stated with some degree of certainty is that the intense counter-propaganda campaign being waged by the Soviets may be in response to a real or imaginary danger of ideological contamination as perceived by the Kremlin. Ironically, this makes the Soviets look much more realistically at the viability of the traditional approach to questions of ideology, not only in the context of foreign propaganda influence upon the mood and consciousness of the people, but from the point of view of internal problems linked to the economic situation. The real issue confronting the leadership is the state of the Soviet economy and its effect on the Soviet people – an issue examined in earlier chapters of this study. While formerly Soviet domestic policies, as a function of centralised planning, did not take into account the social and political consequences of the economic situation, there appears to emerge a growing trend in Soviet political literature to investigate the factors which may influence the mood and attitudes of the population. Contrary to the widely shared view in the West that Soviet public opinion has little political significance for the regime, the evidence presented in this chapter suggests that this may no longer be so.

A new trend in Soviet propaganda can also be detected in the way the Soviets address themselves to Western public opinion. Gone are the days when Soviet broadcasts to the West were full of stereotype phrases and slogans. News and commentaries are being presented in a fashion not much different from Voice of America or the British news services. A much greater number of Soviet diplomats and representatives of Soviet agencies abroad are quite fluent in English.

Since Mikhail Gorbachev came to power the role of propaganda has become even more predominant as the new leader attempts to introduce drastic changes in the economic order of the country. This time, as on previous occasions, the whole state and Party apparatus of propaganda has been set in motion for the purpose of reorienting people's thinking in the direction of the new policies adopted by the Kremlin. In this respect the new policy of *glasnost* did not mean freedom to express opinions that are contrary to the ideological line now being promoted. According to Gorbachev, openness is limited to publicity of the new rules and 'should not be used to undermine socialism'. Spontaneity in forwarding new ideas is still forbidden within the functioning of the Soviet system.

Whether the more realistic approach to economic and social problems by the new leader will bear fruit in the form of higher productivity, is too early to judge. The history of the USSR is not really a guide for drawing definite conclusions, for what we see today cannot be compared with anything that happened in the Soviet Union in the past. What we ought to do is to attempt an analysis of the changes taking place within the USSR in the context of what we know about the operation of the system and the state of Soviet society. Such analysis should allow us to determine, at least, whether the new policies are a revolutionary change or a continuation of earlier trends. The next chapter will be devoted to such an attempt.

10 Perestroika and Glasnost 1985–1987

Following Mikhail Gorbachev's succession to power in March 1985 after Chernenko's death, speculations began to circulate among Western observers as to the likely direction of the Soviet Union under the new leader. As with previous changes in the Soviet leadership, widely differing opinions were offered in the West, each commentator attempting to unravel the intricacies of the Soviet political system and at the same time trying to predict how the new leader would tackle the economic problems that have accumulated since Brezhnev and his successors. Initially, Western analysts saw the new leader in the same light as they saw Yuri Andropov when he won the top job in the Kremlin. After Gorbachev made his inaugural speech, most Western observers agreed that his priority would be a drastic transformation of the Soviet economy – an almost identical assessment made about Andropov when he became leader. Zbigniew Brzezinski, Jimmy Carter's National Security Council chief predicted at the time that Andropov would try to reform the Soviet economic system, not through drastic decentralisation but by an effort to stimulate technological innovations and improvements in efficiency. Although Andropov did not launch an attack on central planning, he made a few attempts to decentralise economic decisions by legislating workers participation in factory management. His rule was all too brief to make an impact on the Soviet economy, but it was during his term of office that Soviet economists and social scientists quite openly discussed the best way to overcome economic stagnation. The debate continued with undiminished vigour during Chernenko's leadership and there were reports in the Soviet press about economic experiments in a number of designated enterprises. (We have referred in the preceding chapters to some of the ideas discussed and the experiments performed during that time). As for Gorbachev, there were serious doubts in the West about the possibility of even modest reforms of the Soviet bureaucratic machine. In the words of one Western political scientist, 'there was no feeling the reforms are ever likely to be applied on a countrywide scale'. Other experts cautioned, however, against underestimating the capacity of the Soviet system to modernise when the power of the Party is perceived to be at stake.

More than two years have passed since the last change in the Soviet leadership, and if at the early stage of Gorbachev's rule questions were being asked as to the direction in Soviet policies, it was becoming increasingly clear that the Soviets were adopting drastic measures which, they believed, would enable them to solve the difficulties facing the Soviet economy. In the context of the tentative conclusions reached in the preceding chapters, we shall now attempt an examination of what has occurred so far in the USSR and the ramifications of those changes for Soviet domestic and foreign policies.

For those who have followed events in the USSR for the last decade or so, and especially the internal debate about economic problems and their suggested solutions, the publication of the new policies could not have come as a surprise. While it is generally assumed that the reforms introduced since Gorbachev came to power are an expression of his personality and political make-up, there is evidence to suggest that the new direction in Soviet domestic and foreign policies is simply the result of various trends in Soviet economic thought and experiments that have been tried for a number of years. Within the context of this proposition, Gorbachev can only be seen as attempting to put into practice ideas promoted by a number of Soviet economic and social scientists. This would be nothing else but the embodiment of a pragmatic approach adopted by the Party leadership in response to the adverse, from its point of view, trends within Soviet society (issues examined in the earlier chapters of this book).

Well before Gorbachev took office, there were many who began to question whether the development of the Soviet Union followed the theoretical Marxist path and advocated drastic steps to remedy the economic situation. E. A. Ambartsumov, in an article published in April 1984 (*Voprosy Istorii*, no.4), quite openly admitted that the socialist revolution and the subsequent attempts at social transformation of society had not succeeded. Economic difficulties had brought about a degree of general dissatisfaction, and this in turn had put serious obstacles in the way of their solution. He made a comparison with the situation as it existed in the early twenties and by insinuation suggested a solution similar to that of NEP under Lenin.

As soon as the successor to Chernenko was publicly announced, it became clear that the party leadership had embarked upon drastic changes in domestic policies and designated Mikhail Gorbachev as the member of the Politburo most likely to make a genuine attempt at reforming the economy. There are sound reasons to believe that the election of Gorbachev's predecessor, Chernenko, was only a stop-gap measure while the leadership debated the reforms that were considered necessary to improve the operation of the Soviet economy. For simultaneously with the announcement of the election of the new leader, came the appeal to the Soviet people which, among other things, spoke about 'intensive work being done in anticipation of the forthcoming XXVII Party Congress and the preparation of a new Programme of the Party' (it was at this Congress that the details of the restructuring of the economy were made public).

A *Pravda* editorial published the next day quoted extensively a speech by Gorbachev to the Plenary Meeting that elected him as the new leader, in which he disclosed the strategy of the Party for the speeding up of the socio-economic development of the USSR and the improvement in the life of Soviet society in all its aspects. The main lines in the new strategy included 'the restructuring of the technological base of production, improvements in the system of social relationships, above all economic, as well as the development of the [Soviet] man himself, improvement in his material conditions of work and life'. It was to be attained through a higher degree of independence and responsibility of Soviet enterprises, as well as through further 'development of democracy' in the whole system of socialist self-government and through widening of openness (*glasnost*) in the activities of Party, government and public organizations. 'The more people are informed, the more consciously they will act, the more actively they will support the Party, her programme and objectives' (*Pravda*, 13 March 1985). In retrospect it can be seen that Gorbachev's speech contained broad outlines of the new policies and reforms introduced later as well as the basic concepts on which the reforms were based – *perestroika* and *glasnost*.

In his report to the April 1985 Plenary Meeting of the CPSU, Gorbachev spelled out in more detail a plan of the proposed reforms. The main thrust of the changes was to be in the substantial improvement of management and of the economic mechanism as a whole. While Gorbachev was still insisting on the principle of centralisation, he gave a clear indication that the restructuring of the economic mechanism will necessarily require the broadening of the rights of the enterprises to act more independently by going over to the cost-accounting system. At this stage, Gorbachev did not specify the practical application of the cost-accountancy principle and the scope of managerial responsibility for its enforcement.[1]

There can be little doubt that at the time final touches of the new methods of management were still in the process of being worked out. They were most certainly based on the experiments performed in some enterprises. In the words of Gorbachev: 'It would seem that the results of the large-scale experiments carried out along this line are not bad. But a stage has been reached when we should go over from experiments to setting up an integral system of economic management' (*Pravda*, 26 February 1986) – a clear pointer that the reforms were seriously considered well before Gorbachev's rule.

He also hinted that effective measures are being worked out to 'eliminate from the distribution mechanism the practice of levelling, and of unearned incomes'. The first was designed to make income dependent on results, the second to combat the 'black' market. Finally, Gorbachev introduced the concept of *glasnost* which he defined as a necessity for the Party Committees to ensure publicity, see to it that the channels of communication with the masses are working, and that attention is being given to public opinion. 'It is important', said Gorbachev, 'that the Soviet people should feel a change for the better as soon as possible'. Above all, he emphasised the importance of labour productivity as the most vital factor of economic growth.

Between the April 1985 Plenary Meeting and the XXVII Congress of the CPSU in February–March 1986, the whole Party apparatus of propaganda was put into motion in order to explain to the population the new course in Party policies. Articles in which Soviet economic and political analysts attempted a theoretical justification of the new policies appeared almost daily. There was also a flood of letters from individuals who either expressed full support for the Party or serious complaints in many areas of economic and social activities or enterprises. This was to be the concrete expression of *glasnost*.

The XXVII Congress formally approved the decisions taken by the intermediate Plenary Meetings and put forward proposals for a number of concrete reforms, which, when transformed into law, would enable the country to embark upon a concerted effort to improve the economy. The Congress declared that the main objective of the reforms was to make the system more efficient in order to raise productivity. At this stage the emphasis was still on reinforcing the role of the Gosplan, in the realisation of the objectives of the economic strategy through better planning (*Pravda,* 23 March 1986). The basic instrument of this strategy was to be a genuine self-accounting method, recoupment and self-financing whereby the level of earnings would be in direct relation to the effectiveness of the operation of a given enterprise and the quality of its production. An important feature of the reforms was also the improvement in the pricing system – an issue widely discussed in the USSR for a number of years.

In its final resolution the Congress underlined the necessity for a change in the ideological–theoretical approach to economic problems. It recommended a drastic change in the ideological education, particularly an end to the underestimation of the role of product–money relationship, economic interests and profits. It recognised that for the reforms to be successful material incentives were most needed as well as business ability.

Following the XXVII Congress, the Central Committee of the CPSU appeared to be in permanent session. Its deliberations were reported almost daily and decisions about various aspects of the country's economic life were adopted. Once a resolution had been adopted, one could almost detect an assumption that the objective of the new measures would be achieved and were spoken of in these terms. Shortly afterwards a formal law would be proclaimed that would put the Resolution of the Central Committee into force.

In May 1986, the Central Committee and the Council of Ministers considered new guidelines for the light industry. The adopted decision 'about the improvement in planning, economic stimulation and improvements in the administration of enterprises in the light industry producing consumer goods', presented a much more detailed outline of the proposed reforms and constituted a blueprint for the Law of State Enterprises (Associations), officially proclaimed in July 1987.

The most important reform was in the area of planning and control of the activities of enterprises. The practice of minute scrutiny by planning authorities of the production processes was to be amended so as to allow greater decision-making authority for the enterprise. Consequently, there will be a drastic reduction in the number of directives issued by the central planning authorities. It will be left for the enterprise itself to submit its own plan of production, including the assortment of goods and their quality. The volume of goods to be supplied will be determined by the enterprise, taking into account the sale of similar goods through wholesale markets as well as orders received from trading organisations – an indication of the increased importance assigned to market forces. In this respect, a significant change is to take place in the sphere of links between enterprises. There will be increased emphasis on horizontal links (an issue discussed in Chapter 8) between related enterprises and trade organisations. Such links will be formalised by agreements to remain in force for a number of years.

One significant aspect of the proposed reforms, that of price formation, did not indicate a marked change from previous practices. As we have pointed out earlier, the question of price formation within a command economy has been a subject of much debate in the Soviet Union for a number of years. But of all the reforms introduced so far price formation remained basically unchanged. Since cost-accounting involved in the first place the principle of profit-making, it would have been impossible to leave price determination entirely to the enterprise. For under conditions of goods shortages it would have resulted in substantial price increases to compensate for any losses or to show bigger profits. Such a possibility was clearly foreseen and it was decided that prices should still be under the control and determination of central planning authorities.

Another radical reform, which on the surface appears to be a return to private enterprise reminiscent of NEP, was the Law of Individual Labour. It provided a legal framework for some productive activities widely practised within an underground economy. Although the law was proclaimed in November 1986, it should be viewed in conjunction with a resolution adopted by the Central Committee and the decree by the Supreme Soviet made public on 18 May, regarding the fight against corruption and other illegal activities of not only ordinary citizens but some in high positions. While the facts of gross corruption and punishment meted out to those caught were publicised in the Soviet press for quite some time, it was only in May 1986 that this issue has become the subject of close scrutiny. On 28 May 1986, *Pravda* reported that the Central Committee of the CPSU considered 'measures for the strengthening of the fight against unearned incomes'. This time the scope and nature of unearned income was defined as income derived from 'embezzlemnt, speculation, bribery and other illegal activities'.

At the same time, stricter control was to be imposed over the usage of raw materials and fuel by way of special documentation. These measures were to be supervised by the Ministry of Finance and the Central Statistical Office. Other measures for combating corruption were in the area of private incomes and assets. Citizens concluding deals in amounts of over 10 000 rubles or building a house (*dacha*) of a value exceeding 20 000 rubles, will be obliged to furnish a declaration about the sources of their financial means. Simultaneously with the above decisions by the Central Committee, a decree was proclaimed by the Supreme Soviet of the USSR which provided for severe penalties ranging from fines to imprisonment and, in extreme cases, capital punishment for illegal commercial activities.

In contrast with earlier disclosures on that subject, the Central Committee openly declared that a close connection exists between the phenomenon of corruption and shortages of goods and services. It proposed a study of the causes of shortages of some goods and services and of restrictive practices such as the refusal to provide accommodation in hotels and speculations in the sale of transport tickets. As for the elimination of such practices, it was proposed to reinforce the system of control over incomes and the application of the principle of compensation for losses sustained by the state by imposing fines in multiples of the loss. The fight against corruption is to be fought in the social sphere as well. The Ministry of Culture, in conjunction with its affiliated organisations – cinema, theatres, literary associations – is to concentrate its efforts on producing artistic works, films and plays that would highlight and promote high morality, and respect for work and honesty among the Soviet people. But the main task was to 'devote constant attention to profound study of conditions that favour the committing of such crimes'. In this respect, the production of goods and services and the elimination of shortages were of prime importance. They were to be alleviated through individual work activities – subject to a special law proclaimed some months later. Regarding food production, it was proposed to consider the removal of some restrictions on the number and kind of domestic animals that a private plot holder may possess.

Only a few months later, the project of a new law on Individual Labour was published in the press (*Pravda*, 20–21 November 1986). In a speech to the Soviet Parliament, the President of the State Committee for Labour and Social Affairs, Gladkov, introduced a project for the above law. Referring to Gorbachev's speech of June 1986, in which he said that the solution to the problem of shortages lay in the search for new forms of assistance for individual work activities, Gladkov suggested that the success of overcoming these difficulties depended on the ability to come up with new non-standard approaches and decisions. The new law was meant to be just that.

Although Article 17 of the Soviet Constitution clearly 'permits individual labour in handicraft, farming, the provision of services for the public, and other forms of activity based exclusively on the personal work of individual citizens and members of their families', it has not been applied in practice. At this stage it was estimated that about 100 000 individuals were involved in these activities, but Soviet research in this area revealed that their number was far greater. This situation – said Gladkov – created favourable conditions for some parts of the population to obtain unearned incomes and also for the emergence of private property trends alien to the Soviet system. The primary purpose of the proposed law was to legalise these activities and to define their scope and limitations. He added that benefit was derived from the experience of 'fraternal countries' in the preparation of the Law. All the work involved in putting the law into practice was to be conducted under widest publicity (*glasnost*). However, he emphasised, 'all these measures did not signify a return to any sort of private enterprise activities, therefore the suppositions and assumptions on this account by some bourgeois analysts were absolutely without foundation'.

The Law was to come into force on 1 May 1987. It defined in some details the kind of individual activities that would be allowed, and the legal obligations of those who would pursue them. The field of individual labour activities was rather wide and included not only production of goods but the provision of services as well. All incomes derived from individual work would be subject to taxation but assistance in the form of finance and the supply of raw material would be provided when appropriate.

A cynical view of this law would be to consider it as a measure whose objective was to bring the underground economy under state control. A more charitable view would be to see it as no more than an attempt to tap the hidden reserves in the economy in order to supplement the existing supplies. We have mentioned earlier the discussions on that subject among Soviet economists and suggestions by some of them to legalise such practices. Since both opinions are not mutually exclusive, one would also be justified to adopt the view that the law is nothing else but an expression of an economic realism that has become a feature of Soviet thinking over a number of years.

Simultaneously with the succession of disclosures about proposed reforms, the Soviet press began to publish articles by Soviet economic and ideological writers in which they analysed the new situation and suggested new approaches that would conform with the new Party line. One article in a Party publication (*Kommunist*, no.5, March 1987, pp.30–9) contained an admission that Soviet economic science often oriented itself on ideological principles that were in direct contradiction with the real needs for the development of Soviet society. Some of these principles were linked to a tendency for running forward and had a utopian character (ibid., p.36). This was reflected in the way certain subjects were taught – economic theory was totally isolated from real economic problems.

Some comments in the press became quite bold and outspoken. An editorial published in *Kommunist* (No.4, 1987 pp.3–20) referred to the January 1987 Plenary Meeting of the Central Committee during which the causes of the present economic situation were analysed. Such analysis revealed that the domination of a dogmatic approach to the theory of economic development constituted a breaking mechanism on the socio-economic progress. As a result 'our opponents were eagerly saying things about which we chose to remain silent. Furthermore, the attempt to keep silent about negative trends in the USSR, undermined the faith of the people in what the Party had to say' (ibid., p.6). For a Western observer this may appear as a radical turnaround in Soviet practices but it would be difficult to draw a conclusion that the Soviets were heading toward a sort of Western-style democracy. Whenever a Soviet commentator steps into a kind of analysis that might be interpreted as a turn towards a Western-style democracy, he would invariably add a qualification refuting such speculations.

> Foreign observers increasingly ask the question 'how they would like to see the Soviet Union in 20 or 30 years time?' Some of them put their hope on 'liberalisation', on a change in the Soviet system that would lead to the destabilisation of the Soviet

society. But Western analysts must see that the programme of democratisation in the USSR does not foresee the creation of a bourgeois democracy of a Western kind. (*Kommunist*, no.4, 1987, p.19)

The January 1987 Plenary Meeting of the Central Committee considered the suggestion to conduct multicandidate elections. Gorbachev expressed the view that this would allow each citizen to express his choice within a far wider circle of candidates. Such a method would be a better indicator for the Party and the Government of the 'mood and the will of the population'. He even foresaw the possibility of secret ballots but was quick to point out that the principle of democratic centralism must be preserved at all times.

Another feature of *glasnost* was the publication of economic results at quarterly intervals which began almost immediately after Gorbachev came to power. The scope of the statistical information and the critical comments that they contained, indicate that the preparation for their publication took place prior to the public announcement of the new policy. The task of compiling the data at quarterly intervals must have put considerable pressure on the resources of the Central Statistical Office, and it would be fair to assume that the number of the personnel engaged in this task must have been considerably increased in good time. References to the growing importance of statistics were made quite often before their frequent publication began. These were usually contained in calls for the reorganisation of statistics, for a widening of the area of published data and qualitative improvement in their presention, 'to increase their reliability. To wage a struggle against eyewash and upward distortions'. In this respect a vast improvement can indeed be observed.

The report on the performance of the Soviet economy for the first quarter of 1987 (*Pravda*, 24 April 1987), for example, points to some very serious shortcomings. At the end of February selective surveys indicated that in a number of enterprises and production units of the Ministry of Machine-building industry, some 40 per cent of industrial robots installed the previous year did not operate. The percentage of idle robots in the agricultural machinery industry and that of the electrical industry was 33 and 24 per cent respectively. Despite the introduction of the rules of cost-accounting and self-financing, a number of enterprises did not fulfil the plan for profits and allowed the cost of production to rise.

There were also many instances of violation of contractual obligations on delivery time. Output in most enterprises of the above mentioned industries actually fell in comparison with the corresponding period of the previous year. In only a few selected enterprises of the machine-building industry and in those producing non-food goods has the plan been fulfilled. By contrast, agriculture showed an increase in output of 8.7 per cent relative to the previous year and productivity in this sector grew by 9.5 per cent.

Although the purpose of collecting statistical data, according to the Soviet Statistical Office, was to serve the needs of Soviet planning authorities, its frequent publications in the daily press was clearly directed to the public at large and to managers of enterprises in particular. A significant feature of these reports was the tendency to show the shortcomings in industrial production rather than achievements. This can be interpreted in the context of *glasnost*, of publicising the true situation rather than its idealisation. It also points, once more, to the new direction in Soviet domestic policies based on realism and pragmatism.

A final step in the series of reforms that have been introduced since Gorbachev came to power was the Law of State Enterprises (Associations), announced on 30 June 1987. It contained precise guidelines for the restructuring of the economy. There was to be a radical change in planning, price fixing mechanism, finance and credit management, a changeover in the sale of means of production to wholesale trade, and in foreign trade links (we shall devote special attention to the latter aspect in the final part of this chapter).

The Law defined in much detail the new relationship between government planning authorities and enterprises, on the one hand, and between enterprises themselves. It drastically reduced excessive central planning and provided more freedom for the enterprises to fix independently their five-yearly as well as yearly plans. However, planning is still to remain the basic instrument of government economic policies. For while in principle an enterprise will be free to determine the kind of goods it proposes to produce and the volume of production according to demand and direct orders from other enterprises, it will have to consider in its planning the social necessities of society and orders placed by government authorities. 'Government orders will guarantee the satisfaction of the basic necessities as well as the supply of certain goods essential for the strengthening of national defence and for securing of economic independence' (*Izvestia*, 1 July 1987). The independence of the enterprise will also be reflected in the self-financing which will eliminate government budget financing of an enterprise, except in some basic and very large undertakings. The use of existing assets will be subject to payment to the government and the provision of finance will be subject to interest charges.

The question of horizontal links between enterprises, which has been the subject of some considerable discussions for a number of years, was finally resolved within the various reforms included in the Law. Enterprises will be free to enter into direct negotiations and conclude agreements on delivery time, price and other conditions. The supply of machinery and equipment will no longer be subject to planning but through wholesale trade in means of production. In practice it would mean that machinery and equipment will be available through a free choice of sources of supply among different producers and wholesalers. This will also contribute to the development of individual production activities as it will enable an individual to obtain the supply of some equipment from state wholesale outlets. The wholesale trade in means of production will be introduced gradually over a period of four to five years.

One other aspect of the reforms, that of price fixing, was also incorporated into the Law. It determined the limit of the autonomy of the enterprise to fix independently the prices for its products. Generally, prices will be subject to strict government control and the administration of state price fixing will determine the procedures for establishing contract prices and will supervise its application. Enterprises will be obliged to be guided by the centrally fixed prices and those determined by Ministries and its branches. But it will have the right to apply prices according to a contract entered into with a buyer of technical equipment produced according to special specifications for a new item. The Law provided for the possibility of widening in due course the area of free price determination.

At a first glance, it can be seen that the objective of the reforms incorporated in the new Law was to make the operation of the economy more efficient by allowing more independence for the management of enterprises, while at the same time maintaining strict control by the state apparatus. But while the reforms are based on the 'analysis of the situation that emerged during the 1970–1980s and on the various past economic experiments', the outcome of this gigantic experiment seems to be uncertain even for the Soviets and will no doubt require some adjustment. In the words of the Soviet economist G. Popov:

> [T]he difficulties in restructuring the economy are due to the fact that we do not possess sufficient knowledge about practical steps needed to put into practice the strategies outlined at the XXVII Congress. We do recognise the obstacles but it is not yet clear to us how to overcome them. (*Pravda*, 20 January 1987)

Such uncertainty also exists in the area of price fixing. Since profit or income will be the general indicator of the operation of an enterprise, it will be practically unavoidable for the enterprise to fix prices at a level that will secure its profitable operation. The Law foresees such eventuality and this is probably the reason for the retention of central price determination and control. In the long run, however, the Law assumes that the restructuring of the economy will eliminate the shortages of goods and services and economic competition rather than socialist competition will determine the natural price level. 'This will be used as a means against monopoly and the dictatorship of the enterprise over the consumer'. Furthermore, unjustified profits accrued to an enterprise as a result of violation of 'state discipline' will be excluded from the reported result of its operation.

On the other hand, an enterprise that shows constant losses could be declared insolvent by the bank that provides credits and may inform all suppliers about this fact. The creditors, in their turn, may stop the supply of goods and services. On the basis of incurred losses or a lack of demand for its products, an enterprise can be closed down. It is interesting to note that for the first time in Soviet history a kind of unemployment benefit will be available for those who might lose their job as a result of the closure. They will receive their average income for three months.

So far we have examined the reforms that determine the operation of the domestic economy. We shall now turn to those economic activities over which the Soviets have only partial control – that of foreign trade. It is in the area of international trade relations that a certain ambiguity seems to exist and Soviet policies are not so clearly defined. Over the years, the subject of foreign trade has been debated within the context of comparative advantage and most Soviet economists agreed that foreign trade would be beneficial for the USSR, in that it would supplement the supply of goods to the Soviet domestic market and provide access to Western technology. But as we have pointed out earlier, Soviet foreign trade is subject to the availability of hard currency for the purchase of foreign goods which necessarily limits the scope of trade. In addition, the fear of dependence on the West is still a powerful factor limiting trade activities. It is probably for this reason that sometimes views expressed by the leadership are in direct conflict with the changes introduced in Soviet foreign trade regulations.

Mikhail Gorbachev, in an interview with the Western press, stated that having won technological independence after the Revolution, the USSR has long been enjoying the status of a great scientific and technological power. This has enabled the Soviet Union to acquire a reliable defence potential. The Soviet Union is counting on accelerating scientific and technological progress not through a 'transfer of technology' from the United States to the USSR, but through 'transfusion' of discoveries and innovations from Soviet science to Soviet industry and agriculture. 'The USSR will survive', he added, 'because it has a first class science of its own and because the United States is far from having a monopoly on scientific and technological achievements' (*Time*, 9 September 1985, p.13).

This statement by Gorbachev, as indeed by others, confirms the conclusion reached earlier that full economic and technological independence of the USSR still remains a long-range goal. Yet the restructuring of the Soviet economy that is to be based primarily on the introduction of modern technology, requires Western know-how.

As a first apparent step in developing foreign trade, Moscow announced in September 1986 the breaking up of the monopoly held by the Ministry of Foreign Trade in conducting foreign trade activities. From 1 January 1987, a number of Ministries and enterprises would have the right to enter foreign markets and to establish direct links with foreign partners. The details of new regulations were to be incorporated in a Law to be proclaimed at a later date

Another solution to the conflicting objectives of technological self-sufficiency and foreign trade relations appears to be the decree 'On the order of creating on the territory of the USSR of enterprises with the joint participation of Soviet organisations and firms of capitalist and developing countries' proclaimed by the Presidium of the Supreme Soviet on 13 January 1987. It was directed toward further development of trade, economic, scientific and technological cooperation with capitalist and developing countries, and covered the activities of joint enterprises on the territory of the USSR. The funds for the joint enterprise would consist of buildings, equipment or other assets, and intangibles such as property rights, inventions and know-how, as well as funds in convertible currency, but the share of the Soviet participant in a joint enterprise must not be less than 51 per cent. A joint enterprise will have the full freedom of production activities and will not be subject to directives by Soviet planning authorities. Finally, foreign assets will be guaranteed against requisition or confiscation through administrative orders.

In a later comment, Gorbachev clarified somewhat his views on foreign trade as a source of acquisiton of technology. While he supported the purchase of Western know-how, he qualified his support by stating that in the past imports of technology were often excessive and that purchases of equipment and many other goods from capitalist countries were not always justified – a reference to the difficulties experienced by Soviet enterprises in absorbing imported Western technology. One could safely assume that the joint enterprises decree has as its objective to obtain practical assistance from Western specialists in the absorption of technology, and where possible to build new plants in conjuction with foreign managerial personnel. The motive behind this last move is to make the acquisiton and absorption of new technology more efficient.

Our survey of the main reforms introduced in the USSR since *glasnost* and *perestroika* were launched, clearly indicates an acute awareness by the Soviet leadership of the poor state of the Soviet economy and a definite trend towards economic realism. However, a fundamental question that many observers ask is whether these reforms herald a new Soviet era or are just a temporary situation which, like NEP and other periods of domestic relaxation, will in due course revert to a more strict regime. The answer to this question depends obviously on the outcome of the new policies but predictions in this field would be purely speculative and would not serve any practical purpose. More relevant is to analyse the situation from a Soviet perspective rather than apply Western criteria. *Glasnost*, for example, which was proclaimed by the Soviet leadership as democratisation of Soviet society, can be seen as a means to achieve the main objective of the reforms – that of economic efficiency. It is only if we look at the changes taking place within the USSR from a Soviet perspective that we can grasp the implications of these changes for East–West relations; whether a unique opportunity presents itself for integrating the Soviets into the world economy as a condition for lessening the intensity of the superpower conflict. We shall elaborate on this point in the concluding chapter of the book.

11 Neither War nor Peace

In the introductory chapter we have made a brief survey of the contrasting positions from which the Soviet Union and the United States view the ongoing conflict between them, as well as of their mutual perception of their rival intentions based on an assessment of the respective military and strategic forces. We have adopted the assumption that while an element of uncertainty about the effective use of military power as an instrument of foreign policy exists, the deterrent factor is still operative. No attempt has been made to assess the actual balance of military and strategic forces of the two adversaries; this area of study being beyond the scope of the book. The prime task, to which reference was made in the introductory notes, was to develop a better understanding of the USSR as a political and economic entity totally different from the Western system of government and the implications of these differences for East–West relations.

We have argued that the arms race in its military aspect is only one facet of the conflict between the superpowers, that while the arms race continues it has other than military implications. This is the economic aspect which in turn involves a number of issues, especially those perceived by the Soviet Union as being linked to its military power and internal policies. We have also expressed the view that the Soviet approach to the question of war appears to be a function of Russian history and tradition, of what we have subsequently defined as Russian ideology on the one hand, and of a large degree of pragmatism, that is, of an increasingly realistic attitude to military, economic and social issues on the other. But the study would not be complete and would remain merely a subject of academic interest only unless it drew some conclusions about the implications of the Soviet views on the arms race, and looked at them in the context of the objectives which the study contained in the book has set out to attain.

Although our main objective was to obtain a better understanding of Soviet behaviour through an investigation into the Soviet mode of thinking and into the functioning of the Soviet system, this would also be relevant within the context of the United States' strategic and political objectives directed towards the use of the arms race in all its aspects as an instrument of foreign policy. We shall, therefore, turn first to the question of the nature and effectiveness of American strategies.

AMERICAN FOREIGN POLICY; ITS OBJECTIVE AND STRATEGY

Looking at the superpower relationship throughout the post Second World War period one could characterise it as mainly one of conflict. A common thread that passes through all presidencies and their foreign policy objectives is the desire to contain communism. This was to be pursued in defence of Western values and freedom. At the same time, each president since the end of the Second World War has expressed a willingness to cooperate with the Soviet Union provided that it conforms to certain rules of international behaviour. President Reagan was no exception and he announced shortly before his inauguration: 'the Soviet Empire should know that there will be no further concessions from the United States unless there is a concession in return'. This was to be known as linkage, whereby American agreement to conduct negotiations on arms control and other issues would be dependent upon acceptable Soviet behaviour in the Third World and elsewhere (Caldwell, 1985, pp.6–7), including the area of human rights within the USSR. More recently, prior to his meeting with Gorbachev in Reykjavik, the US President restated his attitude towards the Soviets in these words: 'the ultimate goal of American foreign policy is not just the prevention of war but the extention of freedom – to see that every nation...enjoy the blessing of freedom'.

Shortly after taking office, President Reagan initiated a hard line policy in relation to the USSR, which he subsequently defined as an 'evil Empire'. This led to a further deterioration of superpower relations. The proclaimed objective of Reagan's policy was to create a situation where the United States could negotiate with the Soviets from a position of strength and it was to be accomplished through an intensive programme of rearmament.

A number of political thinkers interviewed in 1985, prior to the Geneva Summit, offered a variety of views on what ought to be the 'ultimate objectives of American policy in the conflict with the Soviet Union'. These ranged from a modest objective of achieving a balance of power and persuading the Soviets to accept the rules indispensable for its retention, the limitation of Soviet encroachment, the prevention of the takeover of world civilisation by Marxist–Leninist ideology, to the more extreme ones such as 'the dissolution of the Soviet external empire...the subsequent withdrawal of Soviet military forces to the boundaries of the Soviet Union, and the long-range objective to frustrate the permanence of the Soviet system in order to alter its world outlook (Beyond Containment, 1985, p.19),...to change the nature of the Soviet system'. According to Richard Pipes: 'what we want is to induce changes in the Communist system, for it is the system, as presently constituted, that causes aggression' (ibid., p.36).

It is interesting to notice that all the leading political thinkers who were interviewed – liberals and conservatives, Democrats and Republicans - were in agreement that a major war between the United States and the Soviet Union is most unlikely. This would indicate that a military option to achieve the above objectives did not enter into consideration and confirms the view expressed earlier that deterrent is still operative. However, one idea that appeared common to most of the political analysts was to exploit vulnerabilities in the Soviet Union: 'it is an important but usually neglected dimension of American foreign policy...American strategy has to focus upon Soviet weaknesses' (ibid., p.20–1). This did not refer to a military weakness but to internal problems that exist within the USSR.

One area of vulnerability to be exploited was the economic situation of the USSR. Some within the Administration expressed the belief that the United States could literally drive the Soviet Union into the ground in an all-out economic and military competition. One of the strongest proponents of the economic option is Richard Pipes, who believes that economic sanctions against the Soviet Union would force Soviet leaders to reform its economic system (Caldwell, 1985, p.8). Other radical thinkers were opposed to all trade and to all aid to the Soviet bloc, including the supply of grain. Most important, the Soviets should be denied any access to Western technology; this is the area which 'requires maximum control and utmost vigilance' (Beyond Containment,p.23).

According to Richard Allen, former National Security adviser to President Reagan, the United States should constantly work towards making Eastern European nations unreliable allies of the USSR. It should also exploit the demographic trends within the Soviet Union whereby national minorities are growing at a faster rate than Russians. The resistance of these groups against the attempt by the Soviet leaders to eradicate their cultural and linguistic inheritance would be an important and fertile ground for American policy. Generally, it was suggested, everything possible should be done to encourage the forces against socialism in the Eastern European countries, to make things difficult for the Soviets in ruling and controlling their empire – and especially to raise questions in the Soviet mind about the reliability of the Eastern European armies in the event of a war.

Broadcasts to the Soviet Union should help to increase awareness among non-Russian nationalities of their situation. Free movement of ideas should be encouraged through a greater use of America's most advanced technologies in broadcasting to the peoples of the USSR. Secretary of State Shultz, in an address to the United Nations General Assembly in September 1985, criticised 'those political systems that try to stand in the way of the free flow of knowledge and information...the communication revolution will be a truly liberating revolution, for it threatens the monopoly of information and thought upon which tyrants rely for absolute control' (Shultz, 1985, p.11) – a clear reference to the Soviet Union and American foreign policy.

To summarise our brief survey of opinions, we can say that while the main goal of the United States in relation to the Soviet Union appears to be a change in the latter's international conduct, there are three major options open to American policy-makers. The first one, linked directly to the arms race, is the attainment of a military posture which will allow the United States to negotiate from a position of strength. The second option is the economic one; an attempt to affect the Soviet Union economically either by forcing it to continue an arms race 'which it cannot afford', or through other means of economic pressure. Finally, there is the ideological warfare option through a propaganda campaign which, it is hoped, will reach the population of the USSR and influence public opinion to the point of destabilisation of the Soviet regime.

The analysis of the military, economic and ideological aspects of the arms race, as perceived by the Soviets, is an indication of their approach to matters of national security in their totality. The survey of the various issues connected with the arms race and of the perspective from which the Soviets view the conflict is, therefore, essential if we are to have a better understanding of the Soviets. But since the core of international tension is largely the relation between the superpowers – a fact we have emphasised earlier – we must analyse Soviet perceptions of the international situation and their reactions within the context of American foreign policy and American strategies. We shall now turn to the question of the effectiveness of American strategies and at the way the Soviets are meeting what they perceive as the American offensive. It is in the Soviet response to American strategies that we can detect the basic reasons and underlying motives of Soviet behaviour. An examination of their responses and of the roots and sources of Soviet thinking might also lead to a better understanding of the Soviets.

SOVIET RESPONSES

The military–strategic challenge has been met, so far, through an effort by the Soviet Union to equal or to exceed the United States' armament programme – consequently, it is generally assumed that the balance of terror still exists. On this crucial point Soviet military thinking, as expressed in the military doctrine, does not leave any doubts that regardless of any costs and economic sacrifices, the buildup of Soviet military power will continue. The former Soviet Minister for Defence, S. L. Sokolov, expressed the Soviet position in this respect by saying that

> since the United States have not given up their long-standing and unrealisable goal of military superiority, it is necessary to state clearly that not one threatening challenge will remain without due response...Today the Soviet Union has the ability to resolve any scientific or technological problem so as not to allow the United States to achieve military superiority either on earth or in outer space. (*Pravda*, 23 February 1986)

The increase in the 1985 defence budget from 17 to 19 billion rubles (up about 12 per cent), and a further increase in 1987 to 20.2 billion rubles, appears to be another pointer to the Soviet determination to pursue the arms race regardless of costs.

The assumption that the United States may be able under certain circumstances to negotiate with the Soviets and impose political concessions in favour of the US, also runs counter to the historically rooted traditions to which we have referred in the beginning of this book. One important factor influencing Soviet thinking, which was examined in Chapter 2, is the traditional Russian militarism rooted in her past. The reliance on massive military power as an expression of national aspirations is still relevant at the present time, as it was all through most of Russia's history. The progression to superpower status may be linked to the militaristic tradition which even today may imbue the Russian people with a feeling of national pride, and which is also exploited by the leadership as a powerful instrument of indoctrination to show the achievements in the military field.

Another feature of Soviet behaviour which has its roots in Russian history, to which reference was made earlier, is the tendency to keep Russian society isolated from foreign influence. Due to her geographical location and to the cultural and social differences, Russia has remained outside the mainstream of European ideas for most of her history. The clash between the Slavophiles and Westernisers which occurred in Russia in the middle of last century was a clear indication of an attempt by some elements within Russian society to come out of isolation and to find a solution that would enable Russia to take her proper place in the world, and at the same time allow her to retain a typical Russian identity.

Isolationist trends can still be observed today and the constant debate between those in the Soviet Union who would like to develop stronger ties with the West and absorb Western technology and know-how, and those who see in such proposals a danger to the regime, is reminiscent of the problems Russia faced in the past. On another level, the outright rejection of Western culture and anything that smacks of Western 'decadence' may also be interpreted in terms of Russian isolationism rather than revolutionary principles. The isolationist tendencies are being reinforced, on the one hand, by American policies and Washington's attitudes which the Soviets perceive as aimed towards ostracising the USSR politically, and by the developments within the Communist bloc, on the other. On the Far–Eastern borders of the Soviet Union, the rapprochement between China and the United States is perceived by Moscow as a threat to its security, while the situation in Eastern Europe points to separatist trends among the Warsaw pact allies and indicates that the Communist bloc is not as monolithic as in the past.

Soviet isolationism is also enhanced by an ideology which

reinforces the perception of being surrounded by imperialist enemies. Marxism–Leninism, which has been always useful to the leadership as a means of legitimation of Soviet power, serves at the same time as a powerful instrument to isolate the Soviet Union and its society from outside influences. The fusion of ideological and historical factors that are conducive to the isolationist traits in Soviet behaviour, and the resulting suspicions about Western intentions, have certainly contributed to the mutual distrust between the United States and the USSR – a distrust that is at the core of international tension.

The question of Soviet intentions is also foremost on the minds of many Western political analysts and their opinions are formed by their perception of what the Soviet Union really is. George Kennan identified two images of the USSR. According to one perception the Soviet Union is dominated by men 'animated primarily by a desire to achieve further expansion of their effective power...at the expense of the stability, and perhaps the peace, of international life'. Another view of the Soviet Union is of a state dominated by a group of leaders, 'prisoners of both the Russian and the Soviet past and of a Marxist–Leninist ideology. Like the Russian tsars who ruled before them, they have a sense of insecurity, a passion of secrecy and a paranoid fear of attack' (Kennan, 1982, p.160).

Chapter 3 of the book examined the link between such diverse factors as history, nationalism and ideology and their imprint upon Soviet military thought as expressed in the Soviet military doctrine, not only on the theoretical level but on their practical application to the armed forces and strategy. The reconciliation of history and nationalism with Marxism–Leninism serves as a theoretical foundation for Soviet military thought and embraces the problems of war in their widest scope – the nature of war, the role of the armed forces and their link with politics, ideology and economy. On a more practical level, dealing with a potential situation when military operations might be conducted under conditions of nuclear warfare, Soviet military strategy reveals a classical approach to war operations which can be found in military textbooks of times long past. This can be partly explained by Russian military history when the reliance was mainly on sheer numbers and fire power. The relative importance of ground forces and conventional weapons within the Soviet military strategy seems to indicate that the Soviet military have a clear perception of their decisive importance; that the sheer number of troops, military hardware and fire power are a condition of a victory in a potential European war. As far as a global nuclear war goes, the analysis reveals that, despite their declarations to the contrary, the Soviets do believe in deterrent as long as an approximate balance of nuclear strategic forces exists. The clearly separate roles of nuclear strategic forces and of conventional weaponry of ground troops – the former as a deterrent, the latter to be used on the European theatre of war, should one occur – reflects a compromise between the trends in Soviet military thought to which reference was made in Chapter 3, dealing with ground forces versus nuclear missiles.

Events that took place in the last few years or so, especially since Gorbachev took over the reins of power in the Kremlin, indicate that the Soviets' main concern is to retain the strategic balance on which deterrence rests. This would explain apparent Soviet eagerness to come to terms with the United States in the area of nuclear disarmament. The propositions put forward by Gorbachev to reduce gradually the number of missiles is not only, as some claim, an exercise in political propaganda, but an indication that what the Soviets want to avoid is an acceleration of the arms race in its technological aspect. It could be taken as a reflection of a concern that in the technological competition the Soviets may come out as the losing side, given Western superiority in high technology. What the Soviet Union is facing at the moment is not so much the economic problem of the defence burden, but limitations of a different nature – technological inferiority. It is important to note that, so far, the Soviets have not come out with a clear military response to the latest American SDI project. Statements of a general nature such as, 'the other side will not sit on its hands...it will produce appropriate weapons in reply' (*Star Wars*, 1985, p.9), do not offer any clues. But the Soviet Foreign Ministry spokesman Gennadi Gerasimov expressed the Soviets' fear that in the course of the SDI research process the US would stumble on some technological breakthrough. The Soviets are therefore concentrating their efforts towards the elimination or, at least, limitation of American research in anti-missile defence.

Thus, for reasons suggested so far, for the US to attain a situation of negotiating from a position of military strength is still in the realm of speculation and doubtful assumptions. The Soviets have the will and capacity to retain an aproximate strategic parity which would be sufficient, in their view, as an effective deterrence.

The second option of US policy, that of economic pressure, is more complex and requires a much deeper and extensive scrutiny.

The capacity of an economy to sustain its military effort during war operations has always depended on the resources at the disposal of the participating country; but even in peacetime, as long as there exists a perception of the danger of a military conflict, economic resources are vital for the maintenance of an adequate level of military strength. The extent of a military budget is of utmost importance in this regard, but in relation to the Soviet military effort it assumes additional importance in view of the political and economic system which places the exclusive control over economic and military policy in the hand of one supreme authority – the CPSU. It can decide to allocate additional resources for military purposes and divert scientific and technological research from other areas to those connected with development of new military technology.

In the introduction to the book we have argued that the perception by the Soviets of the present conflict is not confined to its military–strategic aspects, but also includes an economic element – a perception of an attempt to destabilise the Soviet Union economically through the arms race and other means of economic pressure. In Chapter 4, we have examined the role of the Soviet economy in the implementation of the objectives set out by the military doctrine and strategy of the USSR. Particular attention was devoted to the link between defence and availability of economic resources and the way that economic problems impinge upon Soviet military thought.

The relationship between the Soviet economy and defence, analysed in Chapter 4, is also important for the purpose of assessing the Soviet military effort. Leaving aside the question of intention to use military power, the evaluation of Soviet military capabilities, which figures so prominently among Western analysts concerned with growing military power of the Soviet Union, can also be made through an examination of Soviet economic resources. This would appear a much easier task than strategic assessment attempted by military experts. For while the latter necessarily calls for assistance from military intelligence, the former can be readily ascertained through a survey of Soviet economic activity and of the share of the military sector in the economic pie. Simple as it sounds, the task of assessing the Soviet military effort by looking at the budget allocation also has severe limitations that makes it difficult to arrive at a definite conclusion about the real level of military expenditure. Chapter 5 scrutinised all the various methods used for the estimation of Soviet military expenditure and it would appear that their findings were inconclusive.

There remains the domestic aspect. For if the evaluation of the Soviet military effort in monetary terms is the subject of a wide range of assumptions and much guesswork, to which reference was made in Chapter 5, the assessment of Soviet economic performance would be more relevant to the question of how much can the Soviet Union spend on armament and maintenance of its armed forces. The answer to this question has important political implications for East–West relations and for the arms race in particular. Is the defence burden becoming a serious obstacle for Soviet economic development generally and for the civilian sector in particular? This question is linked to the economic option which is based on the assumption that the Soviets will not be able to sustain continued and rising military expenditure. The effects of devoting an excessive share of GNP to its military effort combined with a low rate of economic growth, it is assumed, will tend to destabilise the Soviet economy and force the leadership to make less weapons in order to satisfy the needs of the population. Proponents of this line of thought would point to the fact that Western economies are far more developed than is that of the Soviet Union, and that military expenditure is, so far, not as important an issue in budgetary considerations as it would be for the USSR. Chapter 6 discusses in much detail the connection between domestic policies and Soviet military effort. The tentative conclusion that it offers is in variance with the widely shared view that the Soviet GNP, being slightly more than half of that of the United States, will only be able to sustain a continued military buildup at the price of severe restrictions in the civilian sector and at the expense of the living standard of the average citizen. It also differs from the view that the only viable alternative for the Soviets is to cut their defence budget and divert resources for civilian use. We have argued that transferring resources from military purposes to civilian use will not materially improve the economic situation because of the inefficiencies that are inherent in the Soviet system. The Soviet leadership is, therefore, preoccupied with the problem of productivity rather than defence spending. Yet, many political thinkers in the United States are of the opinion that 'anything the United States can do economically, will have a critical effect on Soviet high policy' (Beyond Containment, p.27).

This is certainly relevant to trade relations between the superpowers, for in the area of mutual trade the American administration has a certain degree of control as to the type of goods it is willing to allow to be sold to the USSR as well as on the granting of credit. From the Soviet point of view foreign trade is essential as a source of consumer goods and of new technology. In Chapter 7, we have examined a number of issues connected with foreign trade relations; their role in the Soviet economy as well as the problems faced by the Soviet Government in trading with the West, particularly in their attempt to acquire Western technology. The latter is, as was said earlier in the study, an important political and military issue for the American Government, especially for those who advocate a complete embargo on trade with the Soviet Union on account of its military significance and the implications for the Soviet domestic economy. In the opinion of some political economists, an economic war against the Soviet Union contains a real danger to peace. For while an economic war tends to escalate it may invoke a military alternative for the losing nation (Wolfson and Farrell, 1986).

However, the effectiveness of an economic war is severely limited by the reluctance of some American allies to participate fully in such a course of action. This, combined with the fact that the Soviet Union is endowed with sufficient economic resources that would enable it to sustain an economic war for the foreseeable future, makes the economic option of doubtful value.

The conclusion reached in the study is that given the nature of Soviet society and in the absence of any visible signs of popular discontent, the defence burden may be sustained for as long as Soviet society is prepared to bear it. On the other hand, as has been shown in Chapter 6, the domestic economic situation may be remedied, to some extent, through radical economic reforms which will improve efficiency and increase productivity of available resources. As this study indicates, the inefficiencies that exist in the operation of the Soviet economy are the subject of discussions among Soviet economists. A number of suggestions have been offered over a number of years but the implementation of effective reforms was always bound up with the political constraints imposed by the Soviet political and economic system examined in Chapter 8.

It is the 'burden of inefficiency' rather than the burden of defence that is the issue on which the Soviet leadership has been, and still is, concentrating its attention in recent times. The implication of this conclusion, which the analysis contained in Chapter 8 suggests, is that the view about 'Soviet economic vulnerability which undoubtedly gives the West a degree of leverage that can be used to moderate Soviet behaviour' (Sokoloff, 1980, p.74) may be misguided, and that the possibility of a reduction in Soviet military expenditure on account of economic difficulties and internal pressure appears to be remote.

Of greater concern to the Soviets is that an attempt is being made by the United States to destabilise the Soviet system through radio broadcasts and advanced communication technology. The perception of an ideological and psychological war against the USSR has alerted the Soviet leadership to the possibility that it may be effective in some way. We have fully analysed this aspect of the superpower conflict in Chapter 9 and have indicated how the Soviets, because of their concern, have become more realistic in their assessment of the state of Soviet society.

However, to conclude that the American propaganda offensive has created an undercurrent of opposition to the Soviet regime would be unjustified and certainly premature. Even if we accept the assertion that an ideological opposition within the USSR is slowly emerging (Amalrik, 1970, p.11), which is far from certain, it cannot be said that Western propaganda or the flow of Western ideas has been instrumental in its emergence. A close look at the results of Soviet social research and opinion polls would reveal that the so called 'ideological subversion' and 'ideological contamination' are limited to a simple comparison between the economic conditions in the capitalist world and the USSR. This is expressed in the admiration and appreciation of Western materialism, but there is not the slightest hint of a desire to adopt the capitalist system, and the notions of 'freedom' and 'human rights' are not really an issue for the Soviet population, except for a small group of the more politically aware dissidents. The concept of freedom in the sense of voting rights and alternative governments would be quite incomprehensible for the average Soviet citizen, to say the least. Freedom for the Soviet people means economic freedom, access to consumer goods, a higher standard of living, freedom to pursue some economic activities that are considered illegal, etc.

More relevant to the prospect of change is the process taking place within Soviet society, to which we have referred in Chapter 9

– the steady increase in the population strata defined by the Soviets as intelligentsia. It has been, so far, defined as the educated part of Soviet society but, as we have suggested, it may mean in the long run more than just higher education. It may also bring about the capacity for independent thought. The existence of such a possibility is evident from the recent Soviet approach to ideological education that demands more sophisticated methods of propaganda which must conform to the higher level of education. It is this trend that offers opportunities for a change in Soviet attitudes. But, in the short run, the conformist attitude of the vast majority of the Soviet population precludes the emergence of an effective opposition to the regime. In that sense the success of the American ideological offensive must remain very much in doubt.

Indeed, there are many political thinkers who have been expressing their doubts about the possibility of changing Soviet conduct through various means using some kind of pressure whether military, ideological or economic: 'frontal pressure directed against the system demanding of it steps that go beyond any reasonable scale of feasability...can and does have counterproductive effect' (Sanderman *et al.*, 1979, p.151).

The history of US-Soviet relations is full of examples of Soviet intransigence in dealing with the United States, and of no appreciable change in Soviet policies resulting from attempted pressure. Beside the reasons enumerated earlier, there is also an awareness that economic sanctions never work and, more often than not, it hurts the United States as well. Such was the case with the grain embargo and restrictions of technological transfer – they may have harmed American industry more than they may have harmed the Soviet Union. The attitude of Western European countries in this respect was best summarised in a comment by a Western European statesman, Willy Brandt: 'if we wanted to trade only with democracies, we would certainly ruin our economies very quickly. It is a romantic idea that we would bring the Soviet Union to its knees by economic measures' (*Newsweek*, 30 May 1983, p.39).

So far we have argued that due to the nature of the Soviet Union there is very little hope for the United States to achieve its political objectives through some kind of pressure upon the USSR. Such a conclusion does not really offer any prospect of accommodation between the superpowers given their apparent intransigence. But as Kampelman, the chief negotiator in Geneva said: 'no matter what we think of the Soviets, we have to live with them on this globe...We can't blow them away, we can't wish them away. We have to find a formula by which we can live with them in peace and dignity' (*Time,* 26 May 1986).

There are, indeed, some voices in the United States who suggest the adoption of a different course in dealing with the Soviets. They see the solution to the problem of changing Soviet attitudes in an attempt to bring the USSR into the world economic system, rather than trying to isolate it. In the words of Lawrence Eagleburger, former Undersecretary for Political Affairs, Department of State: 'economic leverage cuts in both directions. Over a long period, there is still merit in the principle that if the Soviet Union is sufficiently integrated into the world economic system, it would face a very complex problem in trying to extricate itself' (Beyond Containment, p.29). The idea of economic integration is closely linked to the concept of interdependence, a subject of some interest among political and economic scientists in the West.

THE FOURTH ALTERNATIVE

The relatively new concept of interdependence between states has arisen following the rapid technological advance in communication, transportation and particularly the enormous increase in international commercial transactions; partly as a result of the activities of non-state actors – the multinational companies. The role of interdependence in international relations has been for some time a subject of discussions among political and economic theoreticians. A view shared by many is that the process of political integration depends to a large degree upon economic interdependence.

Interdependence in its simplest definition means that due to the extensive trading relations and mutual interpenetration of modern technology, standardisation of industrial processes, etc., a point of 'no return' may be reached when economic and technological interdependence becomes too costly, and sometimes impossible, to break. It can, therefore, be assumed that the higher the level of interdependence, the higher will be the cost of breaking and the less likely for it to be broken (Rosencrance and Stein, 1973, p.15). If we accept the above assumptions, then the concept of interdependence would include not only the possibility of economic interdependence but a degree of political integration as well.

The concept of interdependence thus contains descriptive as well as prescriptive elements. On the descriptive level, it assumes that the role of the state is diminishing due to the emergence of other actors whose activities limit the power of the state to take independent decisions. On a different level, interdependence can be seen as a positive development in international relations because it lessens the likelihood of conflict – at least in the military sense. It becomes, in a way, an ideal and a desirable goal, whereby relations between nations are improved and the prospect of peaceful coexistence enhanced. It becomes in fact an objective to be attained (Cooper, 1968, p.151). But while most discussions about interdependence and research in that field put the emphasis on relations between highly industrialised capitalist states whose relations are basically non-conflictual – at least at the level of higher politics of confronting each other militarily – there is less mention about the role interdependence could play in the relations between the superpowers and its relevance to international politics. As one proponent of the idea of interdependence once said: 'complex interdependence seems less relevant to communist states than it does to advanced industrial states' (Keohane and Nye, 1977, p.266).

One possible explanation why the concept of interdependence as a factor in East–West relations has not been given sufficient importance is that interdependence implies economic as well as political integration. The latter cannot enter into consideration for reasons of ideological and government systems differences, which some assert are at the core of the present conflict. Consequently, the possible process of East-West economic integration is being inhibited by political rather than economic considerations. It is said that since interdependence involves increased trading activities between the Soviet Union and the West, it requires an international political atmosphere conducive to mutual trade. In the opinion of some political analysts such was the situation during the short period of *détente*. But while it is fair to say that the policy of *détente* has been a contributing factor in the promotion of East–West trade, it was not the only one and, as we shall see, trading relations did not entirely depend on *détente*.

The policy of *détente* coincided with the perceived parity of strategic forces by both superpowers leading to SALT I. The Soviets, in fact, claimed that *détente* came as a result of the new 'correlation of forces' between the socialist and capitalist camps. The Soviet Union attempted to exploit the international political situation by better trade relations with the West, especially to achieve greater access to Western credits and technology. But at the same time, the Soviets continued steady military expenditure in the 1970s despite arms control negotiations. They perceived *détente* as a factor of cooperation while maintaining the traditional view about the conflictual nature of capitalism and socialism.

Similarly, the American perception of *détente* entailed the hope of restraining Soviet expansion while cooperating in areas of mutual interest. By contrast, in Europe *détente* took a different path of development. Even prior to *détente* there was a trend to settle outstanding disputes with the USSR and Eastern European countries – the *Ostpolitik* initiated by Willy Brandt being a reflection of this trend. At the same time, trade relations with the Soviet Union became much more important for Western European economies, and *détente* was spoken of as the political expression of an economic end – the expansion of markets. Such attitudes were against the political objectives of the United States which since the end of the Second World War, pursued a policy of trade restrictions against the USSR. Legislation passed in 1949 and amended in 1962 prohibited shipments of goods that might contribute not only to the Soviet military but also its economic potential. The Europeans, on the other hand, have only reluctantly responded to the American demand to limit the flow of strategic goods to the East (Pisar, 1970, p.58). Already in the 1960s Western European countries differed from the United States on issues of economic restrictions and have been instrumental in progressively reducing the embargo list. The real setback to the policy of *détente* came in December 1974 when the US Congress approved a trade act that would give the USSR a most-favoured-nation status but conditional on Soviet emigration policies. The Soviet Union has rejected the principle of linkage and has reacted by cancelling the Soviet–US Trade Agreement in January 1975. Thus the policy of *détente* was already under a dark cloud, but its end came with Soviet intervention in Afghanistan.

An analysis of the underlying causes of the collapse of *détente* is not really within the scope of this book, but its link with the course of East–West trading relations is important for the consideration of the concept of interdependence as an alternative. Although, as we have pointed out earlier, there is a connection between economic relations and the policy of *détente*, there does not appear to be a straight correlation between the two. Statistical data (see Table 7.2 in Chapter 7) clearly indicates that despite the end of *détente* and the attempts by the American Administration to influence its

European allies to restrict their dealings with the Soviet Union, East–West trade did not seem to have suffered as much as did political relations. If East–West trade did not grow faster, it was, to a large extent, for economic reasons. It was limited by the amount of Western credits and by the availability of foreign currency in the Soviet Union.

However, the removal of most, if not all, trading restrictions between the United States and the Soviet Union would be a step towards interdependence. This would almost certainly lead to increased trade between the USSR and the United States and could, in the short run, lessen international tension. It would be a process in reverse of that previously attempted: instead of trying a policy of *détente* in order to promote interdependence, steering a course towards the latter might lead to a new form of *détente*. The long-term consequences, however, may be the more important if the Soviet Union could be integrated in the world economic system and if a degree of mutual dependence could be achieved.

A view that prevails among many political scientists is that Soviet economic rate of growth has already become dependent, to some extent, on imports of Western know-how and equipment, a fact admitted even by Soviet economists, and in that sense a small degree of interdependence appears to have taken place. Soviet gas started flowing to Bavaria in October 1973, to Finland and Italy in 1974 and to France in 1975. There has been also an interlocking of production between the East and West through specialisation, co-production and subcontracting (Pinder and Pinder, 1976, p.301). One Soviet source reports that 'according to some estimates, the United States' exports to the Soviet Union alone provide jobs for many thousands of American workers, and since Soviet trade with European capitalist countries is much greater than with the United States, at least two million people in industrial capitalist states are said to owe their jobs to the trade with the USSR' (Lebedev, 1978, p.134).

However, despite the growth in commercial transactions between the USSR and the West, the road leading to increased interdependence is not without serious obstacles. Economic dependence on the West is being avoided by the Soviets as far as economic necessity permits.

The reasons for the objections to closer economic ties with the West go much deeper than just the desire to avoid economic dependence. They lie in the nationalistic and ideologically inspired desire for independent scientific achievements, as well as in the fear of Western influence upon Soviet society. Since increased commercial and trading relations invariably lead to a growing interchange of ideas, cultural exchanges and, generally, to increased travel abroad by Soviet citizens, there is a perception of a danger of ideological contamination (a point discussed at length in Chapter 9). Some Soviet writers stress that the idea of interdependence has been created 'in order to cover up US global hegemonistic plans' (Efremov, 1975, p.73; Sergeev, 1976, pp.103–9).

It may seem that considering Soviet fears about the probable – from their point of view – consequences of closer economic and cultural relations with the West, the possibility of promoting, let alone exploiting such relations, would appear rather problematic. The liberalisation of trade with the Soviets would probably be accepted with strong reservations and with much caution. However, the economic benefits that free access to Western technology and know-how would offer to the Soviet Union as against the threat of ideological contamination, would confront the Soviets with a dilemma: increase contacts with the West or retain ideological purity. Indeed, there are elements within the Party who look at the problem from a more pragmatic point of view and who accept the proposition that the technological advance in the industrialised West makes it imperative for the USSR to entertain links with the capitalist world, lest the Soviet Union fall behind even further.

One well-known Soviet political analyst recognised the opportunities which interdependence offers in the economic sphere, not only for the Soviet Union alone but for the rest of the world as well:

> [D]ue to the present scientific and technical revolution...even the largest industrially developed countries cannot on their own organise economically efficient manufacture of all types of products...[this] gives additional impetus to economic internationalisation, not only to the Soviet Union and the United States, but also to the Socialist countries of Europe...France, FRG and Italy, as well as Japan and other states. (Lebedev, 1978, p.129)

There are indications of a growing awareness among Soviet economists about the opportunities which access to Western production methods offers, and foreign economic relations in general. The analysis of the potential benefits of foreign trade relations is one of the rare occasions when Soviet economists adopt a purely academic approach to an economic problem without any political or ideological connotations (Akademia Nauk, 1977, p.260). Similarly, reports by the Central Committee to the last Congresses of the CPSU spoke of the importance of foreign economic relations for the solution of Soviet economic problems, and of the exploitation of the advantages that they represent. (ibid., p.261). Erik Pletnev, a former director of the political economy department of the All-Union Academy for Foreign Trade, argued that economic contacts between the East and West are an indication of the existence of a universal economy and advocated the expansion of mutual economic ties. During the discussions on the draft of the new CPSU Programme in November 1985, he spoke out for a 'world' economy and expressed his belief that arms control was more likely to succeed if the superpowers were economically interdependent (Ploss, 1986, 53).

The Soviets have recently indicated a willingness to become part of the economic order of the Western World. They have applied to attend the next round of GATT in Uruguay as an observer, as a possible prelude to a formal application for membership. Moscow is also trying to gain access to such supranational Western organisations as the World Bank, the International Monetary Fund, and Pacific Basin Economic Cooperation forums. So far, it has been rebuffed mainly because of Washington's opposition for fear of the possible creation of a communist bloc within these organisations.

It is the existence of such trends within the Soviet Union that offers the opportunities for the lifting of the barriers of distrust through less restricted links between the East and the West. The relatively new realism in the Soviet approach to economic problems, to which reference was made in Chapters 6 and 9, offers a possibility to deal with the Soviets on a more businesslike basis.

But there are also obstacles of an internal nature whose sources lie in the bureaucratic structure of the Soviet state. Although the new Soviet economic policies are aimed at curbing the power of the bureaucracy, Mikhail Gorbachev still speaks of improving the functioning of the national economy through a further strengthening of centralisation, although with some modifications. He still calls for greater discipline and order 'demanding more from everyone, from workers to ministers...a drive against irresponsibility and red tape, to instil labour ethics' (*Time*, 9 September 1985, p.13), etc. Essentially, what Gorbachev suggests is the implementation of past recommendations by Soviet economists, adopted by the Party for some time, but which for lack of determination have not been put into practice. What must be recognised is that what we are witnessing is not a radical change in the Soviet economic system, but an attempt to improve the functioning of the economy, to make it more efficient within the operation of the system. It is an attempt to find an optimal balance between the central administration system and market forces. But, as we have pointed out in Chapter 8, the difficulties in achieving a satisfactory balance must be seen against the constraints imposed by the perceived threat to the political control exercised by the Party. In that sense, it is not a matter of ideology, neither is it a question of the Soviet leadership being prisoners of that ideology; it is rather that they are prisoners of the system they have created and a society they have inherited – a society that needs to be reformed but is stagnating – a fact admitted by Gorbachev himself at the last Congress (*Pravda,* 26 February 1986). But a society that is lacking internal forces cannot reform itself and cannot be reformed by government decree either. It is the nature of the Soviet state apparatus that will make any reforms aiming at improving the system a rather lengthy process.

A feature of the Soviet political system is the so-called 'democratic centralism', to which we referred earlier in the book, whereby any changes in policies are first announced at the very top of the Soviet hierarchy – usually at the Politburo level or at the Congress of the CPSU. Directives are then given to the government authorities or Party organisations about the line to be adopted. These directives filter down the line of the different levels of the Party or government until they reach all those involved in the implementation of the new policy. This is probably the reason why decisions taken at the Politburo or Congress take a relatively long time to be put into practice. At the time of writing, the XXVII Congress of the CPSU is taking place. Among the new directives is the relaxation of the control of the Central Planning, the Gosplan, in order to allow the enterprises to make independent decisions about the types of goods they may produce. But in view of the traditional mode of operation to which Soviet management has been subjected since planning was introduced, it is questionable whether it will be able to act independently, and, most importantly, whether it will be willing to undertake a course on uncharted waters in the absence of clear directives, to which Soviet managers have been conditioned throughout Soviet rule.

Despite the reservations about the importance of Western technology for the Soviet Union expressed by Gorbachev, foreign trade is certainly becoming an important factor in Soviet economic development. The Soviet approach to foreign trade has been dealt with in some detail in Chapter 7. We have argued that the contradictions created by political versus economic considerations are being resolved in favour of the latter and have suggested that the constraints on further development of mutual East–West trade are economic rather than political, especially in the area of availability of foreign exchange. Given the more realistic view on foreign trade relations, one may safely assume that despite objections of an ideological nature, mutual trade, above all transfer of technology, would be readily accepted by the Soviets if it were available without restrictions. But availability of credits is determined by American pressure geared towards its limitation and by the fact that the USSR, to a large extent, is isolated from the world economic system. Which brings us back to the question of integration and interdependence as factors that might be instrumental in promoting better East–West relations.

The reservations which the Soviets may have regarding trade relations with the West have their equivalent among Western political leaders; especially within those circles in the Pentagon which view with considerable suspicion any attempt by the Soviets to gain access to Western technology. They claim that the Soviets are taking full advantage of the opportunities to acquire Western science and technology to strengthen both their military power and military–industrial base. They also assert that the acquisition of militarily significant technologies has resulted in a great reduction in costs, time and risks involved in the Soviet R&D effort (*Soviet Military Power*, 1984, p.107). There are also reservations of a more general nature: 'even if Moscow does not exploit the acquisition of Western technology to enhance its military posture, there is no point in building up the Soviet state into a true economic superpower by improving its technological base and management technique' (Clemens, 1978, p.89). Furthermore:

> the notion that the Soviets will by means of economic ties become 'enmeshed in a web of mutual economic interdependence' is conjectural at best...they...are careful to avoid those steps that would 'enmesh' them...As a result, mutual inter-

dependence can easily turn into double dependence on our part: we could become dependent on their goodwill in repaying debts and shipping key materials such as energy. (US Congress, Commission on Security and Cooperation in Europe, January 1977, p.6)

It is not surprising that a substantial volume of Western technological know-how is being acquired by the Soviet Union through industrial espionage and illegal means. But equally damaging to American interests, according to the Pentagon, is the legal transfer of technology to the USSR. In that sense, the creation of trade barriers is also counter-productive in that the acquisition of Western technology by the Soviets, through illegal means, removes, to some extent, the means of controlling its flow and the source of information that would indicate the extent and nature of the transfer. Furthermore, by denying the Soviets access to advanced technology, the West is forcing the USSR into extensive programmes of R&D and this contributes to the Soviet quest for economic and technological independence regardless of cost.

It would be difficult to deny that there are risks involved in the liberalisation of trade with the Soviet Union, especially in the field of Western technology. But a close examination of the problems of absorption and dissemination of Western technologies by the Soviets suggests that fears of military use of the acquired technologies may be exaggerated. The question of Soviet economic efficiency, analysed in Chapter 8, implies that the erection of economic barriers may be less important given the deficiencies that exist in the operation of the Soviet economy. The Fiat deal, for example, which in the early 1970s was intended to close the automotive gap, did not materialise. The Soviets have failed to update technology or to develop a capability to supply advanced motor industry machinery (Jacobs, 1978, p.201). These and other facts mentioned earlier suggest an answer to the question whether it is in the interest of the West to help modernise the Soviet system, if in the process it creates a more vigorous economic rival to the United States and Western Europe (Clemens, 1978, p.86). 'The prospect that the Soviet Union will match and overtake the West economically, must be regarded as almost visionary' (ibid., p.96).

The Pentagon itself admitted that the Soviets were copying US designs rather than creating original military hardware. 'At the Paris Air Show, the Soviets thoroughly examined the US C-141 jet transport. They photographed the aircraft, measured it and even took metal samples. The resulting structural similarities in a subsequent Soviet aircraft – the IC-76/CANDID – were quite striking. The performance characteristics were almost identical' (*Soviet Military Power,* 1984, p.110). A more up-to-date assessment of the Soviet technological level is that 'although the technological gap between the USSR and the West is constantly narrowing, the West still holds an overall technological lead' (*Soviet Military Power*, 1987, p.111). The Soviets seem to encounter serious problems in developing computer technology needed for modern weapons systems and industry in general. According to the Pentagon, despite efforts to develop or obtain the technology, 'the Soviets remain an average of 10 years behind the West in civil/industrial technology application' (ibid., p.112).

The possible utility of the policy of trade restrictions for the United States is admittedly a matter of controversy. Concern that economic benefits from expanded trade relations would be more favourable to the USSR does not in itself justify the imposition of restrictions given American technological superiority and the Soviet inability to exploit efficiently the advantages of such relations. In any case, the lack of coordination with other Western countries and their reluctance to adhere strictly to the American guidelines makes US policies of limited use.

This course in American policy is not really new – it has been practised by successive Administrations since the end of the Second World War. The Reagan policy may be considered as a variant of the policy of containment which attempted to isolate the USSR, especially economically. Interdependence, if it could be achieved, together with the possible economic integration may, in the long-run, take both sides in the present conflict into an inextricable position when the economic links will be difficult to break. Admittedly, when applying the concept of interdependence to the present international situation, we are invoking a theory for which there is as yet inadequate support, and we cannot use historical precedent, except the relations between Western developed countries to whose non-conflictual nature we have referred earlier. But there is no reason why it cannot be applied to East–West relations.

The relative simplicity of past technologies and the way economic progress took place during the last two centuries did not make economic integration an absolute necessity, and the retention of a degree of self-sufficiency was still possible. This is not the case at the present time. Interlocking of technology and production processes, due sometimes to factors outside state control and sometimes to the limited resources available to any one country, makes economic integration advantageous for all participants.

There are certainly risks involved in adopting a policy of East–West trade relaxation. The concern that this may enhance Soviet military–strategic capabilities is, to a certain degree, a valid one. But on balance it would appear that the benefits arising from the relaxation of trade restrictions between East and West and the long-term prospect of growing interdependence as a factor of international stability outweigh the risks. The introduction of drastic reforms in the USSR and the present state of superpower relations appear to be very favourable for the adoption of a fresh approach towards economic relations with the Soviet Union. Gorbachev may represent a unique opportunity of integrating the USSR into the world economy.

However, any fresh approach still faces the reality of the existence of nuclear weapons and the danger that they represent. Any fresh approach must necessarily accept the fact that we are dealing with states whose mutual suspicions are intensified by a perceived ideological antagonism and who are not going to abandon their nuclear armory. It may also be argued that such action will not reduce the extent of the arms race, but what matters is not the size of the stockpile – one can have stability at a high level of stockpile and instability at a low level. Arms reductions are no guarantee of peace, any more than their increase are necessarily precursors of war.

As we have suggested, the success of military, economic or psychological pressure whose objective is to change Soviet attitudes appears to be rather doubtful. This is due not only to the nature of the conflict itself, but to the inherent forces within the Soviet Union. But any step that would bring the Soviets within the world economic system and would make the Soviet Union in some way dependent upon mutual cooperation would hasten the process of interdependence. The process may already be taking place. In the West, there are non-state actors who for the sake of business interests would be ready to participate in it, and within the Soviet Union the emergence of a social strata of independently thinking individuals who adopt a more pragmatic approach to economic problems may also become a contributing factor.

In the meantime, the international situation can be summed up in the words of the French philosopher, Raymond Aron, who as far back as 1951 asked a question that seems to be applicable even today: 'How will the conditions develop – conditions that render peace impossible to achieve and total war temporarily improbable?'

References

Akademia Nauk SSSR (1977) 'Ekonomicheskaia effektivnost obshchestvennovo proizvodstva v period razvitovo sotsialisma', (Moscow: 'Nauka').

Aktafiev, A. (1978) 'Popytka razmyt'barier mezhdu yadernoi i neyadernoi voynoi', *Mirovaia ekonomika i mezhdunarodnyie otnosheniia*, no.7.

Alexander, A. J., Becker, A. S. and Hoehn, W. E. (1979) *The Significance of Divergent US–USSR Military Expenditure* (Santa Monica, Ca: Rand Corporation). Rand Note, N-1000-AF (Feb).

Alexandrova, E. and Fedorovskaia, E. (1978) 'Rost blagosostoianiia trudiashchikhsia i sberezheniia naselenia', *Voprosy ekonomiki*, no.10.

Amalrik, A. (1970) *Will the Soviet Union Survive Until 1984?* (London: Allen Lane)

Ambartsumov, E. A. (1984), 'Analiz V.I.Leninym prichin krizisa 1921 godu i putei vykhoda iz nevo', *Voprosy Istorii*, no.4(April).

Amos, A. J. Jr. (1960) 'Basic Deterrence and the New Balance of Power', *Journal of International Affairs*, vol.XIV, no.1.

Andropov, U. V. (1982) Speech at the Plenum of the CC of the CPSU 22 November 1982, *Ekonomicheskaia gazeta*, no.48 (November).

Arbatov, A. (1981) 'Strategia yadernovo bezrazsudstva', *Kommunist,* no.6 (April).

Arbatov, G. (1973) *The War of Ideas in Contemporary International Relations* (Moscow: Progress Publishers).

Arbatov, G. (1977) 'Bolshaia lozh protivnikov razriadki', *Pravda* (5 February).

Arbatov, G. (1987). 'Militarizm ı sovremmennoe obshchestvo', *Kommunist*, no.2.

Aron, R. (1951) *Les Guerres en Chaine* (Paris: Gallimard).

Aspaturian, V. (1972) 'The Soviet Military–Industrial Complex – Does it Exist?', *Journal of International Affairs*, vol.26, no.1.

Babosov, E. M. (1984) 'Ideologia v sovremennom mire' (Minsk: Nauka i tekhnika).

Baranov, S. (1971) 'Materialnaia osnova moshchi vooruzhonnykh sil SSSR', *Krasnaia zvezda* (5 March).

Barghoorn, F. C. (1956) *Soviet Russian Nationalism* (New York: Oxford University Press).

Barrington, M. Jr (1965) *Soviet Politics – the Dilemma of Power* (New York: Harper & Row)

Becker, A. S. (1972). 'National Income Accounting in the USSR', in Treml, V. G. and Hardt, J. P. (eds) *Soviet Economic Statistics*, (Durham: Duke University Press).

Becker, A. S. (1977) *Military Expenditure Limitation for Arms Control Problems and Prospects* (Cambridge, Mass: Ballinger).

Becker, A. S. (1979) 'The Meaning and Measure of Soviet Military

Expenditure', in *Soviet Economy in a Time of Change*, JEC (Washington, DC: Government Printing office).
Becker, A. S. (1983) 'Military Allocations and Burden – Overview', in *Soviet Economy in the 1980s, Problems and Prospects,* JEC (Washington, DC: Government Printing Office).
Berger, P. L. (1983) 'Democracy for Everyone', *Commentary*, vol.76, no.3 (September).
Bergson, A. (1972) 'The Comparative National Income of the USSR and the United States', in Daly, D. J., *International Comparison of Prices and Output* (New York: National Bureau of Economic Research).
Bergson A. (1978) 'Conclusion', in *The USSR in the 1980s.* Colloquium held 17–19 January 1978 in Brussels, Nato Directorate of Economic Affairs.
Bergson, A. (1978) *Productivity and the Social System – the USSR and the West* (Cambridge, Mass: Harvard University Press).
Berliner, J. S. (1976) 'Prospects for Technological Progress', in *Soviet Economy in a New Perspective*, JEC (Washington, DC: Government Printing Office).
Berman, R. P. and Baker, J. C. (1982) *Soviet Strategic Forces, Requirements and Responses* (Washington, DC: The Brooking Institution).
Bertram, Ch.(1980) *Prospects of Soviet Power in the 80s* (London: Macmillan Press).
'Beyond Containment? – Future of US–Soviet Relations' (1985) *Policy Review* (Winter).
Bialer, S. (ed.) (1981) *The Domestic Context of Soviet Foreign Policy* (Boulder, Co.: Westview Press).
Bielotserkovski, V. (1980) 'Pourquoi les ouvriers sovietique sont-ils plus passive que leurs homologues polonais?', in *Chronique des Petites Gens d'URSS* (Paris: Seuil).
Birman. I. (1981) *Secret Incomes of the Soviet State Budget* (The Hague: Martinus Nijhoff).
Blechman, B. M. and Kaplan, S. S. (1978) *Force Without War, US Armed Forces as a Political Instrument* (Washington, DC: The Brooking Institution).
Block, H. (1973) 'Value and Burden of Soviet Defence', in *Soviet Economic Prospects for the Seventies*, JEC (Washington, DC: Government Printing Office).
Block, H. (1976) 'Soviet Economic Power Growth – Achievements Under Handicap', *in Soviet Economy in New Perspective,* JEC (Washington, DC: Government Printing Office).
Bode, W. R. (1986) 'The Reagan Doctrine', *Strategic Review* (Winter).
Bornstein, M. (1981) 'Soviet Economic Growth and Foreign Policy', in Bialer S. (ed.), *The Domestic Context of Soviet Foreign Policy,* (Boulder, Col.: Westview Press).
Brezhnev, L. (1981) *Kommunist*, no.9 (June).
Brodie, B. (1966) *Escalation and the Nuclear Option* (Princeton: Princeton University Press).
Brubaker, E. R. (1973) 'The Opportunity Costs of Soviet Military Conscripts', in *Soviet Economic Prospects for the Seventies,* JEC

(Washington, DC: Government Printing Office).

Burt, R. (1979) 'Arms Control and Soviet Strategic Forces: The Risk of Asking SALT to Do Too Much', in Ericson J. and Feuchtwanger, E. J. (eds), *Soviet Military Power and Performance* (London: Macmillan).

Burton, D. F. (1983) 'Estimating Soviet Defence Spending', *Problems of Communism* (March/April).

Brzezinski, Z. (1963) 'Communist Ideology: Key to Soviet Policy', in Graebner N. A. (ed.), *The Cold War: Ideological Conflict or Power Struggle?* (Lexington, Mass: D. C. Heath).

Brzezinski, Z. (1967) *Between Two Ages: America's Role in the Technotronic Era*, (New York: The Viking Press).

Butenko, A. (1982) 'Socialism: Forms and Deformations', *New Times* no.6 (February).

Buzuev, A. (1982) 'Vneshnaia ekspansiia podriatchikov Pentagona', *Ekonomicheskaia gazeta*, no.51 (December).

Caldwell, D. (1985) 'US–Soviet Political Relations: a Regional Assessment', Washington DC.: *AEI Foreign Policy and Defence Review,* Washington, DC.

Caldwell, L. T. and Diebold, W. Jr. (1981) *Soviet–American Relations in the 1980s,* (New York: McGraw-Hill).

Campbell, R. W. (1972) 'Management Spillover from Soviet Space and Military Programmes', *Soviet Studies*, vol.XXIII, no.4 (April).

Campbell, R. W. (1973) 'Methodological Problems Comparing the US and USSR Economies', in JEC.

Castoriadis, C. (1981) *Devant la Guerre* (Paris: Fayard).

Central Intelligence Agency (CIA) (1976) 'A Dollar Comparison of Soviet and US Defence Activities 1965–1975', SR-76-10053 (February), Washington DC.

Central Intelligence Agency (CIA) (1976a) 'Estimated Soviet Defence Spending in Rubles 1970–1975', SR-76-10121U (May), Washington DC.

Central Intelligence Agency (CIA) (1980) 'Soviet and US Defence Activities 1970–1979. A Dollar Cost Comparison', SR-80-10005 (January), Washington DC.

Chapman, J. G. (1963) *Real Wages in Soviet Russia since 1928* (Cambridge, Mass.: Harward Univeristy Press).

Chaze, W. L. (1982) 'The Great Propaganda War', *US News & World Report* (January 11).

Chronique des Petites Gens d'URSS (1981) Colloque International sur la situation des Travailleurs en URSS, Marseille 8–9 November 1980, (Paris: Seuil).

Claudin, F. (1975) *The Communist Movement, from Comintern to Cominform,* (Harmondsworth: Penguin Books).

Clausewitz, C. (1978) *On War* (Harmondsworth: Penguin Books).

Clemens, W. C. Jr (1978) *The USSR and Global Interdependence*, (Washington, Dc: American Enterprise for Public Policy Research).

Cockburn, A. (1983) *The Threat. Inside the Soviet Military Machine* (New York: Random House).

Cockle, P. (1978) 'Analising Soviet Defence Spending: the Debate in Perspective', *Survival*, vol.XX, no.5 (September/October).

Cohn, S.H. (1972) 'National Income Growth Statistics', in Treml, V. G. and Hardt J. P. (eds), *Soviet Economic Statistics* (Durham: Duke University Press).
Cohn, S. H. (1973) 'Economic Burden of Defence Expenditure', in JEC.
Collins, J. M. (1980) US–Soviet Military Balance, Concepts and Capabilities 1960–1980 (New York: McGraw-Hill).
Connor, W. D. (1981) 'Mass Expectations and Regime Performance', in Bialer, S. (ed.), *The Domestic Context of Soviet Foreign Policy* (Boulder, Col.: Westview Press).
Cooper, R. N. (1968) *The Economics of Interdependence* (New York: McGraw-Hill).
Daly, D. J. (1972) *International Comparison of Prices and Output* (New York : National Bureau of Economic Research).
Davis, J. K., Lehman, C. M. and Wessell, N. H. (1974) *SALT II and the Search for Strategic Equivalence*, (Lexington: Lexington Books).
Degras, J. (ed), (1961) *Soviet Documents of Foreign Policy* (Oxford: Royal Institute of International Affairs).
Denison, E. S. (1967) *Why Growth Rates Differ* (New York: The Brooking Institution).
Denton, E. (1979) 'Soviet Consumer Policy: Trend and Prospects', in JEC.
Dexter, B. (1950) 'Clausewitz and Soviet Strategy', *Foreign Affairs* vol.29, no.1 (October).
Documents and Resolutions, XXV Congress of the CPSU, (1978) (Moscow: Politizdat).
Donley, M. B. (ed) (1979) *The SALT Handbook* (Washington, DC: The Heritage Foundation).
Dornan, J. E. Jr (1978) *United States National Security Policy in the Decades Ahead* (New York: Crane, Russak).
Dostal, A. (1977) 'Vneshnaia torgovlia i kredit', *Ekonomicheskaia gazeta*, no.31 (July).
Douglass, J. D. Jr and Hoeber A. M. (1979) *Soviet strategy for Nuclear War* (Stanford: Hoover Institution Press).
Eberstadt, N. (1983) 'Overview', in JEC.
Edwards, I., Hughes, M. and Noren, J.,(1979) 'US and USSR: Comparison of GNP', in JEC.
'Effectivnost oruzhia armii syrii', *Krasnaia zvezda*, 15 July 1982.
Efremov, A.E. (1975) 'Evropeiskaia bezopasnost i krizis NATO', (Moscow: Nauka).
Efremov, A. E. (1976) *Yadernoe razoruzheniie* (Moscow: Mezhdunarodnyie otnosheniia).
'Ekonomicheskaia effektivnost obshchestvennovo proizvodstva v period razvitovo sotsialisma (1977), Akademia Nauk SSSR (Moscow: Nauka).
Engels, F. (1962) *Anti-Duhring*, Foreign Language Publishing House, Moscow.
Engles, F. (1980) 'The Russian Army', 'The Battle of Inkerman', 'The Armies of Europe', in Marx, K., Engels, F., *Collected Works* (London: Lawrence & Wishhart).
Epishev, A. A. (1982). *Krasnaia zvezda* (8 July).

Epishev, A. A. (1983) *Ideologicheskaia rabota v vooruzhonnykh silakh SSSR* (Moscow: Voenizdat).
Ericson, J. and Feuchtwanger, E. J. (eds) (1979) *Soviet Military Power and Performance* (London: Macmillan).
Ericson, J. (1979) 'The Soviet Military System: Doctrine, Technology and Style', in Ericson and Feuchtwanger (1979).
Ermath, F. W. (1981) 'Contrast in American and Soviet Strategic Thought', in Leebaert, D.(ed) *Soviet Military Thinking* (London: George Allen & Unwin).
Faramazyan, R. (1981) *Disarmament and the Economy* (Moscow: Progress Publishers).
Fedoseev, D. (1974) 'Ekonomicheskaia nauka: nekotoryie zadachi eio razvitiia', *Voprosy ekonomiki*, no.2 (February).
Feshbach, M. (1978) 'The Structure and Composition of the Soviet Industrial Labour Force', in *The USSR in the 1980s*.
Feshbach, M. and Rapawy, S. (1976) 'Soviet Population and Manpower Trends and Policies', in JEC (1976).
Feulner, E. J. Jr (1978) 'The Economic Factors in US National Security Policy', in Dornan J. E. Jr, *United States National Security Policy in the Decades Ahead* (New York: Crane, Russak).
Galbraith, J. K. (1981) 'The Economics of the Arms Race – and After', *Bulletin of the Atomic Scientist* (June).
Gallik, D. (1978) 'The Military Burden and Arms Control', in Hunter H. (ed), *The Future of the Soviet Economy: 1978–1985* (Boulder, Col.: Westview Press).
Gantchev, D. (1983) *Izucheniie i formirovaniie obshchestvennovo mneniia* (Moscow: Mys'l).
Garthoff, R. L. (1953) *Soviet Military Doctrine* (Glencoe, Ill: The Free Press).
Garthoff, R. L. (1981) 'Mutual Deterrence, Parity and Strategic Arms Limitation in Soviet Policy', in Leebaert D. (ed), *Soviet Military Thinking* (London: George Allen & Unwin).
George, A. L. and Smoke, R. (1974) *Deterrence in American Foreign Policy: Theory and Practice* (New York: Columbia University Press).
Gide, A. (1950) *Retour de l'URSS* (Paris: Gallimard).
Goldman, M. I. (1972) 'Consumption Statistics', in Treml, V. G. and Hardt J. P. (eds), *Soviet Economic Statistics* (Durham: Duke University Press).
Gorshkov, S. G. (1979) *The Sea Power of the State* (Annapolis: Naval Institute Press).
Goure, L., Kohler, F. D. and Harvey, M. L. (1974) *The Role of Nuclear Forces in Current Soviet Strategy* (Coral Gables, Florida University of Miami).
Gray, C. S. (1978) 'The US and Western Europe: Security Questions, Old and New', in Dornan J.E.Jr.
Grechko, A. A. (1977) *The Armed Forces of the Soviet Union* (Moscow: Progress Publishers).
Greenslade, R. V. (1976) 'The Real Gross National Product of the USSR 1950–1975', in JEC.

Grossman, G. (1976) 'An Economy at Middle Ages', *Problems of Communism*, vol.25, no.2.
Grossman, G. (1977) 'The Second Economy of the USSR', *Problems of Communism* (September/October).
Grossman, G. (1979) 'Notes on the Illegal Private Economy and Corruption', in JEC.
Grushin, B. A. and Onikov, L. A. (1980) *Massovaia informatsia v sovetskom promyshlennom gorode* (Moscow: Politizdat).
Gurov, A. (1982) 'Effectivnost materialnovo obespecheniia', *Krasnaia zvezda* (9 December).
Halperin, M. H. (1963) *Limited War in the Nuclear Age* (New York: John Wiley).
Hardt, J. P. (1961) *The Cold War Economic Gap* (New York: Praeger).
Hilderbrandt, G. G. (1983) 'The Dynamic Burden of Soviet Defence Spending', in JEC.
Hodnet, G. (ed) (1974) *Resolutions and Decisions of the CPSU* (Oxford: Royal Institute of International Affairs).
Hoffman, S. (1968) *The State of War* (New York: Praeger).
Holliday, G. D. (1983) 'Overview', in JEC.
Holloway, D. (1980) 'Decision-making in Soviet Defence Policies', in Bertram, C. (ed.), *Prospects of Soviet Power in the 80s* (London: Macmillan Press).
Holloway, D. (1981) 'Doctrine and Technology in Soviet Armament Policy', in Leebaert, D. (ed.), *Soviet Military Thinking* (London: George Allen & Unwin).
Holloway, D. (1983) *The Soviet Union and the Arms Race* (New Haven, Conn,: Yale University Press).
Holzman, F. D. (1975) *Financial Checks on Soviet Defence Expenditures* (Lexington: D. C. Heath)
Holzman, F. D. (1980) 'Are the Soviets Really Outspending the US on Defence?', *International Security*, vol.4, no.4 (Spring).
Holzman, F. D. (1982) 'Soviet Military Spending: Assessing the Numbers Game', *International Security*, vol.6, no.4 (Spring).
Hook, S. (1984) 'Education in Defence of a Free Society', Commentary vol.78, no.1 (July).
Howard, M. (1984) 'The Nuclear Question and the Problem of Peace', The Alfred Deakin Lecture Trust, Melbourne.
Hunter, H. (1972) 'Soviet Economic Statistics: An Introduction', in Treml, V. G. and Hardt, J. P. (eds), *Soviet Economic Statistics* (Durham: Duke University Press).
Hunter, H. (1978) *The Future of the Soviet Economy: 1978–1985* (Boulder, Col.: Westview Press).
Hunter, H. (1979) 'Soviet Economic Problems and Alternative Responses', in JEC.
Hunter, H., Earl, M. M. Jr and Foster, R. B. (1976) 'Assessment of Alternative Long-range Soviet Growth Strategies', in JEC.
Huntington, S. P. (1961) *The Common Defence* (New York: Columbia Univeristy Press).
Isaev, F. (1949) 'Stalin's Military Genius', *New Times*, no.52, Moscow.

Istoria SSSR (1967) Vol.III and IV (Moscow: Nauka).
Ivanov, V. (1987) 'Bezyadernyi mir i obshchestvennoe soznaniie', *Kommunist*, no.5.
Jacobs, E. M. (1978) 'The Global Impact of Foreign Trade on Soviet Growth', in *The USSR in the 1980s* (Brussels: Nato Directorate of Economic Affairs).
Joint Economic Committee Congress of the United States (JEC) (Washington, DC: US Government Printing Office) (1973) *Soviet Economic Prospects for the Seventies*; (1976) *Soviet Economy in a New Perspective*; (1976a) *Allocation of Resources in the Soviet Union and China, 1975*; (1979) *Soviet Economy in a Time of Change*; (1983) *Soviet Economy in the 1980s, Problems and Prospects*.
Kahan, A. (1981) 'Soviet Agriculture: Domestic and Foreign Policy Aspects', in Bialer, S. (ed).
Kahan, J. H. and Long, A. K. (1972) 'The Cuban Missile Crisis: A Study of its Strategic Context', *Political Science Quarterly*, vol.XXXVII, no.4, (December).
Kaliadin, A. (1973) 'US–USSR Agreements 1971–72', *Mirovaia ekonomika i mezhdunarodnyie otnosheniia*, no.12.
Kaliadin, A. (1978) 'Novoe prepiatsviie na puti k razoruzheniiu', *Mirovaia ekonomika i mezhdunarodnyie otnosheniia*, no.7.
Kampelman, M. M. (1985) 'Can the US and the Soviet Union Coexist?', *USA Today* (Society for the Advancement of Education) (March).
Kaplan, F. M. (1980) *Dubious Specter: A Sceptical Look at the Soviet Nuclear Threat* (Washington: Institute of Policy Studies).
Karamyshev, V. (1965) 'Printzipy sovetskovo voennovo stroitelstva', *Krasnaia zvezda* (12 February).
Katsenelinboigen, A. (1980) *Soviet Economic Thought and Political Power in the USSR* (New York: Pergamon Press).
Kemp, T. (1971) *Industrialization in the Nineteenth Century Europe* (London: Longman).
Kennan, G. F. (1982) *The Nuclear Delusion: Soviet–American Relations in the Atomic Age* (New York: Patheon).
Keohane, R. O. and Nye, J. S. (1977) *Power and Interdependence* (Boston: Little, Brown).
Khachaturov, T. (1977) *The Economy of the Soviet Union Today* (Moscow: Progress Publishers).
Khesin, E. (1975) 'Militarizm i uglubleniie obshchevo krizisa kapitalizma', *Kommunist*, no.12.
Khlestov, O. (1974) 'Venskyie peregovory: zadachi i perspektivy', *Mirovaia ekonomika i mezhdunarodnyie otnosheniia*, no.6 (June).
Khodzhaev, A. (1977) 'Problemy udovletvoreniia potrebiteskovo sprosa', *Voprosy ekonomiki*, no.12.
Khruschev, N. S. (1959) Doklad na zakrytom zasedanii XX siezda KPSS, 'O kulte lichnosti i evo posledstviiakh' (Moscow: Gosudarsvennoe izdatelstvo politicheskoi literatury).
Klochek, V. (1977) 'Vneshnaia torgovlia SSSR v 1976 godu', *Ekonomicheskaia gazeta*, no.18 (April).
Kohn, M. (1983) 'Overview', in JEC.

Kolikov, N. (1980) 'Kursom mira i bezopasnosti', *Mirovaia ekonomika i mezhdunarodnyie otnosheniia*, no.5.

Kolkowicz, R. (1971) 'Strategic Parity and Beyond. Soviet Perspective', *World Politics* (April).

Komin, A. (1967) 'Peresmotr optovykh tzen i priblizheniie ikh k obshchestvenno neobkhodimym zatratam', *Voprosy ekonomiki*, no.4 (April).

Korablev, Y. (1977) *Lenin – the Founder of the Soviet Armed Forces* (Moscow: Progress Publishers).

Korobeynikov, V. (1983) 'Partyiny Komitet izuchaet obshchestvennoe mnieniie', *Kommunist*, no.12 (August).

Kosygin, A. (1980) 'V edinom stroiu zashchitnikov otchizny', *Voprosy ekonomiki*, no.5 (May).

Kovalev, V. (1982) 'Okno uyazvimosti ili yadernaia boynitza', *Krasnaia zvezda* (4 June).

KPSS o vooruzhonnykh silakh Sovetskovo Soyuza (1981). (Moscow: Voenizdat).

Krasovski, V. (1975) 'Obshchestvenny product i konechnyi effect', *Voprosy ekonomiki*, no.6 (June).

Krylov, K. A. (1979) *The Soviet Economy* (Lexington, Mass.: D. C. Heath).

Kubalkova, V. and Cruickshank, A. A. (1980) *Marxism–Leninism and the Theory of International Relations* (London: Routledge and Kegan Paul).

Kulikov, V. (1976) 'Sovetskaia voennaia nauka segodnia', *Kommunist* no.7.

Kuzmin, N. (1982) 'KPSS i voennoe stroitelstvo', *Kommunist*, no.10 (July).

Lagovskyi, A. (1969) 'Ekonomika i voennaia moshch gosudarstva', *Krasnaia zvezda* (25 September).

Latzis, O. (1987) 'Kak shagaet perestroika', *Kommunist*, no.4, (March).

Lavrinenkov, V. (1982) 'Razvivaia initsiativu', *Krasnaia zvezda* (13 July).

Lavrionov, V. (1982) 'Stsenarii neogranichennovo bezumiia', *Krasnaia zvezda* (16 July).

Lebedev, N. I. (1978) *A New Stage in International Relations* (Oxford: Pergamon Press).

Lee, W. T. (1977) *The Estimation of Soviet Defence Expenditure 1955–75: an Unconventional Approach* (New York: Praeger).

Leebaert, D. (1981) *Soviet Military Thinking* (London: George Allen & Unwin).

Lehrman, L. and Fossedal, G. A. (1986) 'How to Decide About Strategic Defence', *National Review* (31 January).

Lenin, V. I. (1964/65) *Polnoe sobraniie sochinenii: Collected Works* (Moscow: Progress Publishers).

Leontiev, A. (1982) 'Velenie vremeni', *Krasnaia zvezda* (6 June).

Levine, H. S. (1981) 'Soviet Economic Development, Technological Transfer, and Foreign Policy', in Bialer. S.

Levshin, L. and Oreshkin V. (1974) 'O politicheskikh issledovaniiakh v sisteme Akademii Nauk SSSR', *Voprosy ekonomiki*, no.5.

Lewis, K. N. and Lorell, M. A. (1984) 'Confidence-Building Measures

and Crisis resolution: Historical Perspectives', *Orbis* (Summer).
Lider, J. (1983) *Military Theory* (Aldershot: Glover).
Lipsey, G. L. (1975) *An Introduction to Positive Economics* (London, Weidenfeld & Nicholson).
Lokshin, R. and Tyukov, V. (1976) 'Uskoreniie obrashcheniia tovarov narodnovo potrebleniia', *Voprosy ekonomiki*, no.2 (February).
Mandelbaum, M. (1979) *The Nuclear Question: The US and Nuclear Weapons 1946–1976*, (Cambridge: Cambridge University Press).
Manevich, E. (1973) 'Problemy vozproizvodstva rabochei sily i puti uluchsheniia ispolzovaniia trudovykh resursov v SSSR', *Voprosy ekonomiki*, no.2.
Marshall, A. W. (1976) 'Estimating Soviet Defence Spending', *Survival* (March/April).
Marshall, A. W. (1980) 'Sources of Soviet Power – the Military Potential in the 1980s', in Bertram, C. (ed) *Prospects of Soviet Power in the 80s* (London: Macmillan Press).
Marx, K. and Engels, F. (1980) *Collected Works* (London: Lawrence & Wishart).
Materialy vsesoyuznovo soveshchaniia statistikov (1979) 'Sovershenstvovanie gosudarstvennoi statistiki na sovremmennom etape', (Moscow: Statistica).
Mayer, V. (1981) 'Narodnoe blagosostoianiie i potrebitelski spros', *Voprosy ekonomiki*, no.2 (February).
McMenamin, R. J. (1978) 'Western Technology and the Soviets in the 1980s', in *The USSR in the 1980s*, Nato Directorate of Economic Affairs, Brussels.
Medvedev, R. (1978) *La Revolution d'Octobre* (Paris: Francois Maspero).
Mendras, M. (1981–1982) 'L'opinion public en URSS', Annuaire de l'URSS, (Paris: Centre National de la Recherche Scientific).
Mickelson, S. (1983) *America's Other Voice* (New York: Praeger).
Migin, M. B. *et al.* (1978) *Ideologicheskaia borba v sovremennom mire* (Kiev: Naukova dumka).
Mikulsky, K. I. (1984) *Problemy sbalansirovaniia sotsialisticheskoy ekonomiki* (Moscow: Ekonomika).
Military Balance, 1978–79, 1979–80, 1983–84, (London: The International Institute of Strategic Studies).
Millis, W. (ed.) (1951) *The Forrestal Diaries* (New York: Viking Press).
Milovidov, A. (1973) 'Filosofski analiz voennoi mysli', *Krasnaia zvezda* (17 May).
Mirsky, D. S. (1942) *Russia: A Social History* (London: The Crescent Press).
Mitchell, R. J. (1982) *Ideology of a Superpower: Contemporary Soviet Doctrine of International Relations* (Stanford: Hoover Institution Press).
Morgenthau, H. J. (1973) *Politics Among Nations*, (New York: Knopf).
Narodnoe khoziaistvo SSSR v 1977 godu. (1978). (Moscow: Statistika).
Narodnoe khoziaistvo SSSR v 1980 godu. (1981). (Moscow: Finansy i statistica).
Narodnoe khoziaistvo SSSR v 1984 godu. (1985) (Moscow: Finansy i statistica).

Nash, H. T. (1975) *Nuclear Weapons and International Behaviour* (Leyden: A. W. Sigthoff).
Nikonov, A. (1978) 'Vyzov politike razriadki', *Mirovaia ekonomika i mezhdunarodnyie otnosheniia*, no.7.
Nixon, R. (1985) 'Superpower Summitry', *Foreign Affairs*, vol.64, no.1.
Ofer, G. (1976) 'Soviet Military Aid to the ME – an Economic Balance Sheet', in JEC.
Ogarkov, N. (1978) 'Voennaia nauka i zashchita sotsialisticheskovo otechestva', *Kommunist*, no.7 (May).
Ogarkov, N. (1981) 'Na strazhe mirnovo truda', *Kommunist*, no.10 (July).
Oleandrov, B. L. (1966) *Ot voiny k miru*, Moscow.
Orlov, Ya. (1969) 'Nekotoryie problemy ekonomiki i torgovli', *Voprosy ekonomiki*, no.4 (April).
Orlov, Ya. (1976) 'Proizvodstvo tovarov massovovo sprosa na predpriyatiakh tiazheloy industrii', *Voprosy ekonomiki*, no.3 (March).
Orlov, Ya. (1978) 'Osnovnyie napravleniia vozdeistvia torgovli na promyshlennost', *Voprosy ekonomiki*, no.7.
Otkuda iskhodit ugroza miru (1983 and 1984) (Moscow: Voennoe izdatelstvo).
Patolichev, N. S. (1978) *Vneshnaia torgovlia*, no.6.
Pavlichenko, V. (1980) 'Gorizontalnyie khoziaistvennyie sviazi', *Voprosy ekonomiki*, no.10 (October).
Petrakov, P. (1987) 'Planovaia tzena v sisteme upravleniia narodnym khoziaistvom', *Voprosy ekonomiki*, no.1, (January).
Pierre, A. J. (1982) *The Global Politics of Arms Sales* (Princeton: Princeton University Press).
Pinder, J. and Pinder, P. (1976) 'West European Economic Relations with the Soviet Union', in Pipes R. (ed.), *Soviet Strategy in Europe* (New York: Crane, Russack).
Pipes, R. (1976) *Soviet Strategy in Europe* (New York: Crane Russack).
Pipes, R. (1982) *Russia Under the Old Regime* (Harmondsworth: Penguine Books).
Pipes, R. (1984) 'How to Cope with the Soviet Threat?', *Commentary*, vol.78, no.2 (August).
Pipes, R. (1984a) 'Can the Soviet Union Reform?', *Foreign Affairs* (Autumn).
Pisar, S. (1970) *Coexistence and Commerce*, (New York: McGraw-Hill).
Plamenatz, J. (1971) *Ideology* (London: Macmillan).
Planning US Strategic Nuclear Forces for the 1980s (1978) The Congress of the US Congressional Budget Office (Washington, DC: US Government Printing Office) (June).
Platkovski, V. (1982) 'Novaia istoricheskaia obshchnost ludei', *Krasnaia zvezda* (14 July).
Ploss Sydney, I. (1986) 'A New Soviet Era?', *Foreign Policy* (Spring).
Podgatovka molodovo lektora (1982) Znaniie, Moscow.
Pogosov, I. (1980) 'Ekonomika SSSR na sovremmennom etape', *Voprosy ekonomiki*, no.4 (April).
Ponomarev, B. N. (1977) 'Splochennost komunistov – vernyi put k uspekhu mira i sotsialisma', *Problemy mira i sotsialisma*, no.7.

Ponomarev, M. (1982) 'London: stavka na yadernyi kulak', *Krasnaia zvezda* (4 July).

Prados, J. (1982) *The Soviet Estimate, US Intelligence Analysis and Russian Military Strength* (New York: The Dial Press).

Prodovolstvennaia programma SSSR na period do 1990 goda i mery po eio realizatsii (1982) *Krasnaia zvezda* (Moscow).

Proektor, D. (1978) 'Oruzhie dlia Evropy ili protiv neio', *Mirovaia ekonomika i mezhdunarodnyie otnosheniia*, no.7.

Pushkarev, S. (1966) *The Emergence of Modern Russia, 1801–1917* (New York: Holt, Rinehart and Winston).

'Razvitie proizvodstva i torgovli predmetami narodnovo potrebleniia v desiatoi piatiletke' (a discussion). (1977) *Voprosy ekonomiki*, no.3 (March).

Reznichenko, V. G. (ed.) (1984) *Taktika* (Moscow: Voenizdat).

Rigby, T. H. and Miller, R. F. (1976) 'Political and Administrative Aspects of the Scientific and Technical Revolution of the USSR', Occasional Paper No.11, Dept. of Political Science, ANU, Canberra.

Rogovin, V. Z. (1984) *Obshchestvo zrelovo sotsialisma* (Moscow: Mys'l).

Rosefielde, S. (1982) *False Science: Underestimating the Soviet Arms Buildup* (New Brunswick (USA): Transaction Books).

Rosencrance, R. and Stein A. (1973) 'Interdependence: Myth or Reality?', *World Politics*, vol.26, no.1 (October).

Rostow, W. W. (1967) *The Dynamics of Soviet Society* (New York: W. W. Norton).

Rush, M. (1983) 'The Soviet Policy Favouring Arms Over Investment Since 1975', in JEC.

Rybkin, V. (1979) *Novoe Vremia*, no.37 (September).

Rzhanitsyna, L. (1977) *Soviet Family Budgets* (Moscow: Progress Publishers).

Sanderman, F. *et al.* (1979) *The Theory and Practice of International Relations*, (Eaglewood Cliffs, NJ: Prentice Hall).

Sarkisiant, G. S. (ed.) (1980) *Soviet Economy: Results and Prospects* (Moscow: Progress Publishers).

Savostianov, V. (1979) 'Obosnovaniie metodik razcheta effektivnosti vneshneekonomicheskikh sviazei', *Voprosy ekonomiki*, no.12.

Sawyer, H. L. (1978) 'The Soviet Energy Sector: Problems and Prospects', in *The USSR in the 1980s*, Nato Directorate, Brussels.

Schinke, E. (1978) 'Soviet Agriculture: An Uncertain Outlook', in *The USSR in the 1980s*, Nato Directorate, Brussels.

Schneider, W. Jr (1978) 'The Military Dimension of US National Security Policy', in Dornan, J. E.

Schroeder, G. E. (1972) 'An Appraisal of Soviet Wage and Income Statistics', in Treml, V. G. and Hardt, J. P. (eds).

Schroeder, G. E. (1983) 'Soviet Living Standards: Achievements and Prospects', in JEC.

Schroeder, G. E. and Severin, B. S. (1976) 'Soviet Consumption and Income Policies in Perspective', in JEC.

Schultz, R. H. and Gordon, R. (1984) *Dezinformatsia: Active Measures in Soviet Strategy* (New York: Pergamon Press).

Schultze, C. L. *et al.* (1972) *Setting National Priorities – the 1973 Budget* (Washington, DC: The Brooking Institution).
Scott, H. F. and Scott, W. F. (1979) *The Armed Forces of the USSR* (Boulder, Cpl.: Westview Press).
Seaton, A. (1976) *Stalin as Warlord* (London: B. T. Batsford).
Semeyko, L. (1979) 'Strategicheskiye Kontseptsii imperialisma, kurs na voennoie prevoskhodstvo', *Krasnaia zvezda* (24 March).
Semmel, B. (ed.) (1981) *Marxism and the Science of War* (New York: Oxford Univeristy Press).
Sergeiev, A. (1976) 'Bourgeois Theories of "Interdependence" Serve Neo-colonialism', *International Affairs*, no.11 (November) Moscow.
Sergeiev, A. (1981) 'The Dangerous Consequences of the Arms Race', *International Affairs*, no.12 (December) Moscow.
Shatalin, S. (1980) 'Metodologicheskiie problemy analiza narodnovo blagosostoianiia', *Voprosy ekonomiki*, no.10 (October).
Shcherbitsky, V. V. (1977) *XXV Siezd KPSS o sovershenstvovanii sotsialisticheskovo obraza zhizni i formirovanii novogo cheloveka* (Moscow: Politizdat).
Sheliag, V. (1974) 'Dva mirovozreniia – dva vzgliada na voinu', *Krasnaia zvezda* (7 February).
Shultz, G., US Secretary of State (1985) Address to the UN General Assembly, 23 September. Official Text, United States Information Service.
Shuvalov, Ye. L. (1965) *Ekonomicheskaia geografiia SSSR* (Moscow: Prosvescheniie).
Sienkiewicz, S. (1981) 'Soviet Nuclear Doctrine and the Prospects for Strategic Arms Control', in Leebaert D. (ed.) *XXV Siezd KPSS, edinstvo teorii i praktiki* (1978) (Moscow: Politizdat).
Snyder, G. H. (1960) 'Balance of Power in the Missile Age', *Journal of International Affairs*, vol.XIV, no.1.
Sokoloff, G. (1980) 'Sources of Soviet Power: Economy Population, Resources', in Bertram, C. (ed.).
Sokolov, S. (1981) 'Pod rukovodsvom Partii, vmeste s narodom', *Kommunist*, no.3 (February).
Sokolovsky, V. D. (ed.) (1963) *Military Strategy, Soviet Doctrine and Concepts* (New York: Praeger).
Soviet Military Power, (1983, 1984, 1985, 1986, 1987) (Washington, DC: United States Department of Defence).
SSSR v tsifrakh v 1979 godu (1980) (Moscow: Statistika).
Stalin, J. V. (1967) *Sochineniia* (Stanford: Hoover Institution).
Star Wars (1985) (Moscow: Military Publishing House).
Stepanov, G. (1981) 'East–West Business Ties: A Sphere of Cooperation , Not an Instrument of Blackmail', *International Affairs*, no.12 (December) Moscow.
Szamuely, T. (1974) *The Russian Tradition* (London: Secker & Warburg).
Talensky, N. (1960) 'On the Character of Modern Warfare', *International Affairs*, no.10 (October) Moscow.
Talensky, N. (1965) 'The Late War: Some Reflections', *International Affairs*, no.5 (May), Moscow.

Tarabaev, P. (1978) 'Neutronnoe Oruzhiie: chto eto?', *Mirovaia ekonomika i mezhdunarodnyie otnosheniia*, no.7.

Tarabaev, P. (1980) 'Vazhny aspekt problemy razoruzheniia', *Mirovaia ekonomika i mezhdunarodnyie otnosheniia*, no.1.

Tchernakova, N. E. (1979) 'Informatsionnyie potrebnosti auditorii gazet, radio i televideniia', in *Sotsialisticheskie problemy obshchestvennovo mneniia i sredstv massovoi informatsii*, Akademia Nauk SSSR, Moscow.

'The Budget of the USSR' (1982) *Ekonomicheskaia gazeta*, no.50 (December).

The Price of Defence: a New Strategy for Military Spending (1979) The Boston Study Group (New York: Times Books).

The USSR in the 80s (1978) Colloquium held 17–19 January 1978 in Brussels, Nato Directorate of Economic Affairs, Brussels.

Thompson, E. P. (1980) 'Protest and Survive', in Holloway, D. *War, Militarism and the Soviet State* (Harmondsworth: Penguin Books).

Tikhonov, N. A. (1981) *Guidelines for the Economic and Social Development of the USSR for the 1981–1985 and the Period Ending in 1990* (Moscow: Novosti Press).

Tiushkevich, S. A. (ed.) (1978) *Sovetskyie vooruzhonnyie sily* (Moscow: Ministerstvo oborony SSSR).

Tolkunov, L. (1982) 'Psikhologicheskaia voina – priznak yadernoi patologii', *Kommunist*, no.4 (March).

Toshchenko, Z. T. (ed.) (1984) *Voprosy teorii i praktiki ideologicheskoi raboty* (Moscow: Mys'l,).

Trapeznikov, S. (1974) 'Ekonomicheskuiu nauku – na uroven sovremmennykh zadach kommunisticheskovo stroitelstva', *Voprosy ekonomiki*, no.2 (February).

Trapeznikov, V. (1973) 'Nauchno tekhnicheskyi progress i effektivnost nauki', *Voprosy ekonomiki*, no.2.

Treadgold, D. W. (1967) *Twentieth Century Russia* (Chicago: Rand McNally).

Treml, V. G. and Hardt, J. P. (eds) (1972) *Soviet Economic Statistics* (Durham: Duke University Press).

Trofimenko, G. (1982) 'Strategiia priamovo protivoborstva', *Krasnaia zvezda* (2 June).

Usachev, I. G. (1976) *Sovetski Soyuz i problema razoruzheniia* (Moscow: Mezhdunarodnyie otnosheniia).

Ustinov, D. (1977) 'Strazh mirnovo truda, oplot vseobshchego mira'. *Kommunist*, no.3.

Valley, B. L. (1985) 'The Ultimate Defence', *Vital Speeches of the Day* (Mount Pleasant, South Carolina, City News Publishing Co.).

Vaneev, V. (1978) 'Gonka vooruzhenii i problema eio ogranicheniia', *Mirovaia ekonomika i mezhdunarodnyie otnosheniia*, no.7.

Vasiliev, V. (1982) 'Kto stoit za kontseptsiei vybora tzelei', *Krasnaia zvezda* (21 July).

Vasiutovich, V. (1980) 'Militarski ugar v S.Sh.A', *Mirovaia ekonomika i mezhdunarodnyie otnosheniia*, no.6.

Vneshnaia torgovlia SSSR v 1981 g. (1982) 'Finansy i statistika', Moscow.

Volchkov, B. (1971) 'Fundament oboronnoi moshchi strany', *Krasnaia*

zvezda (17 November).
Volkogonov, D. A. (1983) *Psikhologicheskaia voina* (Moscow: Voenizdat).
Volkogonov, D. A., Milovidov, A. S. and Tiushkevich, S. A. (1977) *Voina i armiia* (Moscow: Voenizdat).
Voroshilov, K. E. (1951) *Stalin and the Armed Forces of the USSR* (Moscow).
Warner, E. L. III. (1977) *The Military in Contemporary Soviet Politics* (New York: Praeger Publishers).
Wettig, G. (1977) *Broadcasting and Détente* (London: C.Hurst).
Wick, C. Z. (1985) 'The Power of Information in the Quest for Peace', *Vital Speeches of the Day* (Mount Pleasant, South Carolina, City News Publishing Co.
Wolfe, T. W. (1979) *Soviet Power in Europe 1945–1970* (Baltimore: Johns Hopkins University Press).
Wolfson, M. and Farrell, J. P. (1986) *A Framework to Study Economic Warfare Between the USA and USSR* (Corvalis, Or.: Dept. of Economics, Oregon State University).
Yakovetz, U. (1980) 'Tzeny i sovershenstvovaniie planirovaniia khoziaistvennovo mekhanizma', *Voprosy ekonomiki*, no.6 (June).
Yegorov, P. T. Shlyakov, I. A. and Alabin, N. I. (1970) *Grazhdanskaia oborona* (Civil Defence – a Soviet View) (Moscow: Vysshaia shkola). (Translated and published under the auspices of the United States Air Force.)
Zamyatin, L. M. (1985) *Ideologicheskaia borba i voprosy mira* (Moscow: Novosti).
Zhlobin, I. D. (ed.) (1975) *Soviet Finance: Principles, Operation* (Moscow: Progress Publishers).
Zhukov, L. M. (1983) 'Ekonomicheskoe i tekhnicheskoe sotrudnichestvo s zarubezhnymi stranami' (Moscow: Mezhdunarodnyie otnosheniia).

Notes

1 THE POLITICAL ECONOMY OF THE ARMS RACE: AN INTRODUCTION

1. The perception of economic consequences of an arms race imposed by an outside power is not exclusive to the USSR. Eisenhower had this to say at the time on the subject: 'the Soviet leaders hoped that their military threat would force an unbearable security burden leading to economic disaster . . . Communist governments, in this sense, have been aiming at an economic target no less than a military target' (Huntington, 1961, p.66).

2 SOVIET RUSSIAN IDEOLOGY: THE SOURCE OF SOVIET MILITARY THOUGHT

1. The contradiction between communist ideals and Russian nationalism has been always an issue among members of the Communist Party. Lenin once made the following remark: 'Scratch certain Communists and you will find a Great-Russian chauvinist' (Treadgold, 1967, p.203).
2. The reintroduction of tsarist military ranks and pre-revolutionary insignia on military uniforms can also be viewed as an attempt to link the present with Russia's history and traditions.
3. Karl Marx saw the roots of Russian expansionism in her remote past: 'that bold synthesis which, blending the encroaching method of the Mongol slave with the world-conquering tendencies of the Mongol masters, forms the life-spring of modern Russian diplomacy' (K. Marx, 'Revelation of the Diplomatic History of the Eighteenth Century', in Szamuely, 1974, p.70).

3 SOVIET MILITARY THOUGHT – THEORY AND PRACTICE

1. The assessment of a situation within a Marxist idealistic concept is a feature of Soviet political analysis. The Soviets would like to believe that a coalition of socialist states necessarily assumes full solidarity

and cooperation within its camp due to the absence of 'contradictions'. To do otherwise would undermine basic Marxist tenets on which the idea of socialist community of interest rests. The above is an example of a normative statement referred to in the introductory chapter.

2. As we shall see in the later part of this chapter, the dogmatism that prevailed in Soviet literature on the military doctrine gave way to a modified and more realistic approach.

3. A feature of Soviet military analysis is the absence of speculative discussions. Speculations of a strategic nature are usually presented as views reported in the Western press, but when they are not explicitly criticised it can be assumed that they are accepted.

4. The American interpretation of this part of Soviet military strategy is that the Soviets are preparing themselves to fight a nuclear war and for this reason 'Soviet ground forces have been trained . . . for sustained operations in a nuclear environment' (*Soviet Military Power*, 1984, p.50).

4 THE ECONOMIC WAR: ECONOMIC POWER AND NATIONAL SECURITY

1. Just as Soviet military effort is shrouded today in complete secrecy, there is a marked tendency among Soviet historians to emphasise the pre-war high level of Soviet military expenditure.

2. The correctness of this assessment is debatable. It can be assumed that the numerical superiority in weapons of the German army refers to the initial stages of the war when the Soviets suffered huge losses in armament.

3. Contrary to the generally accepted assumption, the full text of the speech was published in the USSR some years later, in November 1959. One million copies were printed, but how many were actually distributed within the Soviet Union is not known. Nevertheless, some original copies of the publication found their way into university libraries in the West ('Doklad na zakrytom zasedanii XX sezda KPSS', Politizdat, Moscow, 1959).

4. These figures by themselves suggest that the contribution by the Allies was of substantial significance to the Soviet war effort despite their claim to the contrary.

5. The extent to which the transfer of Western technology has contributed to the growth of the Soviet economy and to its military effort is the subject of much discussion in the West (see, for example, Schroeder, 1983), and will be examined in chapter 7.

5 ASSESSING THE SOVIET MILITARY EFFORT

1. Although the Soviet Union does not suffer from the same limitations in allocating funds for defence as does the United States, it uses its own estimates of American defence expenditure for propaganda purposes. By comparing America's Defence Bill with the officially disclosed DE in the Soviet budget, Moscow claims that it is the US which spends more on armament than does the USSR (see Kulikov, 1976, Ustinov, 1977; and 'Otkuda iskhodit ugroza miru', 1987).

2. This may well be correct. An indication that civilian R&D may not be included in expenditure on science is a relatively recent policy of 'a gradual transition to financing all outlays in R&D . . . from a single fund created out of profits'. An experiment on setting a single fund for financing all outlays on the development of science and technology in the civilian sector was carried out in the electrical engineering industry and will be also applied in others (Sarkisiant, 1980, p.327). The same Soviet source reports that 'almost five percent of the national income goes to develop science in the USSR' (ibid., p.94).

3. The first substantial increase in defence spending in years occurred in the 1985 budget. Defence expenditure rose to over 19 billion rubles – an increase of some 11.2 per cent. It must have meant a greater share in the Soviet GNP which rose by only 3.1 per cent (*Pravda*, 26 January 1986). Subsequently, the defence budget has been increased to 20.2 billion rubles in 1987.

4. The source quoted above, where the nature of defence expenditure is precisely defined, omits a definition of expenditure on science (Zhlobin, 1975, chapter VIII), but another source (Trapeznikov, 1973, p.75) mentions that only part of military research will be reflected in civilian scientific and technological progress and that 75 per cent of the budget for science will be spent on R&D.

5. Purchasing power parities (ruble–dollar ratios) indicate the number of rubles (dollars) required to purchase the same quantity of goods and services of similar quality that can be bought with US dollars (rubles).

6. An example will illustrate the point: although in 1976 43 US cents bought as much canned orange juice in the United States as did one ruble in the USSR, it took over 5 dollars in the US to purchase the same amount of frozen cod sold for one ruble in the Soviet Union (Edwards *et al.*, 1979, p.374).

7. Past attempts at reaching an agreement between the superpowers on limitation of military expenditure (General Assembly Resolutions 3093A and 3093B of December 1973) have failed due mainly to the difficulties of measurement and valuation of input and output

including price differences (see Abraham S.Becker, *Military Expenditure Limitation for Arms Control and Prospects*, Ballinger, Cambridge, Mass., 1977).

8. This was disputed, not very convincingly, by Igor Birman (1981) who attempted to explain certain inconsistencies in the Soviet budget, particularly the fact that it is always balanced or in slight surplus. Birman claims that DE, far in excess of the budget figure, is financed by a large (hidden) budget deficit.

6 THE DOMESTIC ASPECT AND NEW ECONOMIC REALISM

1. Personal interest and material incentives as motivation for greater efforts appear to have become the guiding principle for better efficiency during the *perestroika* (see Chapter 10).

2. As a result of the economic policies instituted by Mikhail Gorbachev, a form of unemployment benefits was introduced in January 1986. It was followed by an unusual public debate about joblessness in general. This appears to be a policy in anticipation of a modernisation of the economy advocated by Gorbachev that could put a great number of people out of work. *Sovetskaia Kultura* – a Soviet newspaper – in an article on 4 February 1986, reported that officials thrown out of work as a result of the reorganisation were promised full pay for three month if they were unable to find jobs. This principle has been formally adopted and incorporated in a law proclaimed in July 1987 (*Izvestia,* 1 July 1987).

8 THE 'DEFENCE BURDEN' OR THE 'BURDEN OF INEFFICIENCY'

1. One of the basic principles of the economic reforms under Gorbachev is to reduce the role of central planning and to increase horizontal links between related enterprises. We shall discuss these developments in Chapter 10.

2. Such practice is in line with the general tendency within the Soviet economy of avoiding innovations which contain an element of risk. The introduction of new ideas is always risky and the price of failure very high. On the other hand, the reward for success when compared with the danger of failure relatively low.

3. Soviet definition of 'productivity of social labour' is derived from dividing the national income by the number of workers employed in material production (Khachaturov, 1977, p.320).

9 WAR OF IDEOLOGIES – THE PROPAGANDA WAR

1. The forcible repatriation of millions of Soviet citizens and their subsequent re-education in Stalin's vast network of camps is an indication of the extent of fears of ideological contamination.
2. One Soviet source reports that an international symposium on questions of study of public opinion took place in Sofia, in 1981, with the participation of representatives of all Communist Parties of the socialist alliance. (Gantchev, 1983, p.98)
3. East German authorities attempted, at one stage, to limit the possibilities of receiving television programmes from West Germany by issuing recommendations to direct antennae away from the West under the threat of reprimands. The attempt was unsuccessful and consequently abandoned (Wettig, 1977, p.45).

10 PERESTROIKA AND GLASNOST: 1985–1987

1. Cost-accounting is not a new principle in the soviet economic system. It was practiced even during Stalin's rule but due to its narrow scope within the highly centralised system, it was never strictly enforced and consequently ineffective.

Index